Clauspeter Becker
PORSCHE 911 — The Evolution

Design: Anita Ament
Layout and cover design: Andreas Pflaum
Cover photo: Christoph Bauer

Photo credits:
All photos made by **Christoph Bauer**,
GT 1-Chapter by Hans-Dieter Seufert,
Design-Studies: Porsche AG, Archiv Style Porsche

The author and publisher would like the thank the Porsche AG Press Department for its extraordinary support, and heartfelt thanks to Herr Klaus Steckkönig for his tireless efforts.

ISBN 3-613-01851-9

Copyright © by Motorbuch Verlag,
Postfach 103743, 70032 Stuttgart.
A division of Paul Pietsch Verlage GmbH & Co.
First edition, 1997

Reproduction, including excerpts, prohibited. Copyright and all other rights reserved. Translation, storage in a retrieval system, reproduction and distribution, including CD-ROM, Laserdisc etc. as well as storage in electronic media such as the Internet etc. without prior written permission of the publisher is illegal and punishable by law.

Reproduction
and printing: Bechtle Druck, 73 730 Esslingen
Binding: Riethmüller, 70176 Stuttgart
Printed in Germany

PORSCHE 911

The Evolution

Clauspeter Becker

translated by Peter Albrecht

Motorbuch Verlag

Foreword

Thirty-four years ago, felt confident that we had created a milestone automobile. In 1963, the new Porsche – we still called it the 901 – had all of the qualities necessary to establish a new standard in sports car design for the foreseeable future. Indeed, the 911 far exceeded our expectations. It has remained a vital design for three and a half decades. Many competitors have come forward to challenge for this role – several built by our own company – yet among sports cars, the 911 has remained the measure of all things. For this, we can thank the engineers of the Weissach research and development center, who believed firmly in the 911, and worked tirelessly to maintain its youthful vigor. I regard this most recent design, the first complete re-engineering of a timeless concept, in the same way. It endows the 911 with the equipment necessary for a long, successful journey into the future. I am happy to congratulate all the employees of our firm on the result of their efforts; you have created a new automobile, yet one that remains a true 911. It establishes a new benchmark among the sports cars of the world.

Professor Dr. Ferry Porsche

Contents

Fathers of the New 911 — 8
A fireside chat with Horst Marchart and leading engineers

A True 911 — 14
The design of the new Carrera

Close to the Wind — 28
Aerodynamics of the new Carrera

A Virtual Tour of a Powerplant — 36
The engine of the new Carrera

Burning Snow — 50
Cold-weather testing on the Alaska Highway

The Geometry of Good Manners — 58
The suspension of the new Carrera

New Heights — 70
Driving the Carrera through Italy's Monti Sibillini

84   **Getting a Grip**
Wheels and tires of the new Carrera

90   **Once Upon a Time in the West**
Test driving the new Carrera in the American Southwest

108   **Just a Bit More**
The electronic Systems of the new Carrera

118   **Safety First**
Passive safety features of the new 911

126   **Porsche Provençal**
First sorties to southern France: a red Carrera in search of lavender

140   **Super Plus**
Porsche GT1: the ultimate 911

152   **By the Numbers**
Technical specifications

A fireside chat with Horst Marchart and Porsche's leading engineers

Fathers of the New 911

Their mission accomplished, Porsche engineers talk about the high and low points of the 911's development history

It is the late summer of 1997. Work on the new Porsche Carrera has been completed. Like the calm after a storm, a relaxed atmosphere spreads over the Ebnisee, a small Swabian lake. The men who created the new 911 meet at the Schassberger Hotel for a fireside chat and a look back on five very eventful years. How did it all start?

Horst Marchart remembers November 11, 1991 very well. "On that day, we suggested a new joint strategy in which two models, the Boxster and the Carrera, would be built on the same platform. I remember the date because I was appointed to the board of directors that same day." The project was approved in February 1992.

Horst Marchart, age 58, vice president of research and development, has worked for Porsche since 1960.

"The introduction of 'simultaneous engineering' presented us with a steep learning curve."

More than five years later, styling chief Harm Lagaay fondly recalls that "For the studio staff, February 20, 1992 was our Independence Day."

"But that was no simple beginning," says Horst Marchart. "The entire company was restructured, and the economic situation demanded a drastic cut in staff. Many good people left us back then, and with them went a vast amount of know-how. Today, we can honestly say that, in 1992, nothing that we have now was complete, ready to pull out of a drawer."

Project manager Rainer Srock recalls that "At the time, we were still in the intense final development stages of the previous Carrera, the 993. Naturally, not all of our capacity was available for the new project. We could establish the basic outline of a new strategy, but the real work on the Boxster and Carrera did not begin until 1993. From that point onward, everything happened faster than ever before."

Harm M. Lagaay, 51, chief of styling, worked for Porsche from 1970 to 1977, returning in 1989.

"For the studio staff, February 20, 1992 was our Independence Day."

Chief designer Harm Lagaay underscores Rainer Srock's point: "We had the Boxster ready for production in a record time of 34 months; the Carrera followed 12 months later, exactly according to plan."

Horst Marchart reflects on this extraordinary feat. "At the time, we not only revolutionized our technology; we restructured our entire development process. The introduction of 'simultaneous engineering,' encompassing all participants, from the designer to the production experts right up to the purchasing department and our suppliers, presented us with a steep learning curve and countless meetings."

Engine designer Rainer Wüst comments on the most recent work to come out of his department: "The question of whether or not the boxer engine

Rainer Srock, 62, project leader for the 986 and 996, has been at Porsche since 1959.

"In 1992, we were still deeply involved in the final development stages of the previous Carrera."

had a future did not warrant much discussion. The flat-six engine was ideally suited for the design concept of our cars."

Horst Marchart adds that "We were well aware of that, since we experimented with a rear-mounted V8 engine back in the 1980s. And we were glad to shelve the idea of putting a four-cylinder boxer engine in the Boxster."

Rainer Wüst expounds on the changing of the guard in Porsche engine design: "Of course, the shift from air to water cooling appealed to us as engineers. Finally, we could realize four-valve technology, even on the Boxster, and, overall, build a modern, contemporary engine. But at the same time, we had a political problem; despite their unquestionable good qualities, our water-cooled four- and eight-cylinder engines were never fully accepted within the Porsche dealer organization."

Based on his own experience, Harm Lagaay interjects: "But I think that problem is behind us. As soon as somebody drives the new Carrera, they will not need any additional persuasion."

Rainer Wüst glances to his left, and says "The new technology represents more than just higher power and torque from smaller displacement. Exhaust emissions and fuel consumption are considerably lower. The thing is, the good handling characteristics of the Carrera make it difficult to drive in a restrained, economical manner."

Dr. Ludwig Hamm, in charge of body engineering, explains that "Our colleagues in engine design may have felt quite comfortable with water cooling. For us in body engineering, those radiators caused any number of headaches. Finding space ahead of the tires to mount radiators large enough to cool these powerful engines was no small problem."

"There were lots of different experiments," con-

Dr. Ludwig Hamm, 47, in charge of body engineering, has been at Porsche since 1974.

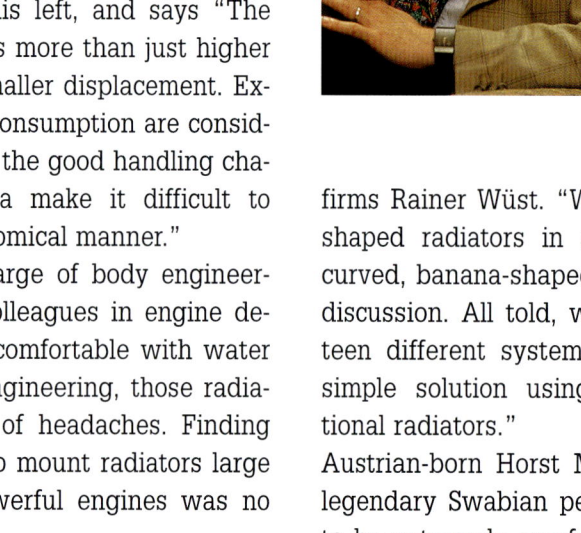

"Finding space for sufficiently large radiators was no simple matter."

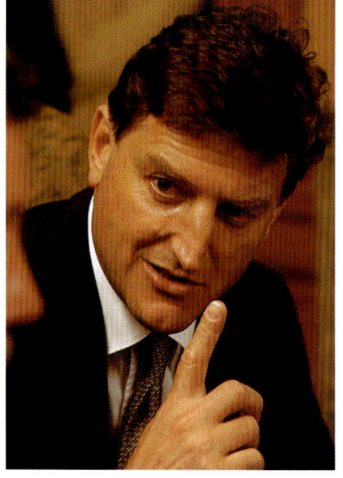

firms Rainer Wüst. "We experimented with ring-shaped radiators in a modified 964 body, and curved, banana-shaped radiators also were under discussion. All told, we experimented with fourteen different systems, but finally settled on a simple solution using flat, lower-cost, conventional radiators."

Austrian-born Horst Marchart elaborates on the legendary Swabian penchant for thrift: "We had to be extremely careful with money, because the project description was very specific about retail prices: 75,000 Marks for the Boxster and no more than the then-current price of 132,000 Marks for the Carrera. We simply couldn't allow the car to get any more expensive – not if we wanted to hold our own in the market."

Dr. Hamm admits his past worries. "With the Boxster, for a long time, we had our doubts about whether we could meet that 75,000 Mark limit. Even with a four-cylinder, it was anything but a sure thing."

"But even for the considerably more expensive Carrera, the situation was no less tense. It is a larger car, with completely new drivetrain technology and groundbreaking improvements in passive safety," adds Horst Marchart.

Rainer Wüst, 49, in charge of engine development, has been at Porsche since 1971, with one short interruption.

"The question of whether or not the boxer engine had a future did not warrant much discussion."

From the Type 356 to the latest Carrera, the entire Porsche model line bears virtually identical facial expressions.

Dr. Hamm points out the central theme of his own department: "The body not only surpasses our previous traditions in terms of its exterior appearance; thirty-four years of progress are also reflected in the load-carrying structure. It is considerably stronger, and its passive safety features set new standards in sports car design. In crash tests, our excellent results are comparable to those of the finest sedans."

Rainer Srock adds that "Although the body is larger and more rigid, it is also lighter, and as a modern design, it is much better suited for partially automated assembly. In other words, its production will be more economical."

Horst Marchart explains that "The fact that we stayed with steel is not unrelated to costs. Increased competition from aluminum has resulted in a surge of development within the steel companies. The new, high-grade sheet steels permit us to build bodies that are quite competitive in terms of weight."

The question of real problems encountered in development of the new Carrera reawakens memories of the early planning stages.

Horst Marchart describes the crisis atmosphere of the planning years. "At the beginning, the prognosis for the success of the previous 911, the 993, was not all that good, and the end of the 928 and 968 models was in sight. The entirely new 996 project was successfully completed under those conditions."

Harm Lagaay continues the story. "But then, the

Carrera, in the guise of the improved 993, sold better than expected."

Horst Marchart picks up the thread. "Had we known that then, it might have been more difficult for us to realize today's model lineup, with two completely new cars, as effectively as we have."

Rainer Wüst, the engine man, puts in the final word: "This is only the beginning."

Seen from above, the new Carrera is unmistakably part of the 911 line. Only the 356 is clearly descended from the VW Beetle.

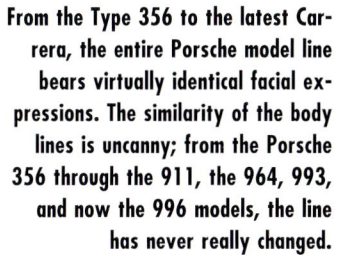

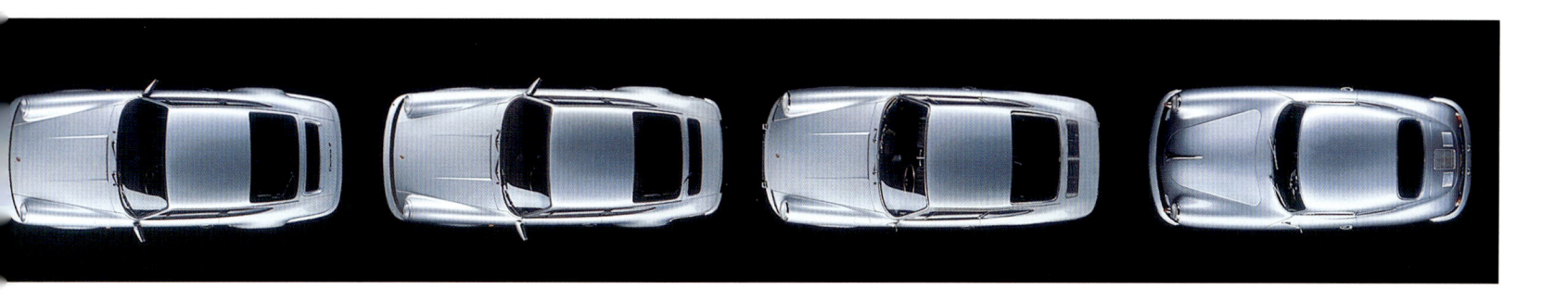

From the Type 356 to the latest Carrera, the entire Porsche model line bears virtually identical facial expressions. The similarity of the body lines is uncanny; from the Porsche 356 through the 911, the 964, 993, and now the 996 models, the line has never really changed.

Six Porsche generations, as the competition sees them. The last three models are equipped with electrically-extended rear spoilers.

13

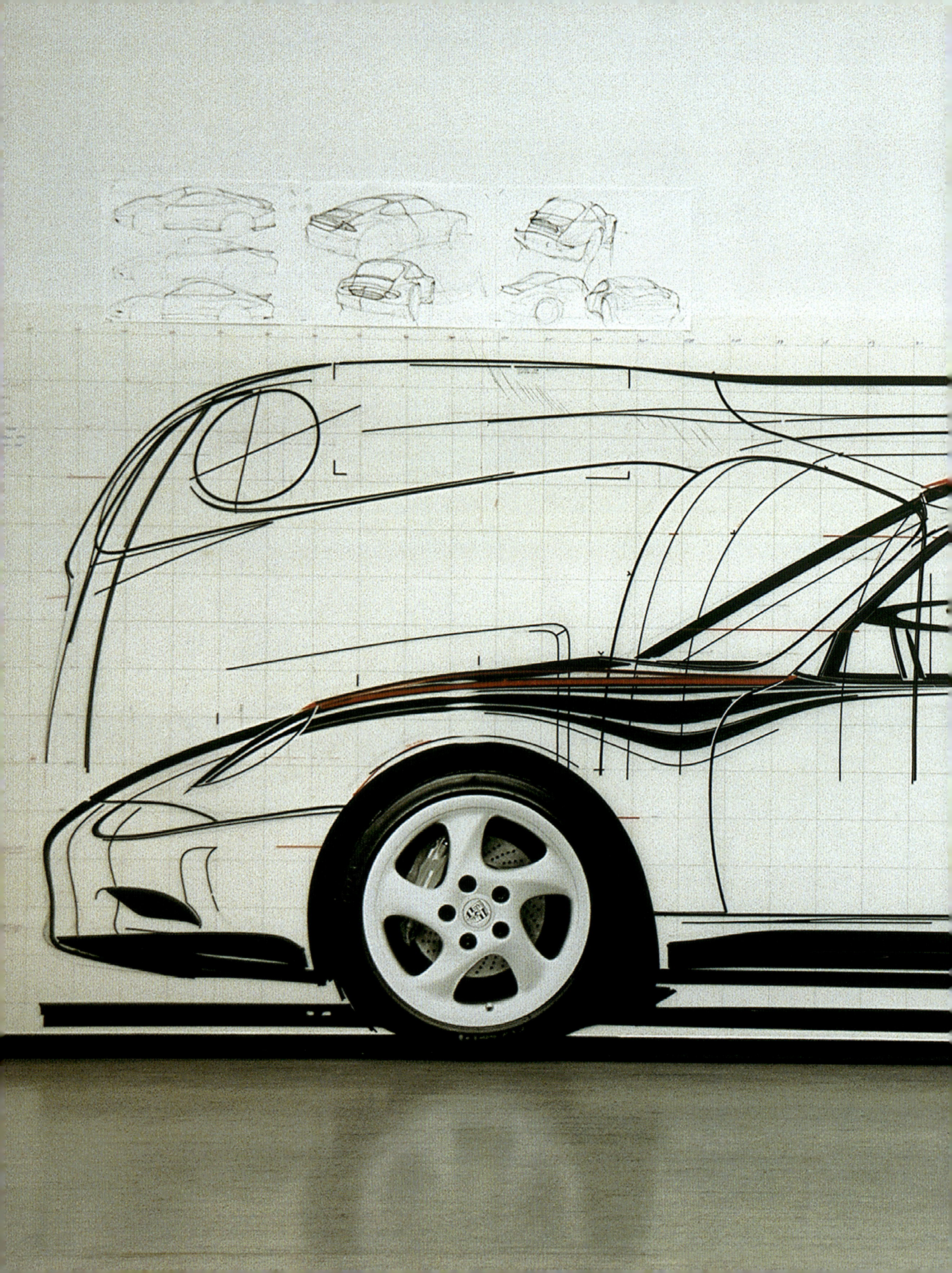

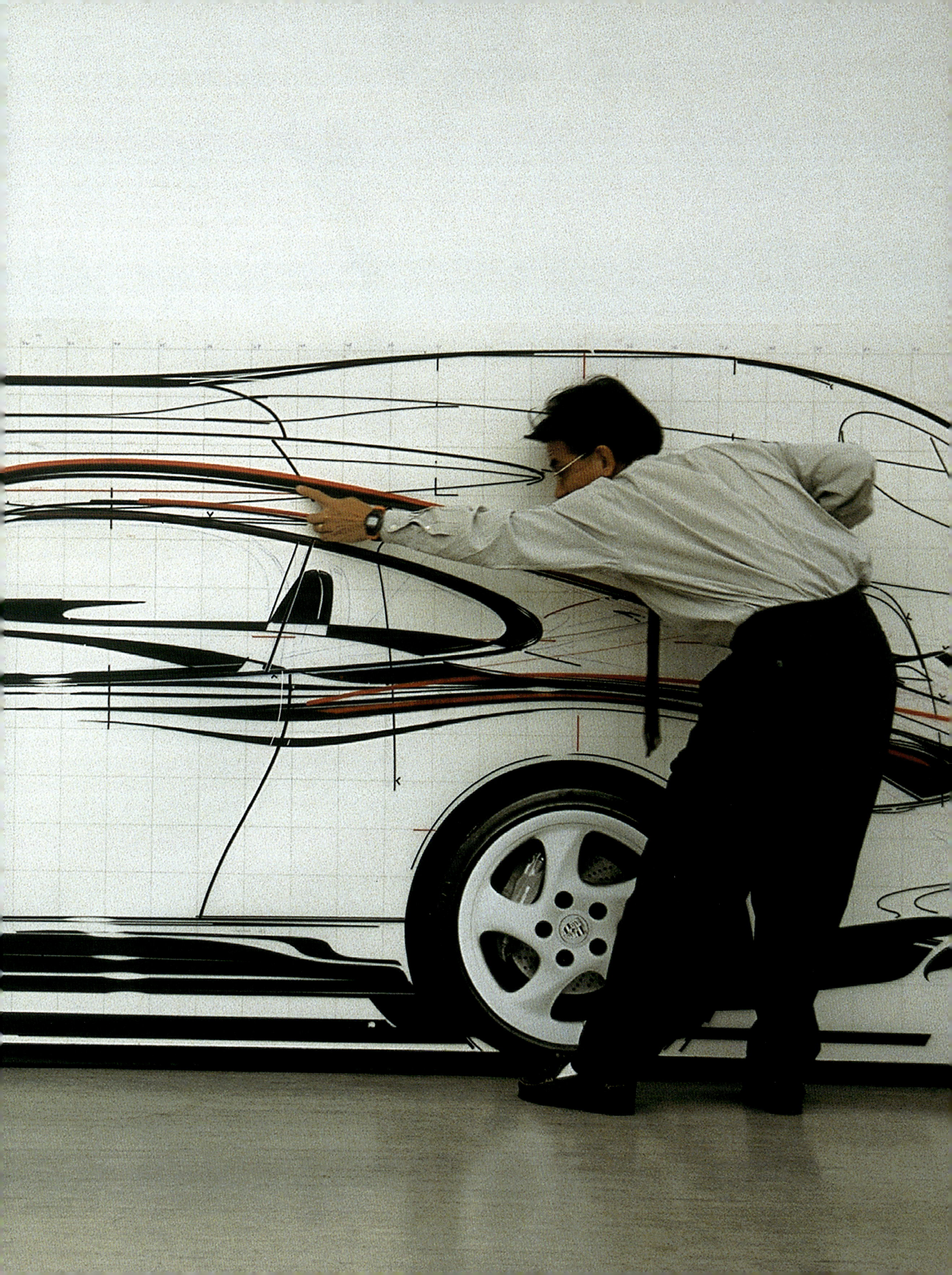

The Design of the New Carrera

A True 911

For the first time since the early 1960s, the styling team, led by Harm Lagaay, was allowed to design an all-new 911

The new Carrera expresses a more formal shape; the prominent fender flares of its predecessors are more subdued.

On this day, the courtyard of the Porsche design studio in Weissach, hermetically sealed from the outside world, resembles a branch of New York's Museum of Modern Art. Fifty years of Porsche design are on display here: the original 356, three generations of 911, and the new 911 – still top secret at this time.

The stylistic harmony of these five magnificent machines is even more intense than we remember. Only when we see, in one sweep, the past half century of automotive design as expressed in Porsche's own dialect, do we realize we are looking at a single car – one that has continued to develop over five decades. Among automobiles, most of which undergo rapid, almost organic evolution, loyalty to one shape over such a long time span can be found nowhere else.

This lineup represents five greater and lesser leaps of styling development. We remember the jump from the 356 to the first 911 as one of the greatest. But today, seen from a distance, yesterday's revolution is a mere family affair, and not a particularly remarkable one at that. The old patriarch has stretched a bit, but not changed his ways.

The three 911s in the center of this group show the effects of a continuous program of bodybuilding. With increasingly wider tires, the bodywork becomes more muscular around the fenders; and for the wide-hipped Turbo of the previous generation, the stylists have put the body on a diet of anabolic steroids.

The second great stylistic leap, the break from this design philosophy of muscular, athletic bodywork, lies in the future represented by the new Carrera. In contrast to its predecessors, the new Carrera exhibits taut flanks; its language of form is restrained, serious and distinguished. The car appears valuable instead of volatile.

Chief designer Harm Lagaay describes the essence of these two generations with two succinct examples: "The old 911 is like sprinter Ben Johnson – musclebound and aggressive. The new 911 is like Carl Lewis, who, for all his athletic ability, has a leaner figure, more elegant and better proportioned."

The design team under Lagaay approached the task of replacing a 34-year-old legend with healthy self-confidence. "This assignment gave us tremendous motivation," recalls Lagaay, "but we never had any apprehensions about the job."

Armed with such self-assurance, they tackled the first all-new body in the long history of the Porsche 911. Despite several successful facelifts over the decades, the 911 had been forced to retain some heirlooms from its earliest days: the shape of the doors had remained unchanged from the beginning, and the roof kept its distinctive form until the very last. All those years, the 911 remained basically the same car. In 1997, while its dynamic performance represented the state of the art, its roots reached back to the early 1960s – a time when manufacturing techniques and materials met completely different standards. The radical renewal of the evergreen Porsche was, in a sense, a technological diet plan, one that fit perfectly into Porsche's corporate strategy. In the early 1990s, chief executive Wendelin Wiedeking had demanded a leaner, more efficient model line. Two basic platforms would herald Porsche's return to success: the Boxster would be the affordable entry-level model, while a considerably improved but not more expensive 911 would represent the classic Porsche – a solid basis for sales and profits.

By their virtuoso application of a new concept – shared components for the two model lines – Porsche engineers redefined the art of producing cars economically in small numbers. Their ambitious goal was to build two cars, each a marketing success in its own distinct price class, with as many shared parts as possible.

This approach provided the stylists with an interesting challenge. "We had to – or perhaps I should say we were allowed to – develop the Boxster and the new Carrera at the same time," recalls Lagaay. The result of these efforts is two cars, identical up to their windshields. Because all major elements are shared, the designers' essential task was to develop a few characteristic differences while keeping the basic family resemblance. Given different front valances, and different headlight lenses, the Boxster and Carrera have related yet unique faces.

The personality of the Carrera still is based on the concept of the sport coupe, achieved here with unprecedented credibility. In the case of the Porsche 911, it remains viable as a sport coupe despite the doubts, indeed the ridicule, of the past decades. In precisely this field – that of the consummate sport coupe – Porsche's stylists were able to refine the classic

The late afternoon sun emphasizes the smoother lines of the Carrera. This underscores not only its more elegant appearance, but also results in aerodynamic detail improvements.

concept to the betterment of the overall design. For example, the windshield, which the old 911 stretched so upright, so proud, indeed so defiantly against the wind, was reshaped; it was raked back farther, still with a distinct curve, but no longer stretched to the A-pillars as had been fashionable in 1964, during the waning days of the "panoramic windshield" era, when the original 911 was designed. At last, windshield and roofline meet in aerodynamic harmony, while the windshield wipers reward the reduced curvature with better cleaning action across a larger area.

The side glass of the new 911 no longer forces the beltline down to the fenders; instead, it is

CARBON/KEVLAR ROCKER!
PORSCHE
PORSCHE
PORSCHE
PORSCHE
"AIR-EXTRACTION"
AIR INTAKE

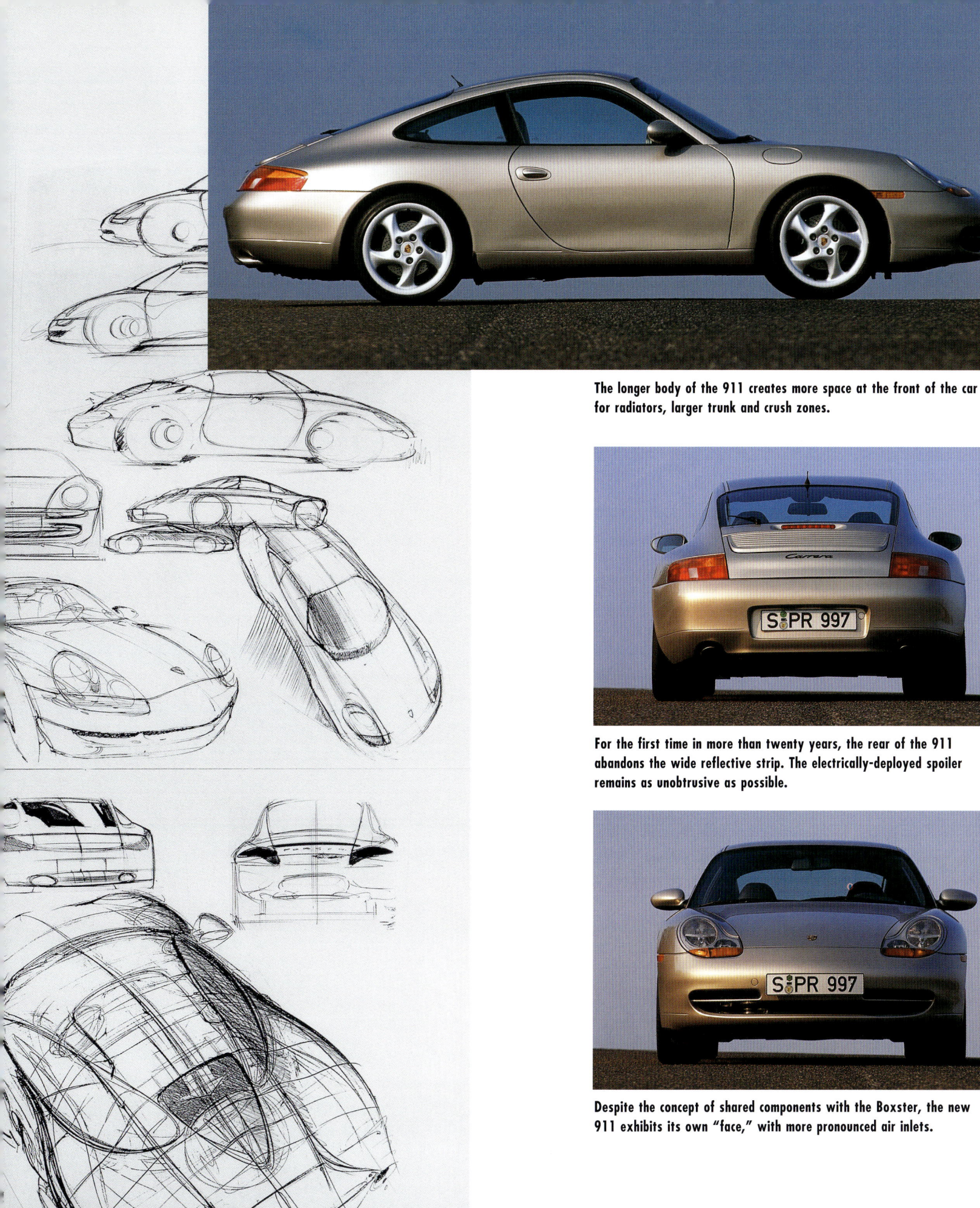

The longer body of the 911 creates more space at the front of the car for radiators, larger trunk and crush zones.

For the first time in more than twenty years, the rear of the 911 abandons the wide reflective strip. The electrically-deployed spoiler remains as unobtrusive as possible.

Despite the concept of shared components with the Boxster, the new 911 exhibits its own "face," with more pronounced air inlets.

The latest variation of the classic 911 theme began with a multitude of concept renderings; despite bold forays into a stylistic fantasyland, they always returned to the solid, unmistakable basis of the 911.

19

- FESTER SPOILER / HECK FENSTER
  AUFKLAPPBAR
- ENTLÜFTUNG

ANDERES HECKLEUCHTE GRAPHICS
PULVER BESCHICHTE "ALU"
OPTIK!

Beginning with their first sketches, Porsche designers strove for smoother flanks and distinctly better aerodynamics.

The lines from the windshield to the roof, with its more pronounced curvature for improved aerodynamics, impart a more harmonious appearance to the design.

an independent element embedded in a calm surface. With a slight upswing at the lower edge, the side windows underscore the shape of the rear, expressing power and emphasizing the presence of the engine.

The new car shares a trademark with all 911s: an electrically deployed rear spoiler, which provides early boundary layer separation and reduced lift at high speeds. Because the raised spoiler covers the third brake light in the center of the engine lid, Porsche is starting a new design trend: a second iteration of the center brake light, located in the rear edge of the spoiler.

The reflective band along the rear edge of the car, a trademark for 25 years, has disappeared. Harm Lagaay finds that this styling element, once premiered by Porsche, "has become a worn-out cliché now found on ordinary sedans." The taut flanks of the new 911 are the styling element that will carry this design far into the future. The father of all Porsches, the 356, had this shape, without padded shoulders or hips. The early 911s maintained this slim form. Reflections could play across both of these bodies in a subtle symphony of light and shadow... the reflected sky traced a straight line down the flanks and ignited dynamic highlights of speed. These virtues disappeared on later 911s, their flared fenders effectively placing chicanes in the path of such reflections.

The new Carrera has that look again, that play of light which sends its message of speed across fenders no longer stretched over bulging muscle. It reflects speed, yet, in a subtle, virtual way, makes the car appear longer.
This new language of design also greets us in the interior. The old, disciplined "engine room" styling ethic has given way to more pleasant tones, while another icon of apparent functionality has simply fallen from its pedestal. The five classic, round instruments have departed, leaving a group of descendants who present their various scales in a more compact, compartmentalized manner. The initial shock upon seeing this onslaught of readouts is followed by the realization that now, for the first time, all of the gauges are visible through the steering wheel. The hard-learned 911 driver's habit of squinting past the rim to read the speedometer won't be missed by those who drive the new Carrera. They will now be able to tell their speed at a glance.
The next experience inside the new 911 is the discovery that everything beyond the instruments has more space. The area surrounding us is a good seven centimeters (nearly three inches) wider. The stylists have successfully emphasized this new expanse as the cockpit has become more open and airy. The strongly arched roof provides adequate headroom, while the large rear glass lets more light into the car – something which younger passengers

Variation 1 – June, 1992

Variation 2 – June, 1992

Variation 3 – June, 1992

Intermediate Design Stage – December 1992

The Porsche styling studio produced full-size models of the five development stages of the new body. Stylistic experiments, practical demands and aerodynamic fine tuning led to the final shape, which lends an even stronger self-image and more pronounced elegance to the 911.

Final Design – June 1993

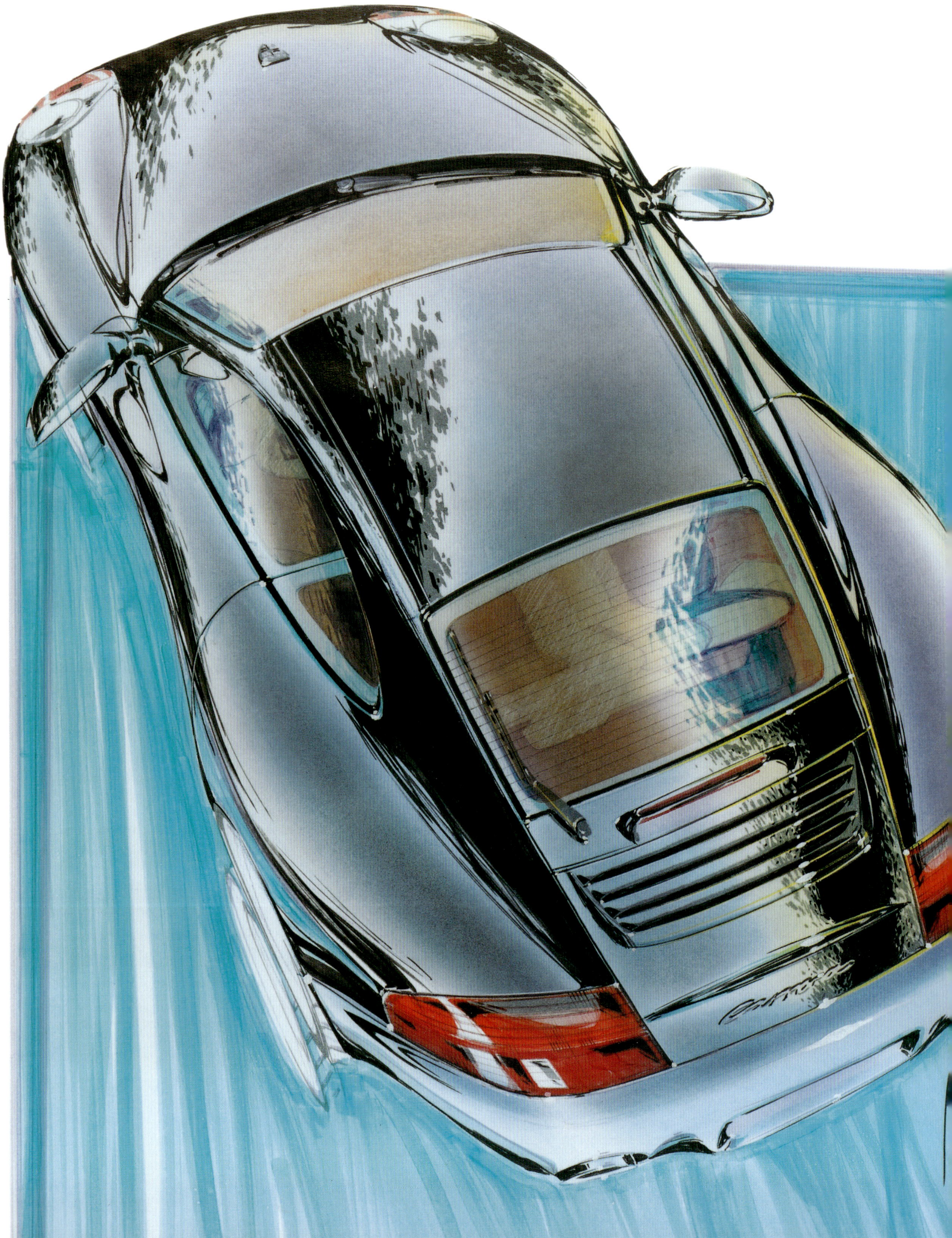

After the sharp-edged functionality of the old 911, the interior of the new Carrera is dominated by bold, sweeping shapes.

riding in the back seats will appreciate. The new Carrera affirms, indeed consummates, the ideal that in this computer age, instrument panels will become user interfaces. For customers with a taste for the ultimate, and willing to pay an additional 4.900 DM, the center of the instrument panel houses the 24 buttons and knobs of the Porsche Communication Management System. This highly integrated means of controlling climate and communication is more than just another exercise in electronic perfection. It is a high-performance assistant in search of an intelligent copilot who, even as we enjoy driving our new Carrera, skillfully operates the radio, CD changer, on-board computer, navigation system, hands-free cellular phone and climate control.

The future has begun. After thirty-four years, we have a completely new 911. How long it will reign, no one can say. In 1964, the designer of the original 911, Ferdinand Alexander Porsche, never would have guessed that his creation would have such a long life span. Harm Lagaay abstains from any predictions. But as a compulsive designer, one whose work is never truly finished, he does know one thing: "We already know what we can improve with the following generation of the new 911."

Sculptors at work: two modellers put final touches on the clay model. Behind the car are designers Pinky Lai and Harm Lagaay.

27

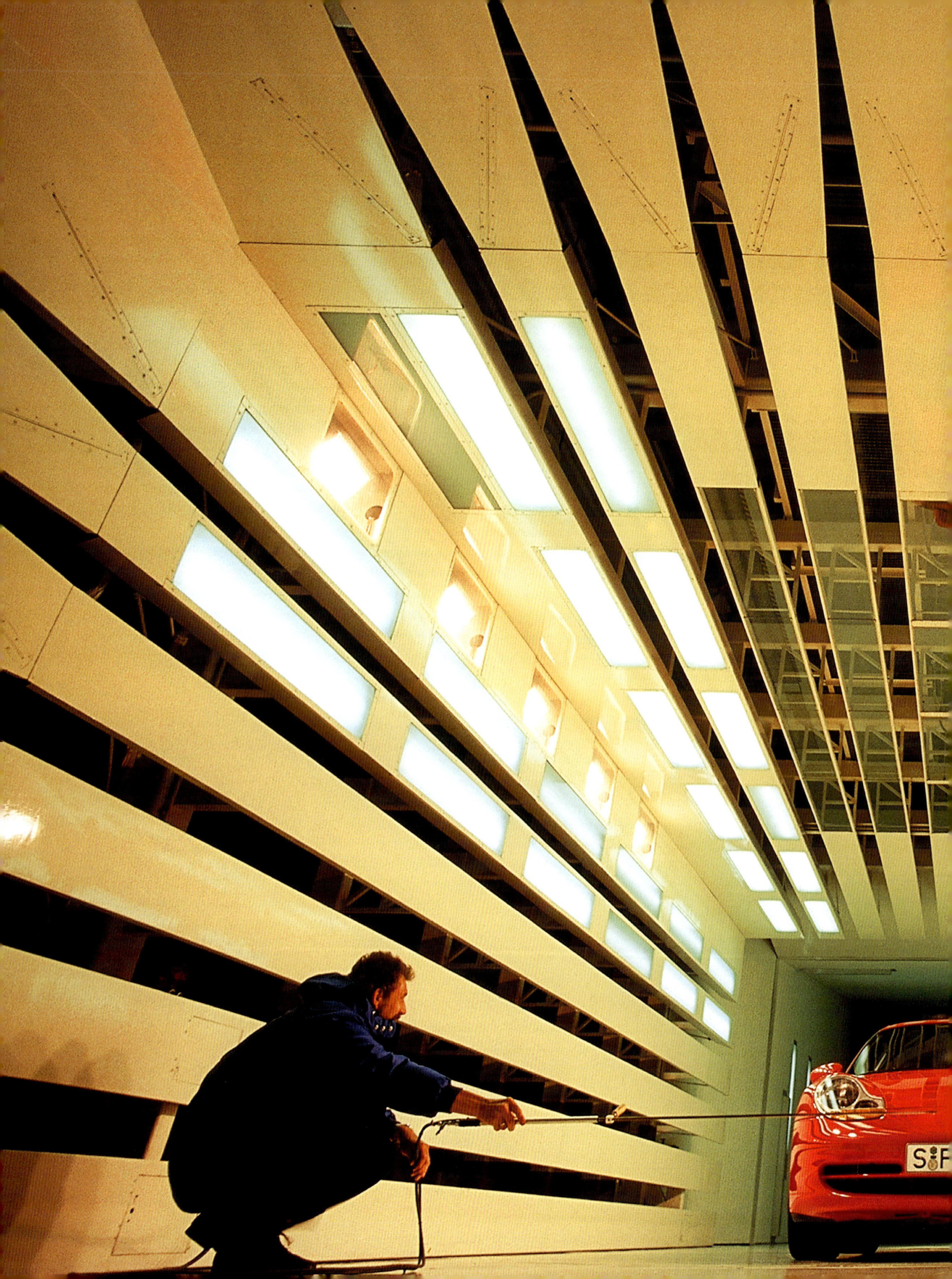

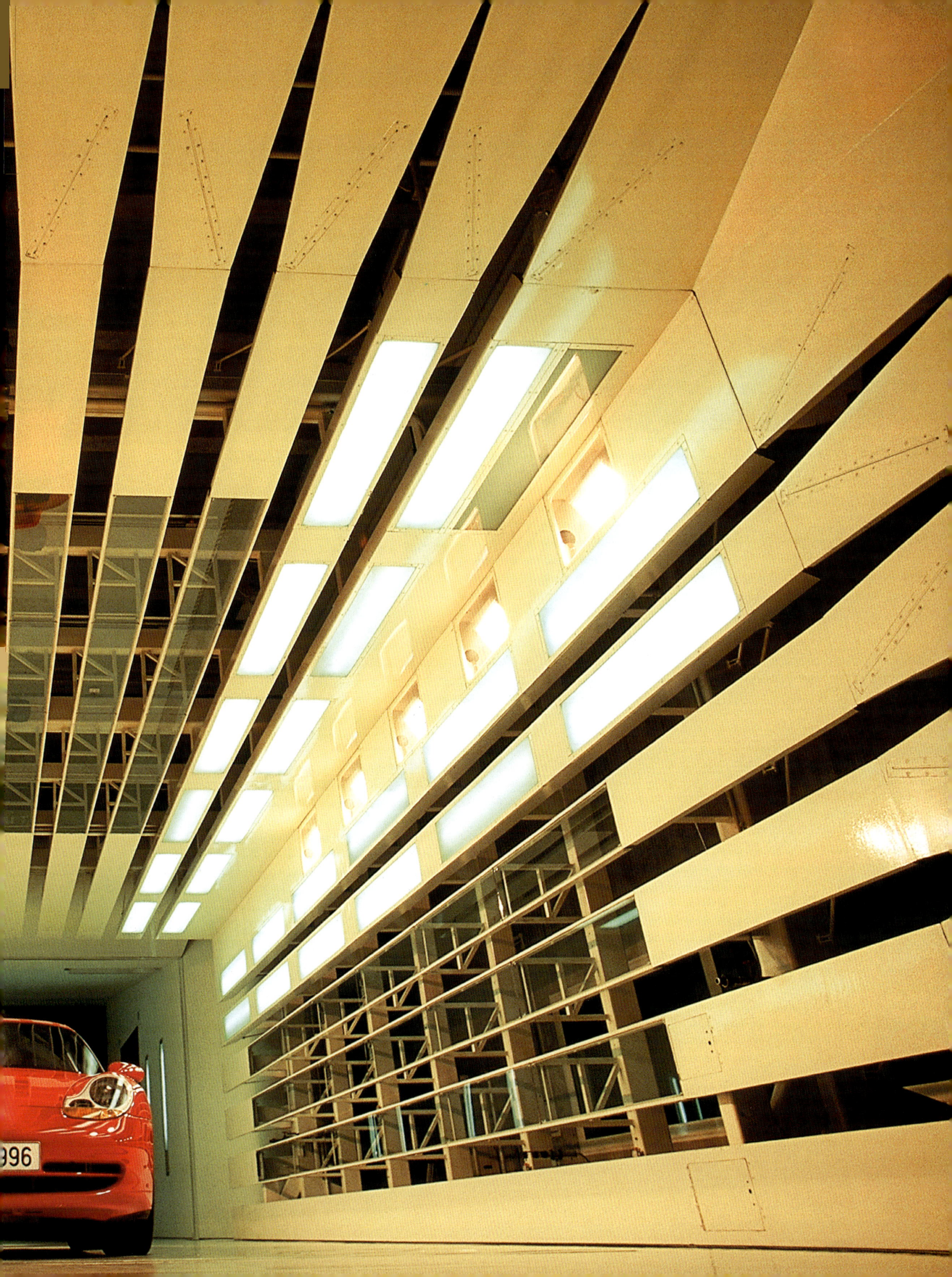
996

Aerodynamics of the new Carrera

Close to the Wind

Porsche's wind tunnel is used not only to reduce aerodynamic drag; safety and adequate cooling are given even higher priority

Whenever a carmaker touts the low drag coefficient of its latest model, Michael Preiss, in charge of the Porsche wind tunnel in Weissach, is once again provoked to deliver a critical commentary on this popular but little-understood parameter. "The drag coefficient is only one of many aerodynamic qualities encompassed by a good car design," explains Porsche's experienced Lord of the Winds.

Preiss sets completely different priorities for the aerodynamic properties expected of a Porsche. "For us, safety and cooling share top priority. We never compromise these in favor of a low c_d."

Safety occupies the attention of aerodynamicists in the form of aerodynamic lift. This unavoidable effect makes itself felt in nearly all normal production cars. As long as the air stream has a longer path over the top of a car than underneath it, the body will exhibit characteristics similar to an aircraft wing; increased speed means increased lift, and the force holding the car to the road is reduced.

This unpleasant side effect of speed may be minimized or even reversed. With their flaps and wings, Formula 1 racers achieve downforce equal to several times the weight of the car. The body of the impressive Porsche GT1 pursues the same objective; at 250 km/h (155 mph), this 1100 kg (2400 lb.) supercar is pressed onto the road by a force of two tons.

Because ordinary consumers, even Porsche drivers, demand cars that are more practical than this winged two-seater, the aerodynamicists must seek a reasonable compromise for downforce on their production vehicles.

With the new Carrera, they have achieved exemplary results. The effective lift is closer to zero than for the majority of production sports cars in this performance class. Like the drag coefficient, these lift figures are dimensionless constants which form part of certain mathematical formulas.

At the front axle of the new Carrera, Porsche engineers have measured a lift coefficient (c_{lf}) of 0.08; at the rear, c_{lr} is 0.045. In such a case, aerodynamicists speak of a "positive pitching moment." This means that the lift at the front is somewhat greater, a desirable condition. Slightly reduced side forces at high speeds make sudden directional changes less dangerous. The steering behavior remains slightly understeering, and potentially hazardous reactions from the rear end – particularly when the throttle is suddenly closed – are reduced,

On the Porsche Carrera, the means to this end of achieving minimal lift are omnipre-

In the wind tunnel, a mist of mineral oil makes streamlines readily visible.

sent. The steeply sloping front is nearly as obvious as the electrically-deployed rear spoiler. Both features have a dual positive effect in that they reduce aerodynamic drag as well as lift. Other measures become apparent only in the shop, when the car is on a lift; then we can see that the underbody is covered by smooth metal and composite panels. The trick to achieving not only low drag but also reduced lift with a flat bottom lies in deliberately admitting a certain amount of air at the front, which is then accelerated below the car.

The consistent application of such measures leads to the result that at 250 km/h (155 mph), the lift generated by a Carrera can be cancelled by the added weight of some luggage in the trunk.

For the aerodynamicists, the problem of ensuring adequate cooling was not a simple one. This challenge was not limited to the 20 liters of water in the cooling system; a sports car's brakes demand cooling air as well, and temperature-reducing measures are needed for the various lubricants in the engine, transmission, and differential.

The airflow to the water radiators, located at the left and right ahead of the front wheels, is particularly convoluted. Its work done, warm air leaves the body just ahead of the

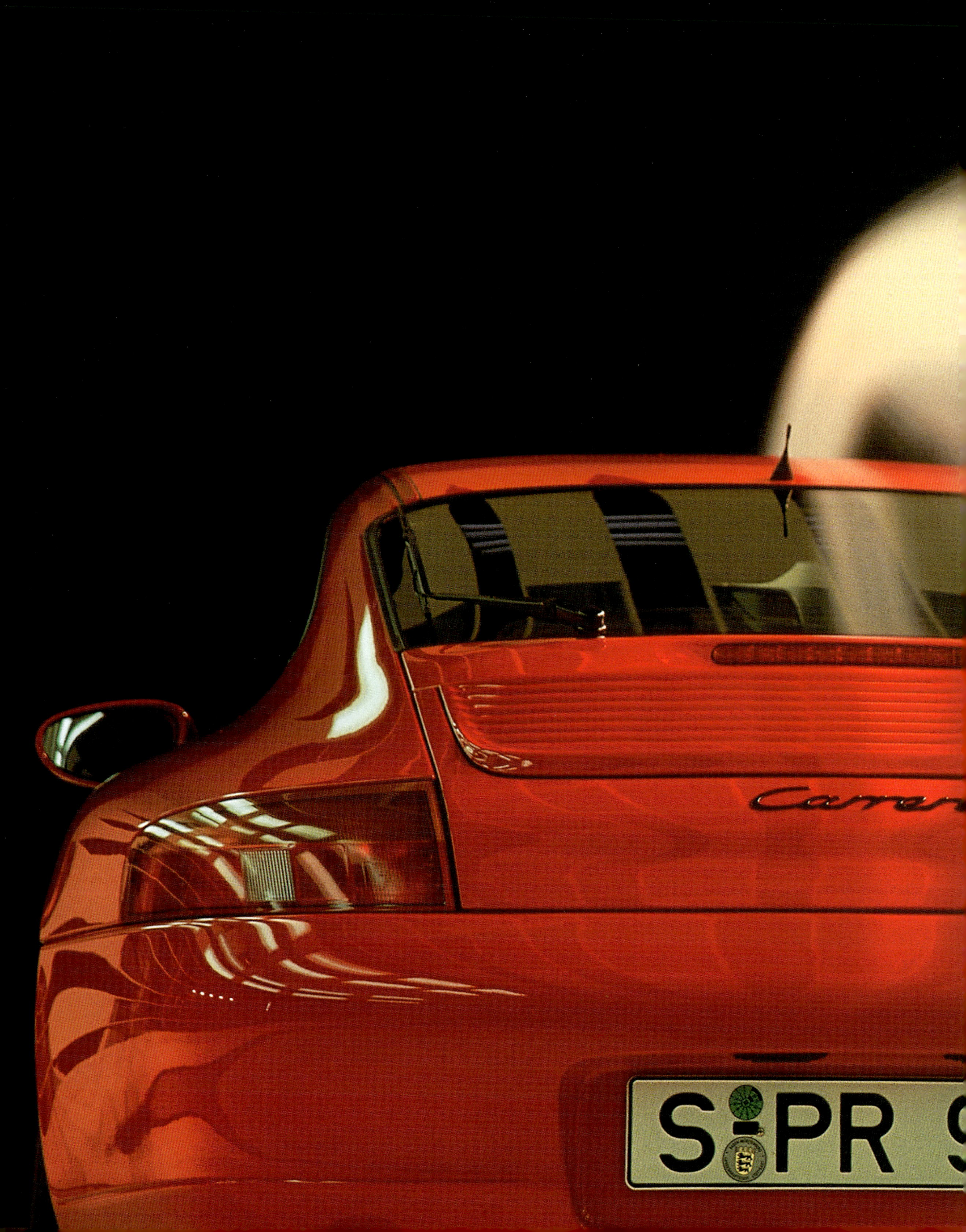

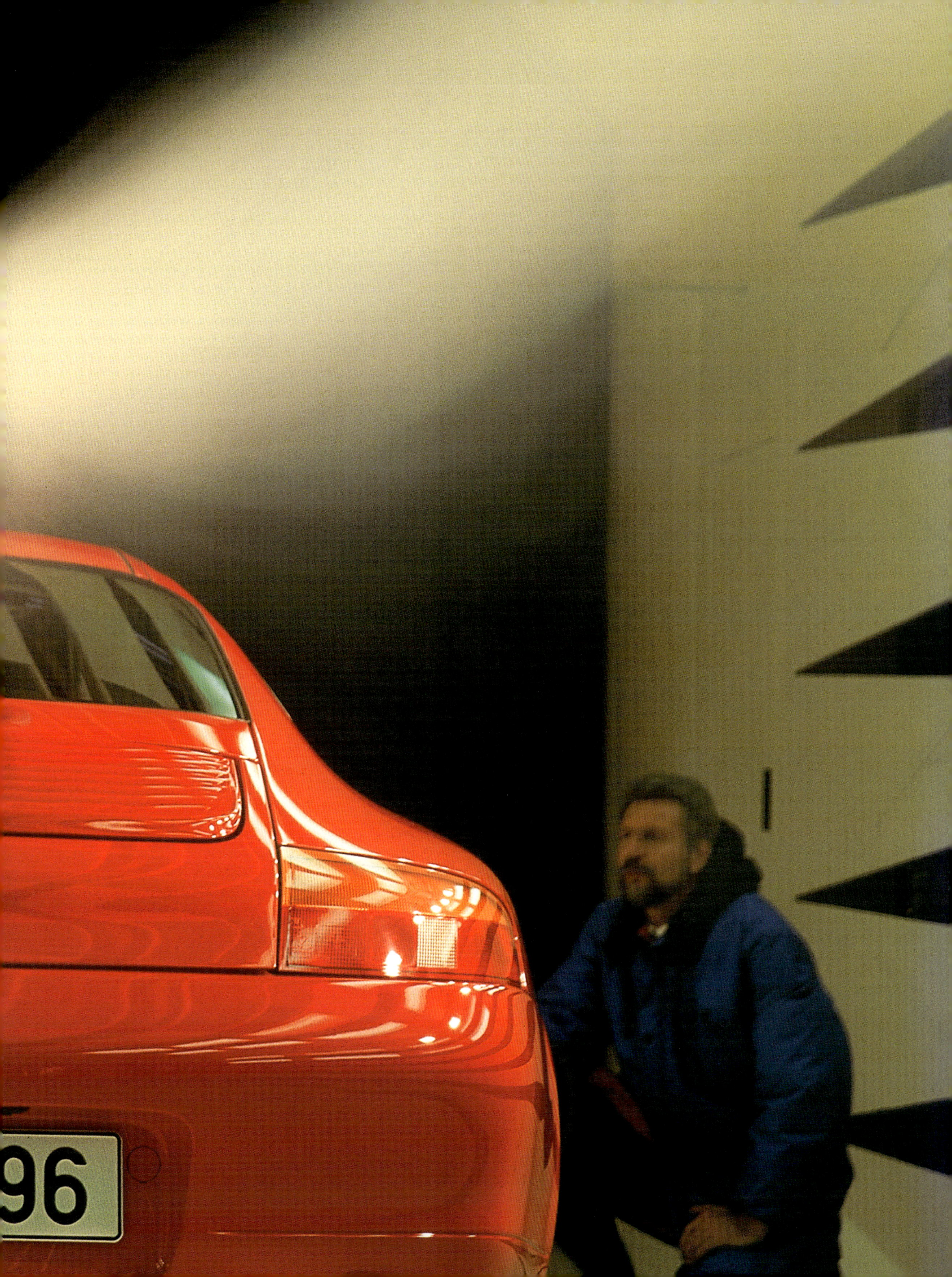
96

The streamlines follow the shape of the body; the boundary layer only separates at the edge of the spoiler.

tires, where it forms a sort of air cushion and reacts against the onrushing air like an enlarged front spoiler.

Without additional aids, the air exhausted downward from the radiators would have a negative effect; it would increase front lift, as it does on the Boxster, which has a c_{lf} of 0.13 from a similar front-end treatment. The faster Carrera, with its effective rear spoiler, demanded a more effective solution. A composite air deflector was inserted in the radiator exhaust flow; a small scoop diverts air outward to reduce c_{lf} to 0.08.

Engine cooling is handled by an oil-water heat exchanger which sits directly atop the powerplant. Heat is rejected by passing it to the engine coolant. In the case of the Tiptronic S, its oil is cooled by a similar heat exchanger using engine coolant to carry off waste heat. Now, with the addition of the Tiptronic oil cooler, the two water radiators at the front of the car are no longer adequate to handle the heat load, so a third radiator must be added at the front. Its airflow had to be precisely managed by the aerodynamicists. A slight increase in lift was unavoidable, but a

by brake cooling: "Nice, smooth wheels – like the ones favored by us aerodynamicists for low drag – are useless in this case. Slim spokes for large airflow are what's needed here."

For low drag and good downforce, a sealed pan below the engine and transmission would be desirable, but without any cooling whatsoever, it wouldn't be possible to ensure proper drivetrain operation under all conditions. The six-speed transmission and the differential, which share the same oil bath, are served by an arrow-shaped NACA duct. The differential of the Tiptronic, with its separate oil supply, needs its own cooling air channel.

Due to a fast sports car's requirements for a high degree of safety through minimal lift, and for cooling a high-output engine which generates 80 kilowatts (107 horsepower) of waste heat, a minimal cd is not possible. Seen in the light of the demands placed on the design, the drag coefficient of 0.30 reflected in the new Carrera's specification sheet is an outstanding achievement. Michael Preiss is absolutely certain when he says that "No comparable sports car has values as well-balanced as those of the new 911. If we wanted to reduce its drag coefficient even more, we would have to build a different car, and that would no longer be a 911."

good part of it is negated by the added mass of the third front radiator and coolant.

An additional, deliberately engineered airflow at the front of the car leads to the brakes, which demand a tremendous amount of cooling air, as they are several times as powerful as the engine itself. Fortunately, because of their greater temperature differential to the surrounding air, cooling them is somewhat easier – though the problem is anything but trivial. With extreme heat transfer rates, everything has to work perfectly. Michael Preiss explains the conflicting goals imposed

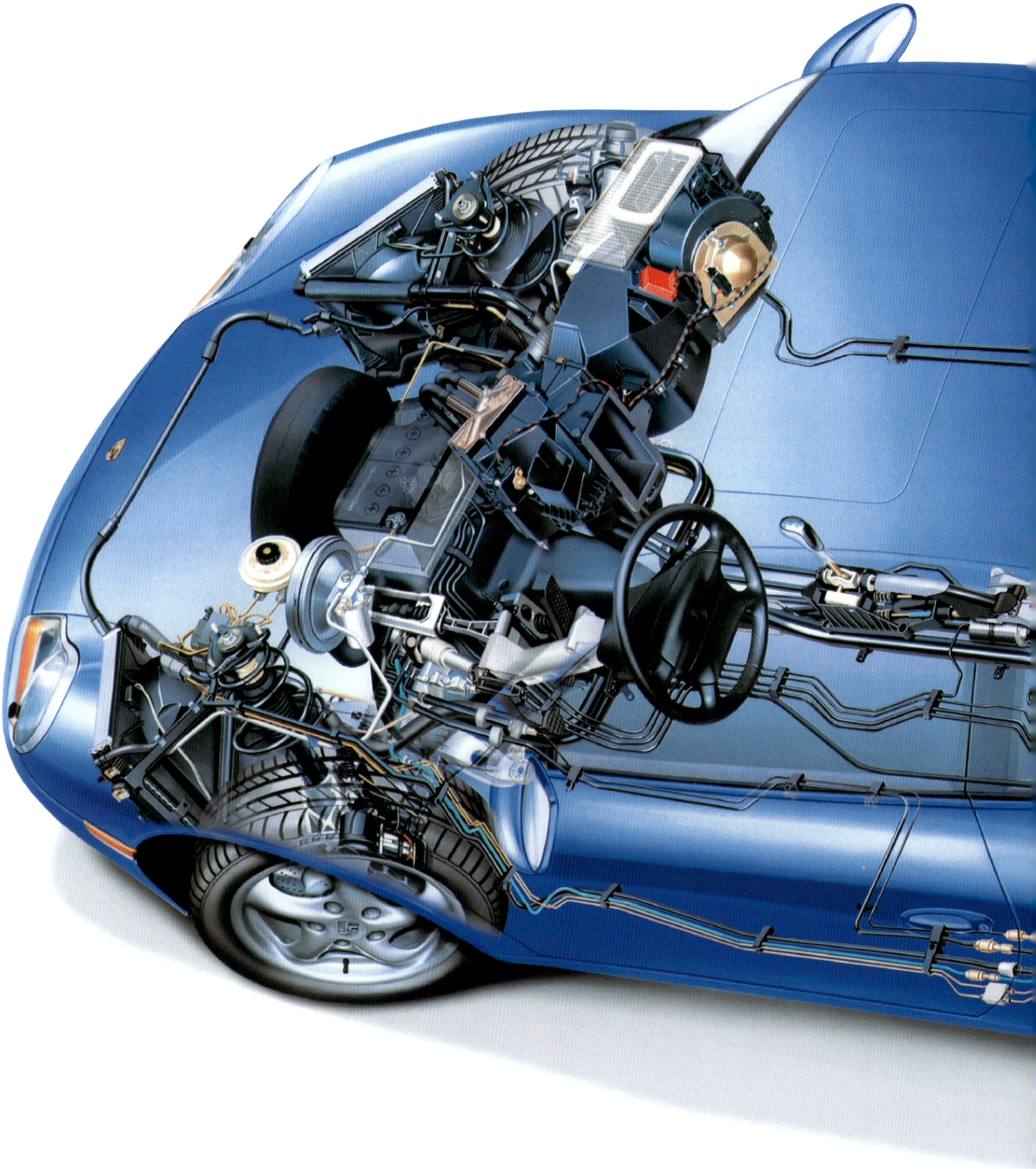

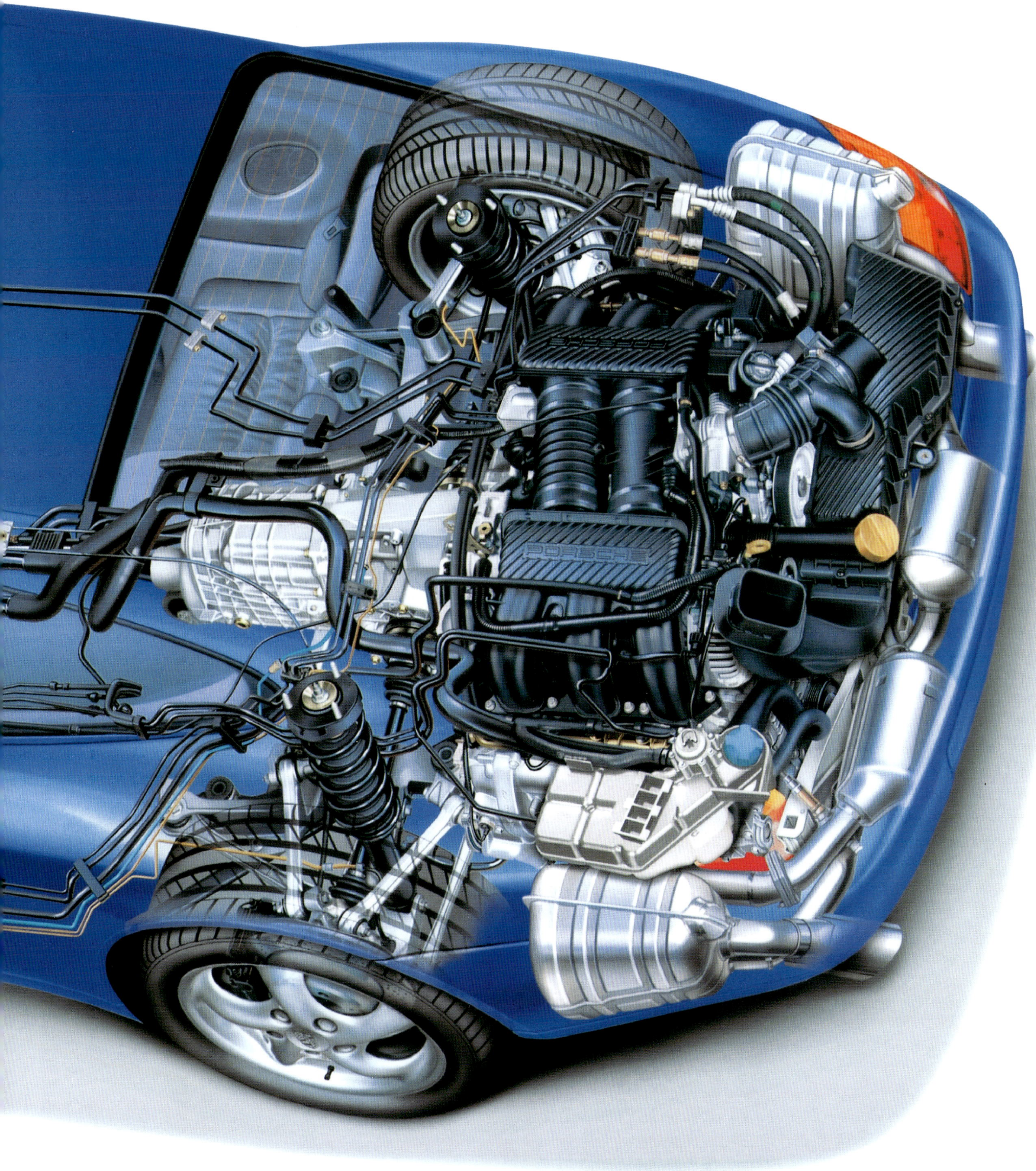
PORSCHE

The Engine of the new Carrera

A Virtual Tour of a Powerplant

A guided tour of a remarkable example of modern mechanical architecture

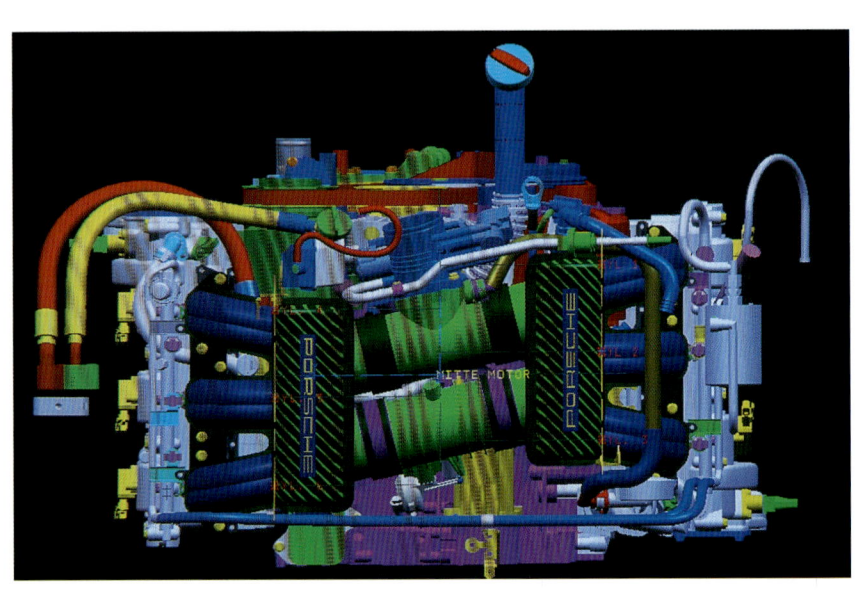

The computer paints a multicolored picture of the boxer engine.

Ladies and gentlemen, we see before us a remarkable example of modern mechanical architecture. The low, compact design of the boxer engine is clearly demonstrated by our new powerplant, which bears the type designation 96/1.

The new design is 70 millimeters shorter and 120 mm lower than its predecessor. Its façade boasts clean, functional lines. Instead of cooling fins, this powerplant exhibits a smooth water jacket. The front face of the engine is dominated by the poly-V belt which drives the alternator, hydraulic pump and air conditioning compressor. Clearly visible channels for coolant and lubricating oil incorporated in its cast housing signal that this design embodies a high degree of functionality.

Climbing to the top, we come to the public entrance of our new powerplant. This is the oil filler neck, which, like the jetways used in modern airports, may be extended for access. I hope you have all donned your protective clothing and brought along your flashlights, as we will soon encounter the finest synthetic motor oil and be engulfed in darkness. Please watch your step as you descend.

Here we are, inside the main structure of our powerplant. All around us, we see the vertically split crankcase. Please note the outstanding surface finish and fine structure of the walls. This is pressure-cast aluminum alloy, which can be worked to such a fine finish at a very reasonable cost.

The large metal component on our left is the central bearing carrier for the seven-bearing crankshaft. It is bolted to the crankcase halves, and absorbs the forces that result when 300 horsepower (221 kW) are generated at 6800 rpm. Naturally, this requires a high degree of rigidity. Behind this wall of aluminum, poured in a permanent-mold process, are sturdy cast-steel bearing webs. The bearing webs of the Carrera engine are even stiffer than those of the Boxster powerplant. Please direct your attention to the openings in the wall; these are oil nozzles for cooling the underside of the pistons.

The three beams high above us are, as you may have guessed, the connecting rods. They have a length of 118 millimeters, and are made of forged steel. The unaided eye will hardly be able to see the parting line on the bottom ends. After forging, the bottoms of the connecting rods are microscopically scored by a laser and then, using a very powerful machine, deliberately broken off. The crystalline surface of the fracture presents an ideal joint when the connecting rod is bolted together again.

If you will direct your gaze farther to the right, you will see that the connecting rods disappear into three large pipes. These are the cylinders on this side of the horizontally opposed, or "boxer" engine. They are made by Kolbenschmidt, using that company's proprietary "Lokasil" process. In contrast to the crankcase walls, the cylinders are made of a hypereutectoid alloy (if I may use the technical term), which simply means that there is a high proportion of silicon in the aluminum alloy. Now look though this magnifying glass and note that the cylinder walls are by no means smooth. In fact they are laced by a network of tiny canyons. This is intentional; aluminum has been etched away, and what remains is a craggy landscape of silicon cliffs. Silicon is hard and wear resistant. And why do we have valleys between the cliffs? Yes, of course, because they

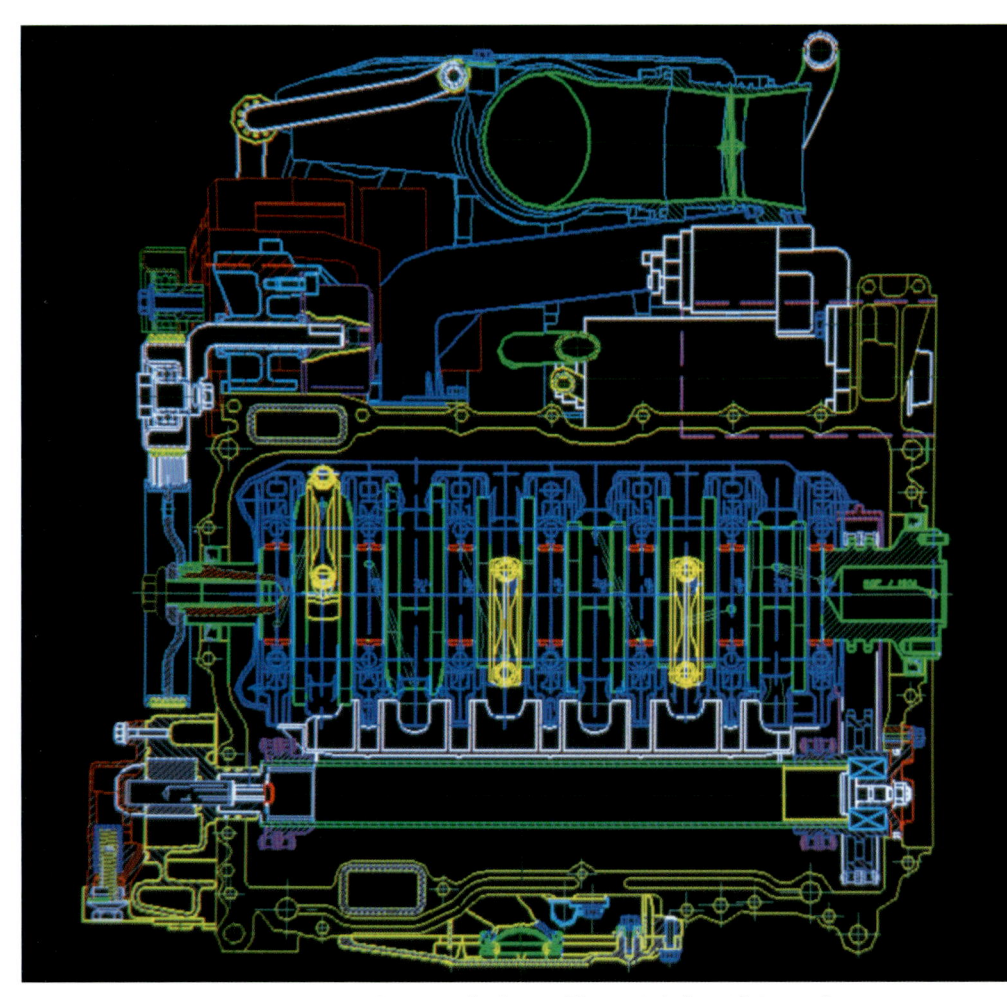

Anatomy of a boxer. The crankshaft, with its twelve counterweights, runs in seven bearings. Below it, rotating at half speed, is the intermediate shaft for the camshaft drive.

hold lubricating oil. How are the crankcase and the Lokasil cylinders joined? The explanation sounds simple: the six pipes are placed in a mold, and aluminum is poured around them. But as simple as it sounds, the process caused a fair number of headaches among the engineers before the method was perfected.

Over here, in cylinder number six, the piston is in a position we call bottom dead center. (Even though we don't have a "top" or "bottom" in a horizontally opposed engine, only right and left). The piston is squeeze-cast of aluminum alloy. It is fitted with three rings, two for compression and one for oil control. Its diameter is 96 millimeters and it covers a distance of 78 mm with each stroke. This gives us a displacement of 3387 cc. For the numerologists among you, the cylinder spacing may be of interest. At the now-traditional spacing of 118 mm, it is identical to that of the previous air-cooled engine. If it ever becomes necessary to increase the displacement of our powerplant, there are built-in reserves to be exploited.

Yes, good, thank you for bringing up the intermediate shaft, which is located below the crankshaft and is driven from it by means of a double chain. This is not visible from our location, nor are the additional double-chain drives to the exhaust camshafts on the left and right. The reason is that the camshaft drive for the left cylinder bank is taken from the back end of the

Every connecting rod is already broken. Splitting the bottom end is achieved by deliberately fracturing the rod.

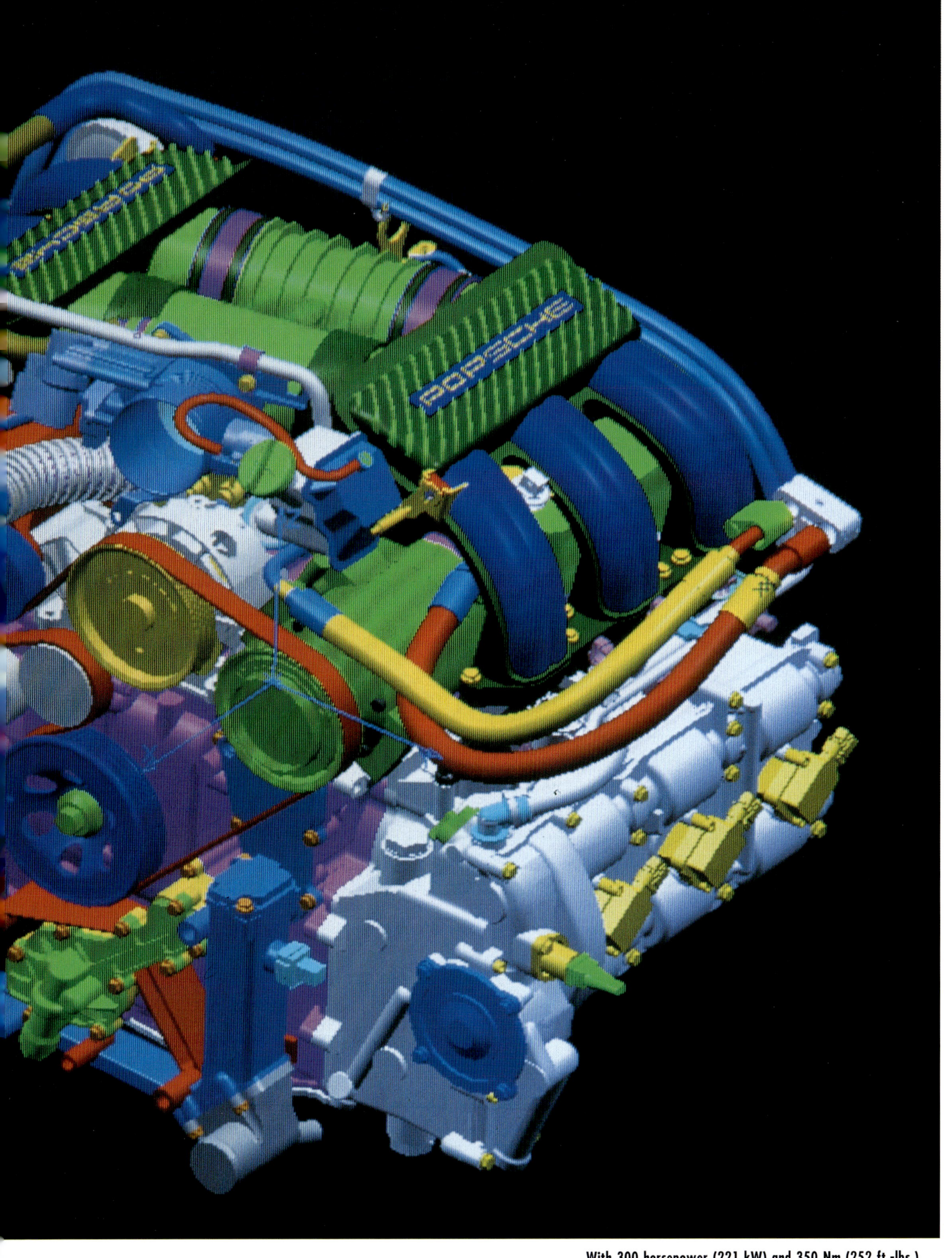

With 300 horsepower (221 kW) and 350 Nm (252 ft.-lbs.) of torque, the new six-cylinder boxer engine outperforms its predecessor, yet is 70 mm (nearly 3 inches) shorter, and 120 mm (nearly 5 inches) lower.

The intake system arches over the engine; its two resonance chambers are connected by a passage which is closed by a butterfly at midrange engine speeds.

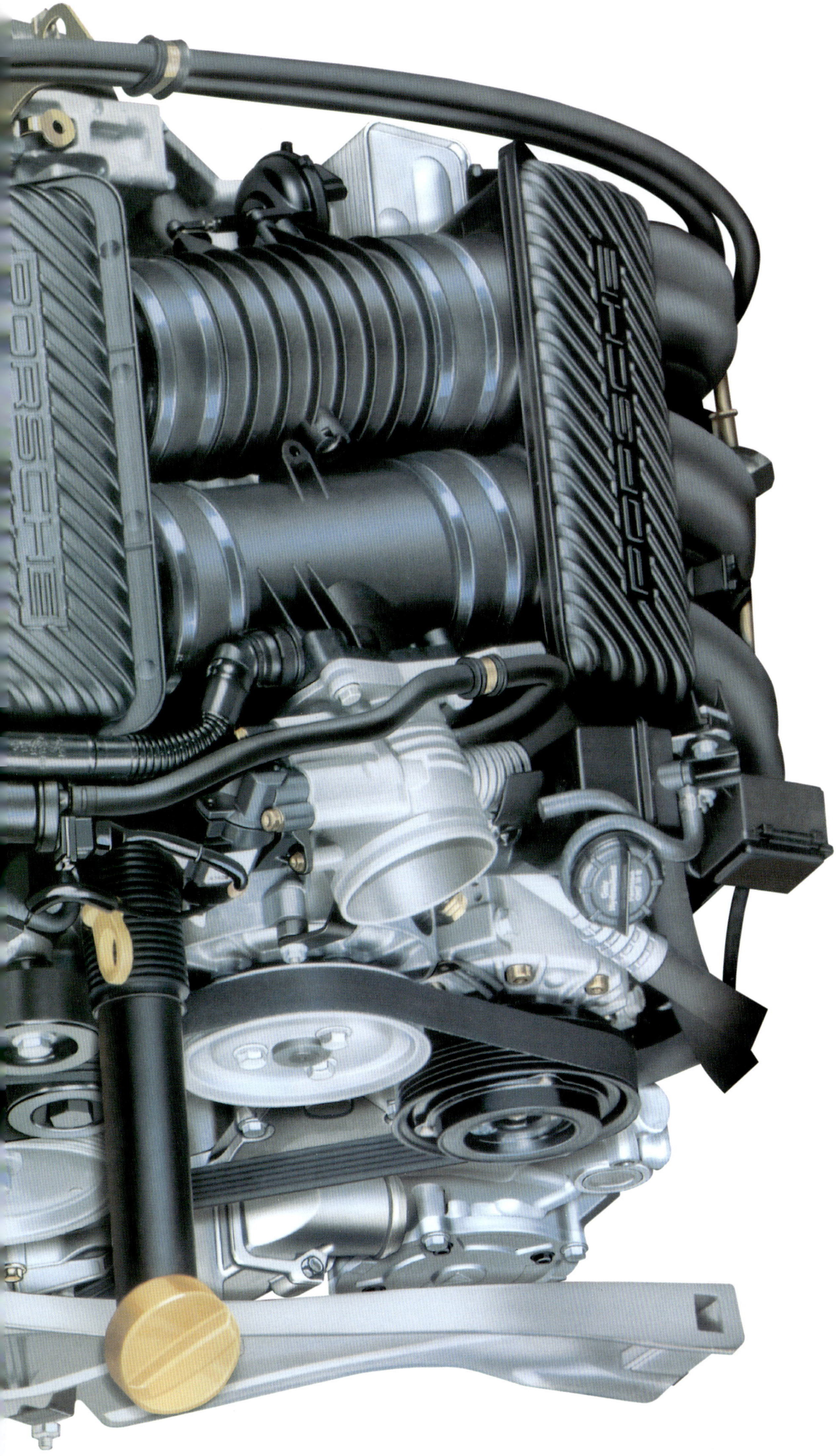
PORSCHE
PORSCHE

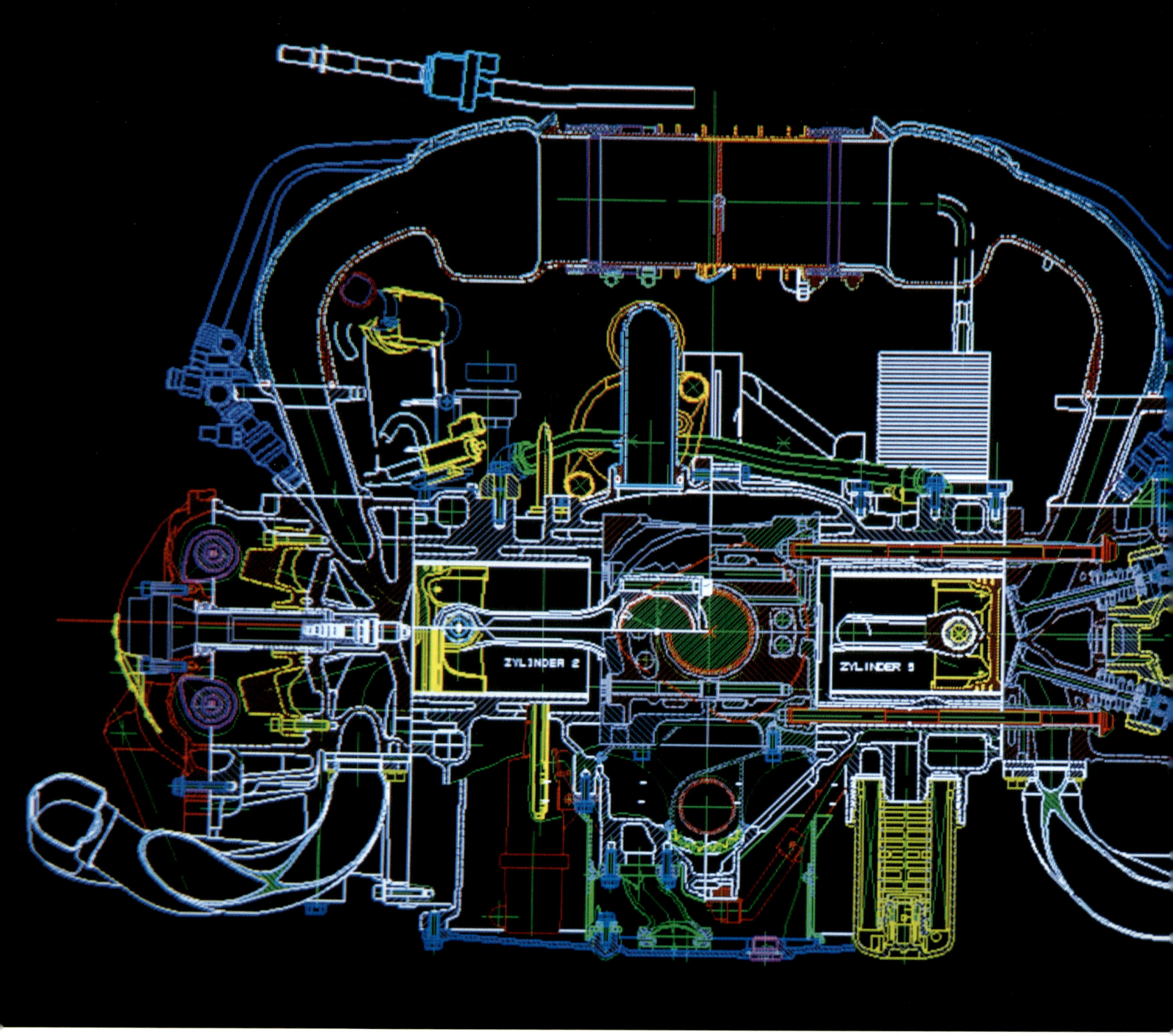

The boxer engine itself is extremely low. The complex intake system above and the integral dry sump below, holding ten liters of oil, give the powerplant a more voluminous appearance.

intermediate shaft, while the cams for the right cylinder bank are driven from the front. This isn't nearly as complicated as it sounds, and is very functional as it permits a more compact engine design. The two timing chains and their housings exploit the space made available by the offset between the two cylinder banks.

By the way, we are now on the ground floor of the boxer engine. Below us is the cellar, with its oil supply. The engineers call this the "integral dry sump lubrication system." They designed it so that oil (more than ten liters of it) can flow out of the bearing carrier directly into the oil tank. We can't get there from here, but then we don't want to take an oil bath right now, do we?

Please follow me through the crankcase ventilation system and into the intake system. You can't hear it now, but we are in a resonant induction system, in which tremendous pressure waves are generated while the engine is operating. Farther forward is a throttle butterfly, which opens when the gas pedal is pressed. On one side you will note a small passageway with a flap of its own. This exploits the resonance effect, opening above 2720 rpm and closing again below 5120 rpm. This changes the resonant behavior of the inducted air mass, and in ideal cases produces volumetric efficiency in excess of 100 percent.

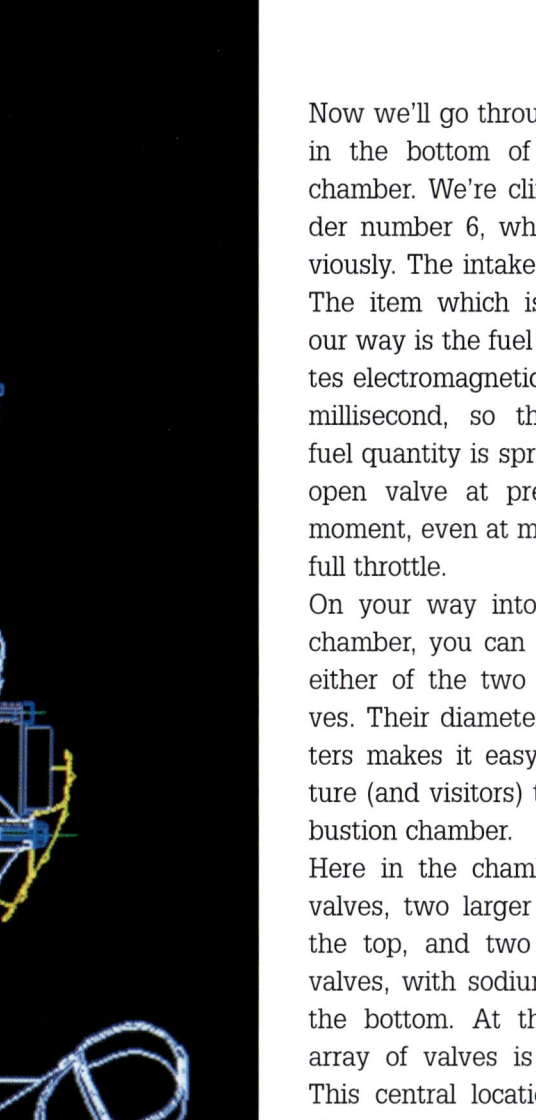

Now we'll go through this trap door in the bottom of the combustion chamber. We're climbing into cylinder number 6, which we saw previously. The intake valves are open. The item which is partly blocking our way is the fuel injector. It operates electromagnetically, timed to the millisecond, so that the required fuel quantity is sprayed through the open valve at precisely the right moment, even at maximum rpm and full throttle.

On your way into the combustion chamber, you can of course choose either of the two open intake valves. Their diameter of 37,1 millimeters makes it easy for fuel-air mixture (and visitors) to enter the combustion chamber.

Here in the chamber we see four valves, two larger intake valves at the top, and two smaller exhaust valves, with sodium-filled stems, at the bottom. At the center of the array of valves is the spark plug. This central location ensures complete, consistent ignition of the mixture. Unfortunately, with the piston in this position, we can't look past the valves into the stainless steel exhaust system. If you're interested, you may do that from cylinder number 3, but I can assure you that you will see nothing more nor less than an oxygen sensor and a highly effective metal monolith catalytic converter.

Here in the combustion chamber, the charge is compressed by a factor of 11.3 to one. (Of course, we wouldn't want to subject our visitors to such pressures!) Here, in the resulting tiny space, is where the fuel is burned. Our engine prefers Super Plus with a research octane rating of 98, but lower octane fuel will also work. Cylinder-selective knock control corrects the ignition timing as necessary, and only for that cylinder which is suffering from irregular combustion. In this way, the engine easily runs on regular-grade fuel, even if such weaker cocktails aren't its favorite brew.

Unfortunately, the path to the timing gear housing is a bit awkward. Unlike castles and palaces, engines aren't made with visitors in mind.

Here, on this side of the cylinder head, we find the mechanical systems which manage the gas flow into and out of the combustion chamber. The lower of these two is the exhaust camshaft, the intake cam is above us. Connecting the two is a chain and a tensioner which can also change the timing of the intake cam relative to the exhaust cam. The intake timing can change by as

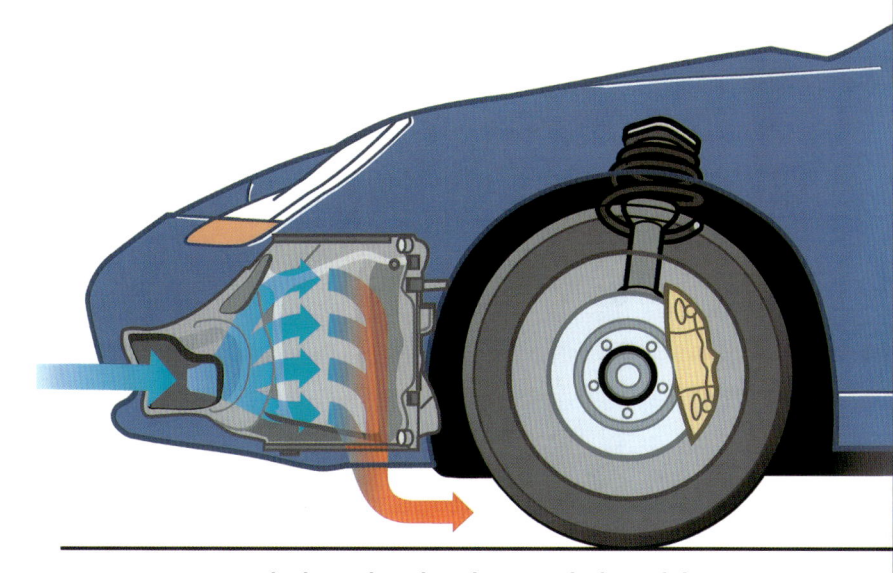

The ductwork to the radiators at the front of the Carrera is extremely convoluted. Twenty liters of coolant circulate through the system.

much as 25 degrees. Like the adaptive intake manifold, this intervention in the normal course of gas flow improves volumetric efficiency in certain engine rpm ranges, resulting in increased power and torque. For the driver, this translates into better "pull" across a wide rpm band. The twelve cams visible here actuate the valves by means of so-called bucket tappets, which really bear a closer resemblance to coffee mugs without handles. Inside these tappets are tiny hydraulic cylinders which use engine oil pressure to take up valve clearance.

Unfortunately, I can't show you these items from here, but my colleague would be happy to show you these when you tour the spare parts department. There you will also have the opportunity to see the conically-wound valve springs and their small spring retainers. This relatively recent engine design practice saves weight and space.

45

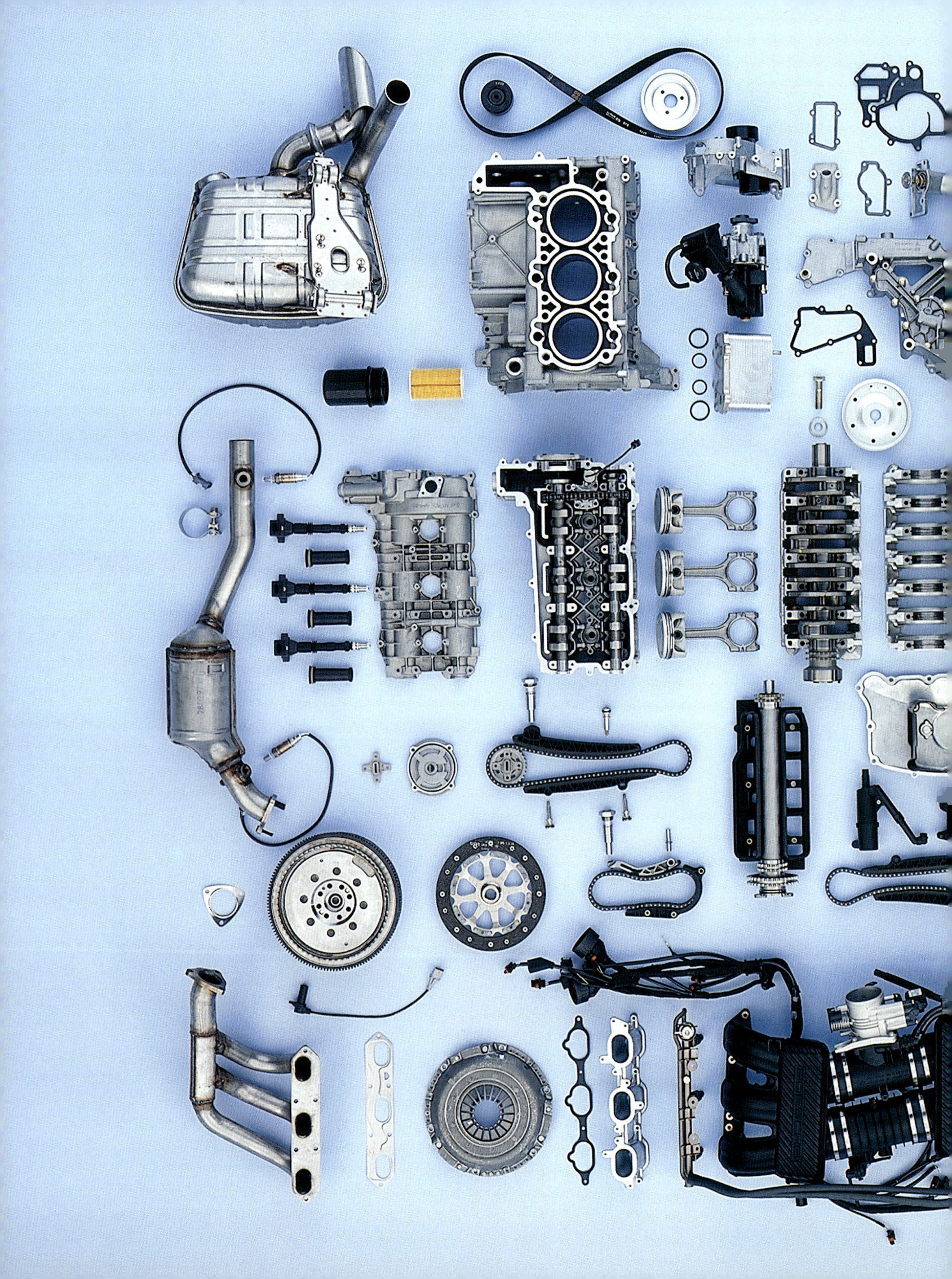

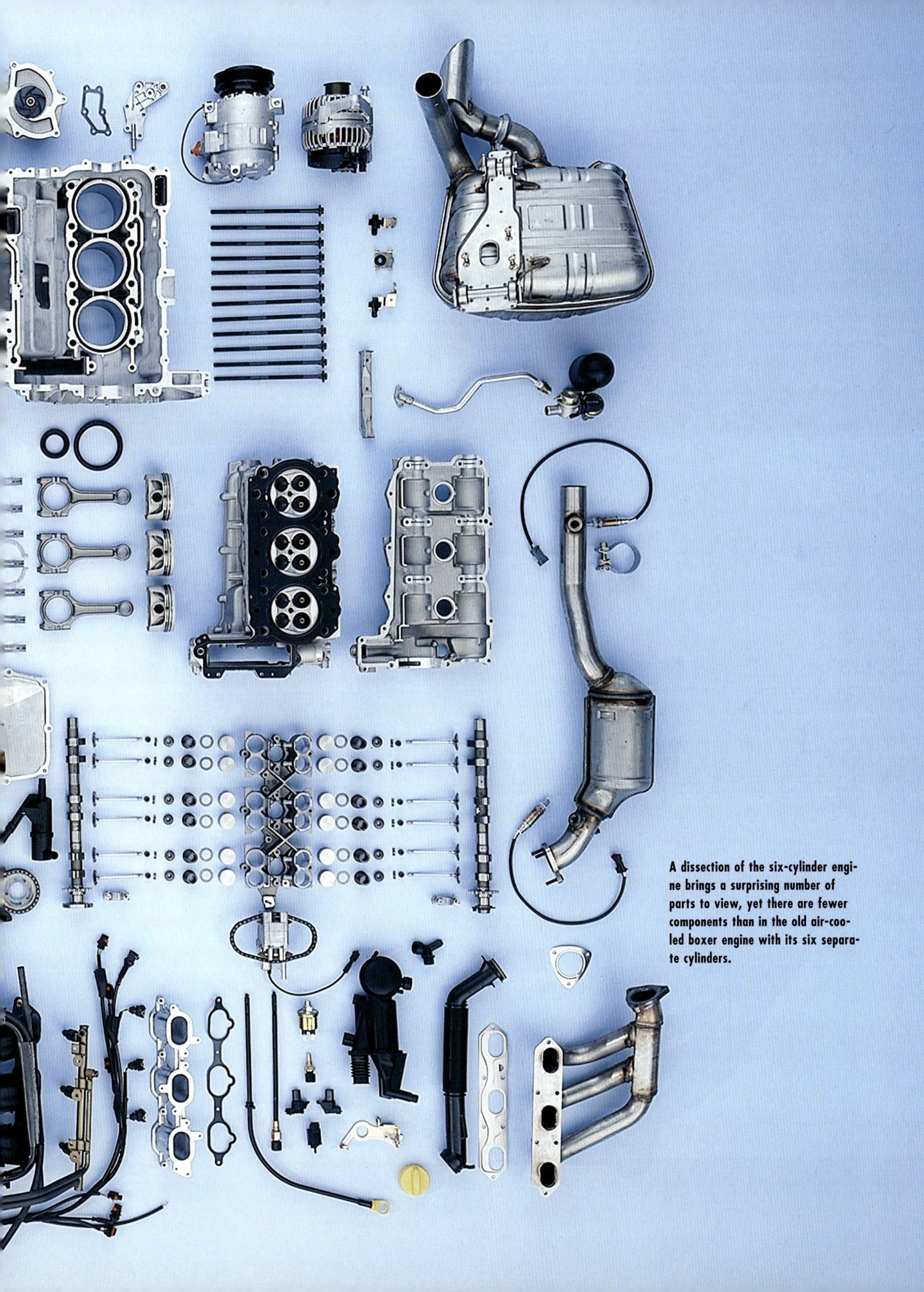

A dissection of the six-cylinder engine brings a surprising number of parts to view, yet there are fewer components than in the old air-cooled boxer engine with its six separate cylinders.

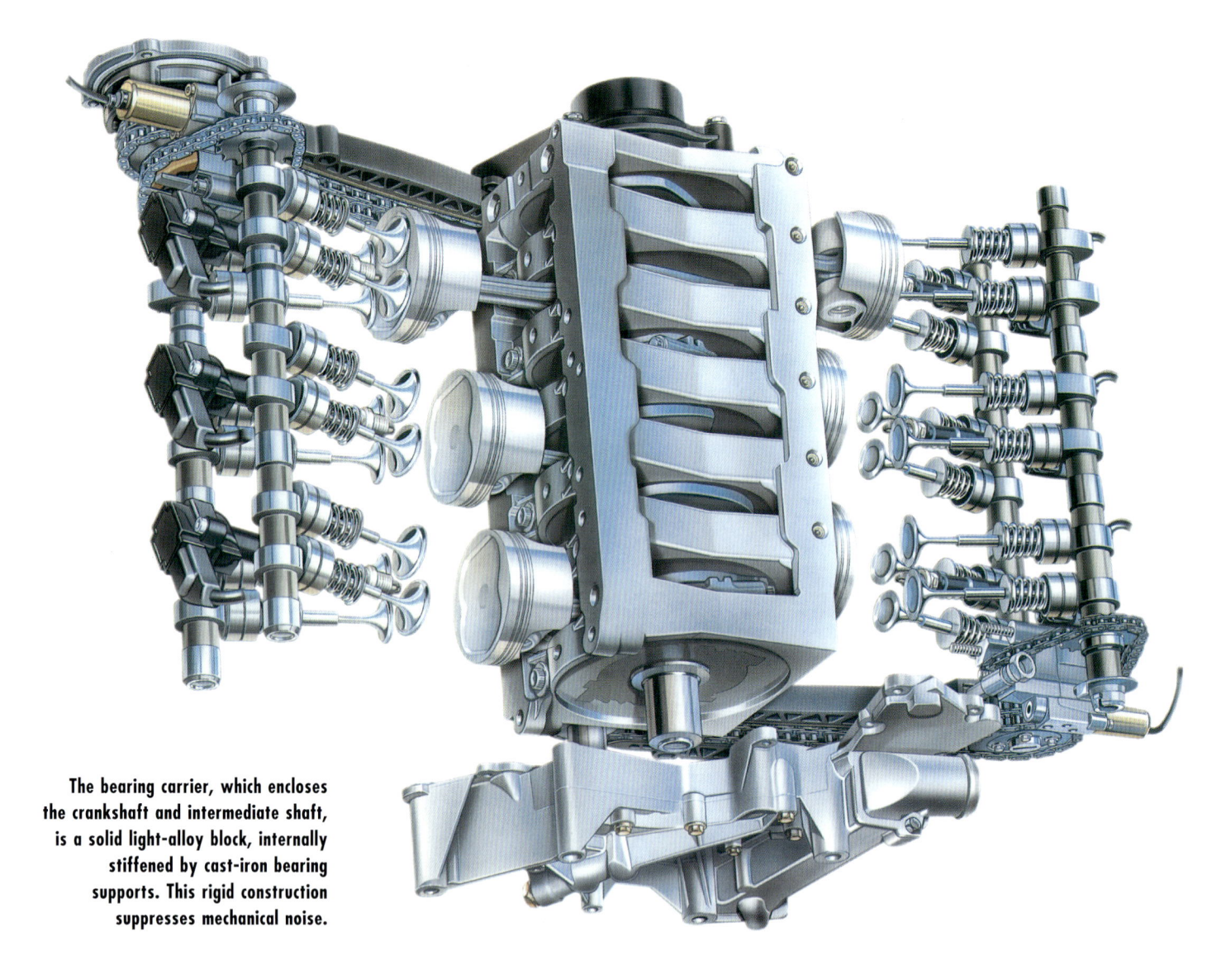

The bearing carrier, which encloses the crankshaft and intermediate shaft, is a solid light-alloy block, internally stiffened by cast-iron bearing supports. This rigid construction suppresses mechanical noise.

The fact that here, too, we find only small amounts of oil on the floor is due to the scavenge pumps, one in each cylinder head, which draw off excess oil and return it to the integral oil sump.

Even while the engine is running, temperatures here in the timing gear case remain moderate, thanks to water cooling. Coolant flows through channels in the wall that separates us from the combustion chambers. After many successful years using air cooling, Porsche's engineers have naturally made every effort to design an especially good water cooling system. As is typical at Porsche, they learned valuable lessons on the race track: three world championship titles in Formula One with the water-cooled TAG engine, plus countless victories with water-cooled boxer engines in endurance racing should put any question of Porsche's competence with water cooling to rest. Porsche did a thorough job, and the new boxer powerplant is cooled like a racing engine.

Unlike normal production engines, the coolant doesn't simply flow down the cylinder bank, from number 1 through 3, or 4 through 6. Instead, it flows crosswise through the engine block. That way, it doesn't transfer heat from one cylinder to the next; rather, each cylinder is supplied with coolant at the same temperature. Cool water reaches the underside of each cylinder bank, and, after passing the cylinders, warmer water is drawn away from the top. To ensure that temperatures remain balanced, the coolant stream is divided as it enters the crankcase; part of the stream flows around the upper part of the cylinders, which run at relatively cool temperatures. The other part of the stream flows through the cylinder heads, reaching the hot exhaust side first.

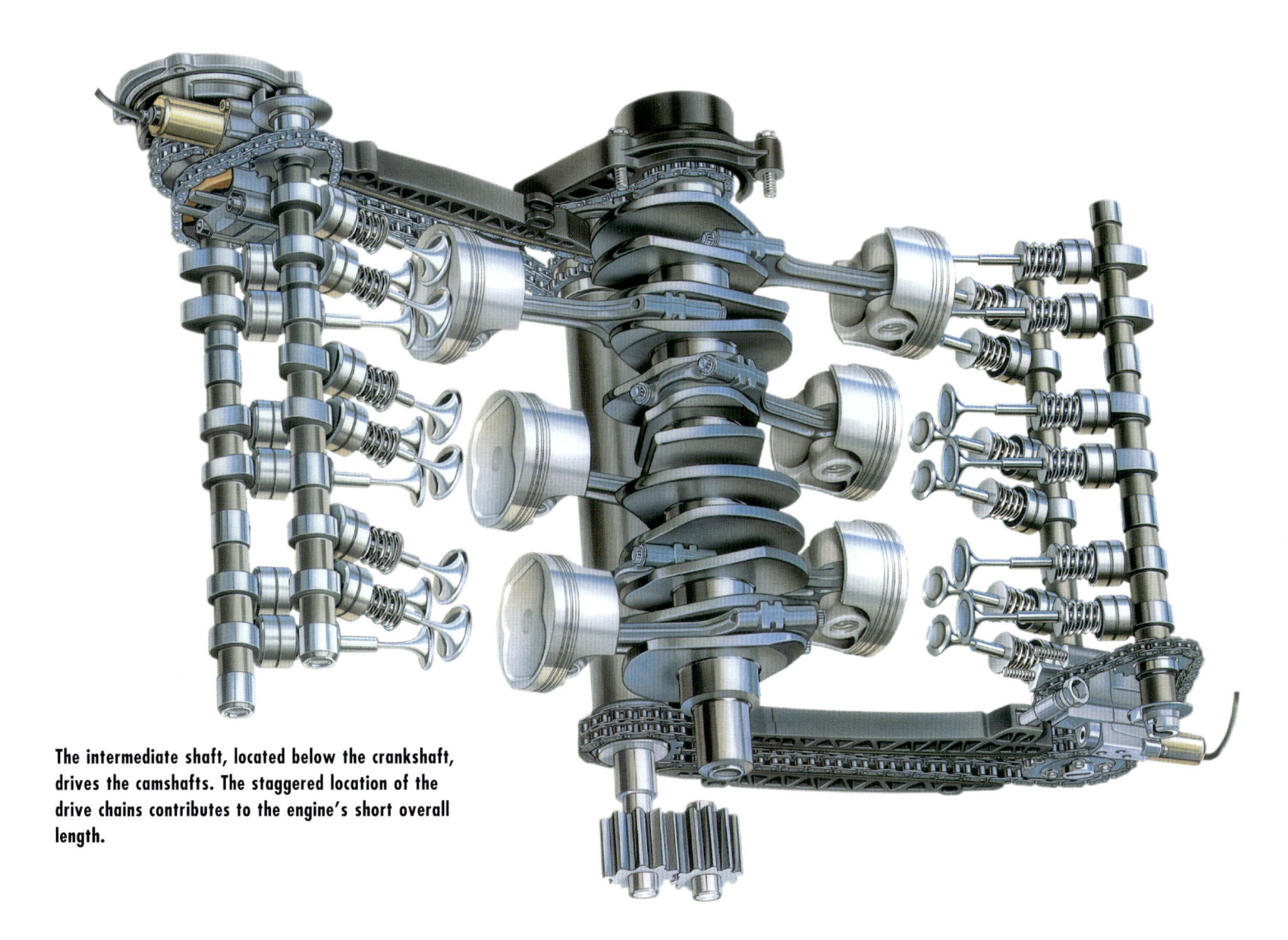

The intermediate shaft, located below the crankshaft, drives the camshafts. The staggered location of the drive chains contributes to the engine's short overall length.

The gentleman in the second row asked about oil cooling. Very simple. We have an oil/water heat exchanger, mounted directly on the crankcase without any hose connections. The neat thing about this design is that the coolant, which warms up quickly, heats up the engine oil until it reaches its operating temperature. If the oil temperature continues to rise above 90 or 100 degrees Celsius (that's 195 to 212 degrees Fahrenheit, for our visitors from the United States), heat flows in the opposite direction, from the oil into the water.

Now we're ready for the dynamometer test. I'd like to ask our esteemed guests to leave the engine and follow me to the control room.

Please observe the torque curve on the monitor. As the computer, which is standing in for our test engineer, applies full throttle at 1000 rpm, the readout already shows a respectable 250 Newton-meters of torque (or 180 foot-pounds, for those accustomed to the American system of units). You may not think 36 horsepower at this low engine speed is much of a beginning, but the Carrera has more than enough power in each of its six gears. As the revs climb, we can see the ideally flat torque curve. Even before the tachometer reaches 3000 rpm, torque rises above 300 Newton-meters (216 foot-pounds), and climbs steadily to its peak value of 350 Nm (or 252 ft.-lbs.) The power curve climbs upward even more steeply. (Even a Carrera would have trouble climbing such a steep grade). As it spins upward through ever-higher speeds, the powerplant reaches its peak output of 300 horsepower (221 kilowatts) at 6800 rpm. To show you what happens if the engine overspeeds, our colleague the computer will stay on the throttle: 7000, 7100, 7200, 7300, that's all she'll do; the rev limiter puts an end to our excesses, without the slightest trace of stuttering from the engine. If we were on the Autobahn, we would be travelling at 300 kilometers per hour, or if you prefer, 186 miles per hour.

That concludes our tour. I'd like to wish all of you a safe journey home, and thank you for your interest.

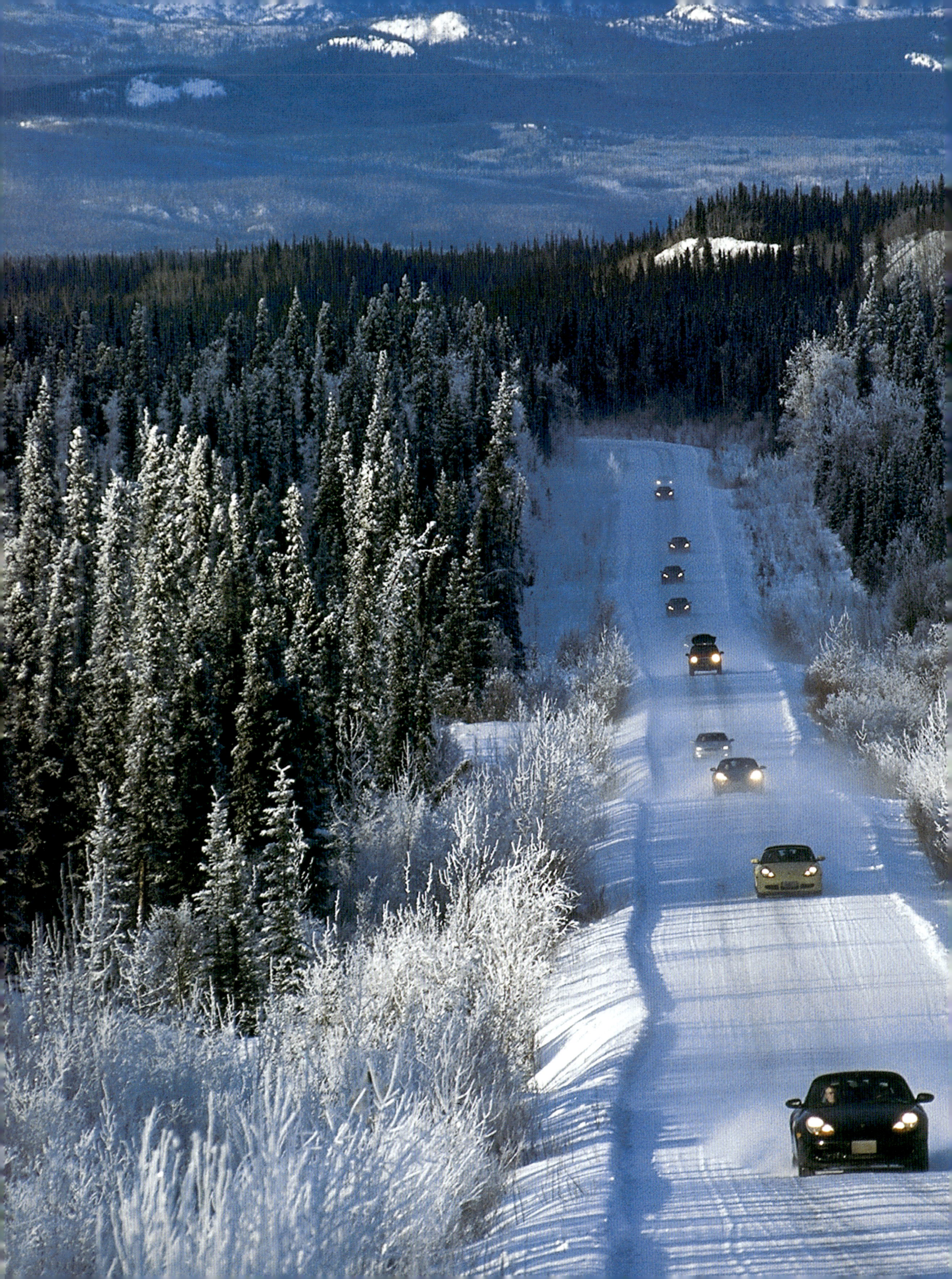

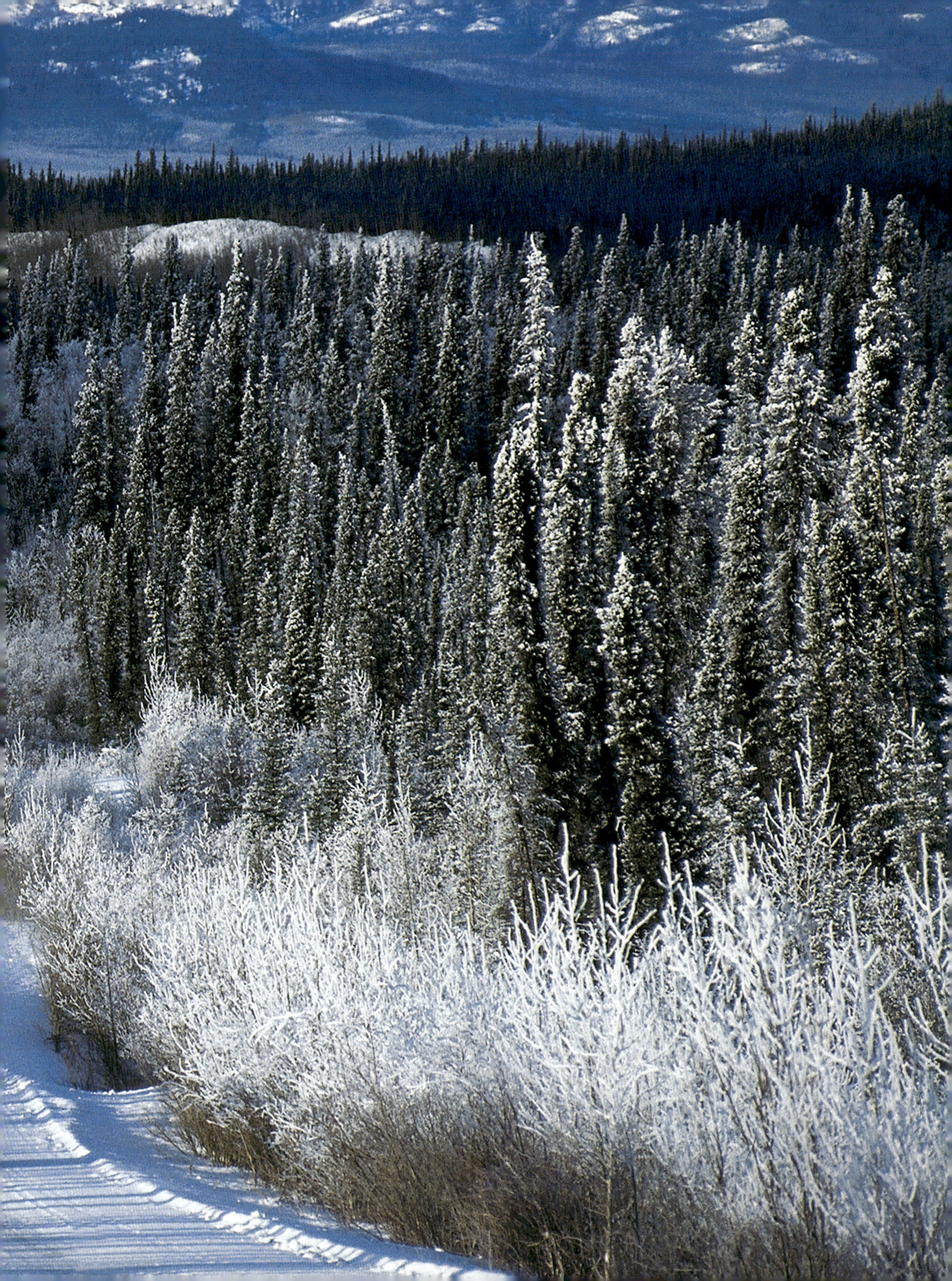

Cold-weather testing the new 911 on the Alaska Highway

Burning Snow

Cold-weather testing the new 911 on the Alaska Highway

Rainer Wüst and Hans-Bernd Weiner check test data stored in a notebook computer.

Wintersport à la Porsche presents an annual challenge for the engineers and test drivers of the Porsche R&D Center. On the icy roads of the Canadian Arctic, every workday lasts twelve hours. Each leg of the test driving route extends about 1000 km, or 600 miles – lonely miles close to the Arctic Circle. For two entire weeks, the crews work every day, no vacations, no Sundays, no excuses.

The eleven Porsche engines recall their ordeal:

"The worst time was at Watson Lake, where for a few hours during the night, the mercury dropped to -32° Celsius (-26° Fahrenheit). It was almost enough to give us engines circulation problems."

Under such conditions, the two circulatory systems of the boxer engine have a much more difficult time than in our milder climes. The engine oil has almost changed its state from a liquid to a solid, it no longer flows but rather lies like a lump of molasses, thick and heavy, in the integrated dry sump. The coolant, too, is turning lumpy, despite being laced with antifreeze. Its consistency resembles that of a light sorbet – only about 35 degrees colder.

As these engines are awakened at 6 AM for the beginning of their work shift, their bearings are not so much lubricated as greased. Movement is difficult, the crankshaft turns without enthusiasm, the pistons struggle against congealed oil on the cylinder walls, the oil pump works more like a grease gun, the water pump churns through slush. The starter motor draws on every one of its 1600 Watts, struggling just to turn the engine over, but the battery refuses to yield the full measure of its power; it is simply too cold, and it excuses itself, citing the laws of physics. Nevertheless, the engineers have taken all this into consideration, and finally the crankshaft turns at modest speed, the valves keep time for the four strokes of the combustion cycle, fuel, so reluctant to vaporize, finally ignites and burns. The engine comes to life, and as warmth begins to flow, suppleness returns to its many bearings.

Heinz Bernhard, leader of the Arctic expedition, recalls that "The adventure of an early morning cold start belongs to the past. In the old days, we used to see glowing starter cables." The test crew recalls that even good quality European jumper cables fell apart in the cold. Bernhard tells us that "At forty below, the insulation was so brittle that it simply cracked and fell off when the cables were coiled up again, so that to jump start a car, we held bare wires in our hands."

In contrast to such tales, worthy of Jack London, the frigid night at Watson Lake in 1997 had no dramatic moments. The eleven test cars, some of them new Carreras, some Boxsters, started willingly, shrouding themselves with dense clouds of steam in the predawn gloom. The eleven Porsches take in Watson Lake with the same otherworldly detachment as Comet Hale-Bopp, standing overhead in the Arctic night.

Watson Lake lies a thousand miles east of Anchorage and 1350 miles north of Vancouver, in the Yukon Territory, along the Alaska Highway. The town is preparing for its centennial in 1998. Here, the vehicles of choice are four-wheel-drive pickups or Chevrolets appropriately named after this Canadian province. Cars park near electrical outlets, and block heaters keep their engines warm at night. The preferred winter sport vehicle is the snowmobile. The local gas station sells a brand called Totem Oil (which in German would mean "Dead Oil.") Hougen's Department Store sells pans and any other equipment needed by gold prospectors. Genuine gold nuggets may be found at Murdoch's. At the Northern Beaver Post, we may be entertained (or perhaps not) by yet another Elvis clone. The pinnacle of luxury is represented by the waterbed suite at the Big Horn Hotel.

The Sign Forest of Watson Lake.

The main attraction at Watson Lake is the Sign Post Forest, which was planted in 1941. The American government sent 1500 troops and 7500 civilian construction workers to build the Alaskan Highway in the incredible time of eight months and twelve days; in the middle of the Second World War, this strategic road from Dawson Creek, British Columbia to Delta Junction and later Fairbanks, Alaska, was of crucial importance. The 1500-mile gravel road through the nearly unexplored Arctic was built to counter a possible Japanese (or, later, Russian) landing in Alaska. The Watson Lake of the 1940s was no doubt a more tranquil place than it is today. For the long winter, there was not yet a floodlit ski area, and in the brief summer, fishing was the only after-hours recreation as the golf course had not yet been built. The troops tasked with building the road had every reason to be homesick. In 1942, Carl K. Lindley of the U.S. Army hit upon the idea of bringing along a city limit sign from his home town of Danville, Illinois. Lindsay's fellow troops soon copied this idea to overcome their own homesickness. Later travellers continued the tradition, and by 1990, the number of signs had risen to 10,000. Of course, Weissach, Germany is represented in the Sign Forest of Watson Lake.

Its sign collection distinguishes Watson Lake from its nearby neighbors Ross River (232 miles

Refueling stop in Watson Lake. Temperature: -28°C, -18°F.

away), Johnsons Crossing (202 miles) or Whitehorse (283 miles), all of which live in the memory of the 1898 gold rush. Such solitude and vast empty expanses add up to long, fast daily runs averaging 60 miles per hour over a solid layer of ice, which, at five degrees below zero Fahrenheit, is hard and grippy. On this day, we've passed Whitehorse, part of the Klondike Highway, and Robert Campbell's winding logging road. This day's short but frigid 475-mile run ends in daylight, even before the early dusk of a winter night at the 60th parallel throws Watson Lake into darkness.

The workday ends with a critique of the day's exercise. Chief engineer Horst Marchart, sojourning at the edge of the Arctic to inspect the progress of the testing program, leads a brief discussion. Bernd Kahnau, project manager of the new Carrera program, is not at all unhappy with the progress. "In the past, we had a lot more to discuss." Now, in their evening sessions, the team discusses mostly minor matters. A slight howling is heard in fifth and sixth gear; the transmission supplier, Getrag, will have to address this. A rattle is coming from the induction system at part throttle; the cold air hardens the thin composite intake runners, and they generate undesirable resonance effects. The production part will have to be molded with slightly thicker sections. At temperatures below -20°C (-4°F), the idle speed is still not where it should be, but this can be corrected by reprogramming the electronic engine management system. On test cars, such corrections can be done on the spot by means of a notebook computer attached to the Motronic control unit.

Each evening's conference is followed by supper in proper cowboy manner; travelling through Canada, the Porsche crew goes from steakhouse to steakhouse. Great slabs of beef are devoured to the accompaniment of potato chips or country potatoes, cubed and pan fried. A bottle of Moose Head beer caps off a long day's work.

The night is shorter than usual – there are 560 miles to cover between Watson Lake and the airfield at Fort St. John. Horst Marchart's flight to the United States leaves at 14:30 – so the morning's testing is advanced to 4 AM. It promises to be a bitterly cold night.

By 4 AM, the mercury has sunk to -32°C (-26°F), and the air almost seems to solidify. Breath hangs as a dense fog. Like every other morning, the first shift goes to work on an empty stomach; this early, there's no hope of finding breakfast anywhere in town. And using the coffee machine in the motel room would have robbed us of five more minutes of sleep.

Bernd Kahnau takes me along in his Carrera. The headlights reflect back from hard, smooth ice. The water-jacketed boxer engine sounds reliable yet eager in its lower rev ranges. Although this is not the time or place for full-throttle blasts to 7000 rpm, winter tires help speed our progress. Bernd Kahnau recalls the bad old days:

"Imagine coming to your car on a morning like this, and all four tires are flat. That happened a lot back then. The cold makes rubber hard and brittle. Tubeless tires simply lost pressure."

I would rather not think about that, preferring to bask in the warmth streaming from the heating ducts, which gradually dispel the cold inside the car's cabin. But for Bernd Kahnau, this comfort seems to reawaken icy recollections of earlier, air-cooled days:

"Thirty years ago, with outside air temperatures like these, we measured a stagnation temperature in the footwells of 3°C (37°F). And it stayed that cold all day long. Today, we turn the climate control to 20 or 24°C (68° or 75°F), and in less than 15 minutes we have a perfectly comfortable working environment."

Our course leads southward. Here, the Alaska Highway is more travelled than it is north of Watson Lake. The road has been spread, not with corrosive salt, but, in the manner of the region, with coarse gravel. On occasion, it rattles against the fender liners. In contrast to the attitude we might expect of most Porsche owners, Bernd Kahnau welcomes this noise:

"The plastic liners in the wheel wells have to hold up even under these temperatures, but that really isn't a problem these days. What still causes us some concern is a mixture of snow and gravel, which packs into the wheel wells and, what's worse, into the wheels themselves. At best, this results in a severe imbalance; in a worst-case scenario, this ring of ice, with its sharp embedded rocks, grinds against the brake caliper. And we can't do anything about it except to install calipers that will survive this treatment."

In the dawn, we can see the northern fringe of the Rocky Mountains, which here rise to a mere 3000 meters (9800 feet). In the summer, this is vacationland, with the Sentinel Range and Muncho Lake Provincial Park, 1100 meter (3600 ft.) Muncho Pass, and 2972 meter (9750 ft.) Mt. Roosevelt in the Wokkpash Recreation Area.

Sometimes, Bernd Kahnau sees the mountainscape from a completely different perspective. "In the valleys, we can run into totally unexpected thermal problems. At Eagle Plains, up near the Arctic Circle, on our way to Inuvik, we once went into a valley at 40 degrees below zero. At first, this had no effect, but then when the cars left this deepfreeze for a warmer zone with higher humidity, the outside of the windows fogged up in seconds. We couldn't see a thing."

But that's not all that can happen to a supercooled car when moisture is allowed to play its tricks. Bernd Kahnau remembers frozen brake pads:

"Even if it's possible to break the rear pads loose when driving off, that doesn't help much, because on the icy road, the car just plows straight ahead, completely out of control, with frozen front wheels." Even more exciting were encounters with throttle icing and an engine that just continued to run at half throttle, no matter what the gas pedal did.

On our southern route, the temperature gradually climbs. We reach Ft. Nelson with its downright tropical -15°C (+5°F) just in time for the second breakfast seating (our first). For hungry truckers, there's a Burger King. A proper American breakfast, with hamburger and hash browns, hits the spot.

Farther south, the highway is flanked by thriving industry. The region is dotted by successful oil and natural gas wells. More than a few molecules of these fossil fuels have escaped into the atmosphere, and provide the area with its unique bouquet. The Motronic system of a Porsche can react to such an atmosphere and correct the fuel injection quantity. It's even possible that the exhaust leaving the test cars is a bit cleaner than it was going in.

The farther south we go, the more frequently we find the ice layer broken. The highway is rougher. In his role as intrepid test driver, Bernd Kahnau doesn't complain about the lack of comfort:

"This is good for judging body integrity. When all of the plastic parts, gaskets and seals have hardened in the cold, we get body noises which we would never hear in our mild German climate." Judging by the new 911's silent acceptance of these Arctic conditions, this is no longer a problem. The perfection I have experienced so far prompts the question whether such an arctic expedition is a routine exercise, or a series of surprises.

"It's the unexpected things that make it all worthwhile," says Kahnau. "During the last winter test, we had some bad experiences with icing in the crankcase ventilation system. When that stops working, pressure builds up in the crankcase, and the whole affair ends with an oily disaster. A relatively simple fix eliminated the problem once and for all."

All Porsche prototypes are painted matte black.

Average speed on snow: just under 100 km/h (62 mph).

The expense of sending a fleet of ten test cars and a Jeep Grand Cherokee service vehicle to the Canadian Arctic for two weeks serves to perfect the product. The program chip of the climate control system received its fine tuning in North America's icebox, perfected to provide optimal air distribution. The selected temperature is expected to remain constant, even if one drives from the tropics to the Arctic.

Fort St. John, British Columbia, exhibits a measure of urbane civility at the edge of the wilderness. With growing prosperity, the former way-station on the road to the Klondike gold fields has expanded into the surrounding countryside. The memory of more difficult times lives on in the annual gold-panning world championships, which take place every August 3 and 4. Otherwise, St. John is mainly concerned with oil and natural gas. But the climate here is mild enough to allow forests of spruce and fir, and in summer, grains are harvested. We have returned to that portion of our planet which is habitable throughout the year. The airport, which Horst Marchart reaches with time to spare, is a reminder of the Second World War; Americans built it as a tactical base, and later sold it to the Canadians. From here, airlines like North Caribou Air fly beyond the edge of civilization to Yellowknife, on the Great Slave Lake, or to Inuvik, on the Mackenzie River.

The objective of the day is Dawson Creek, on the Alberta border. The tallest building in town is a grain elevator. The surrounding prairie lies under a blanket of snow. We have covered just under a thousand kilometers, a good 600 miles. Getting out of the car, Bernd Kahnau summarizes the progress of the last few decades: "When we started doing winter tests, there were days when we only covered ten kilometers – six miles. And at the end, we were exhausted."

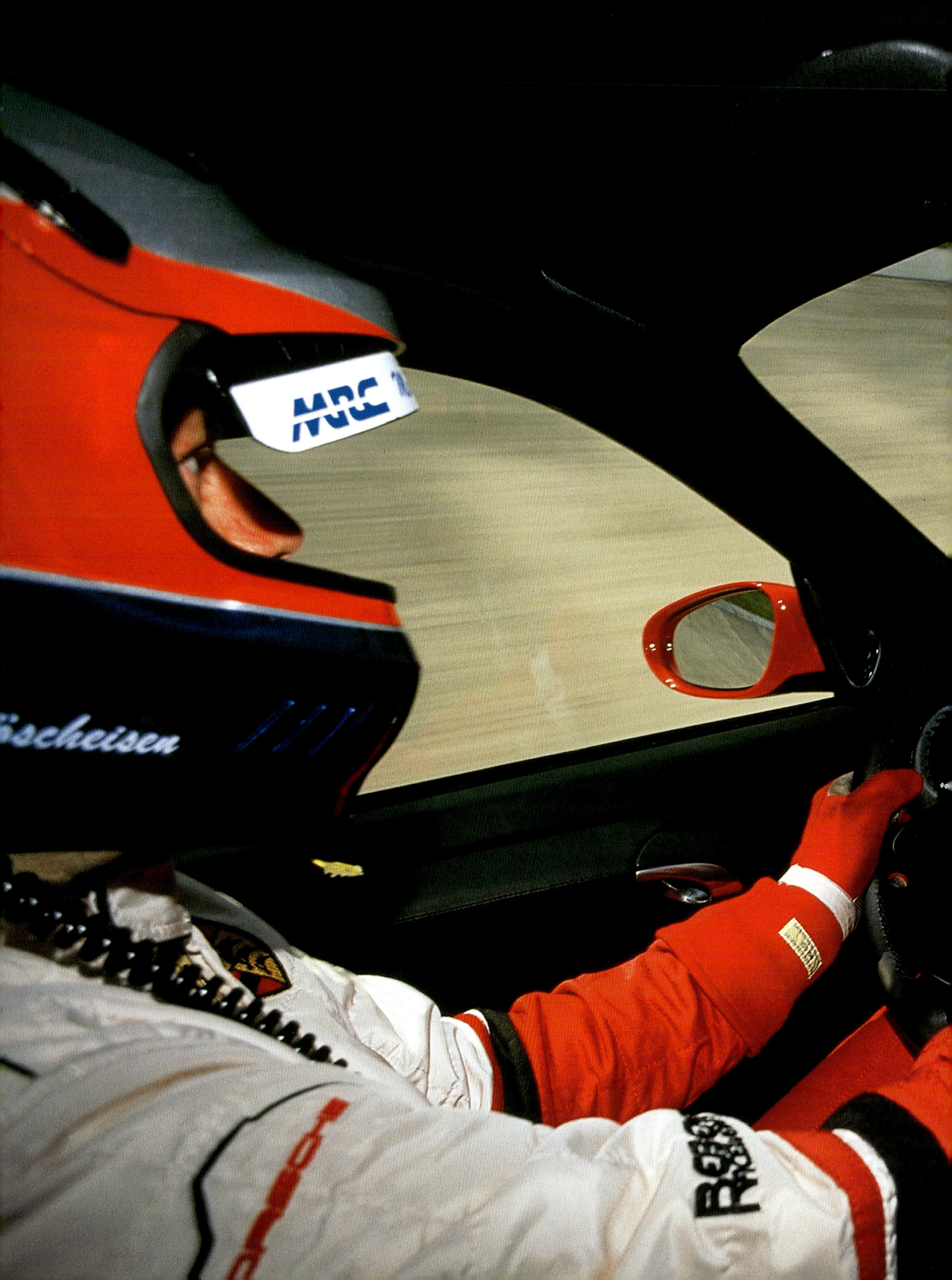
MBC

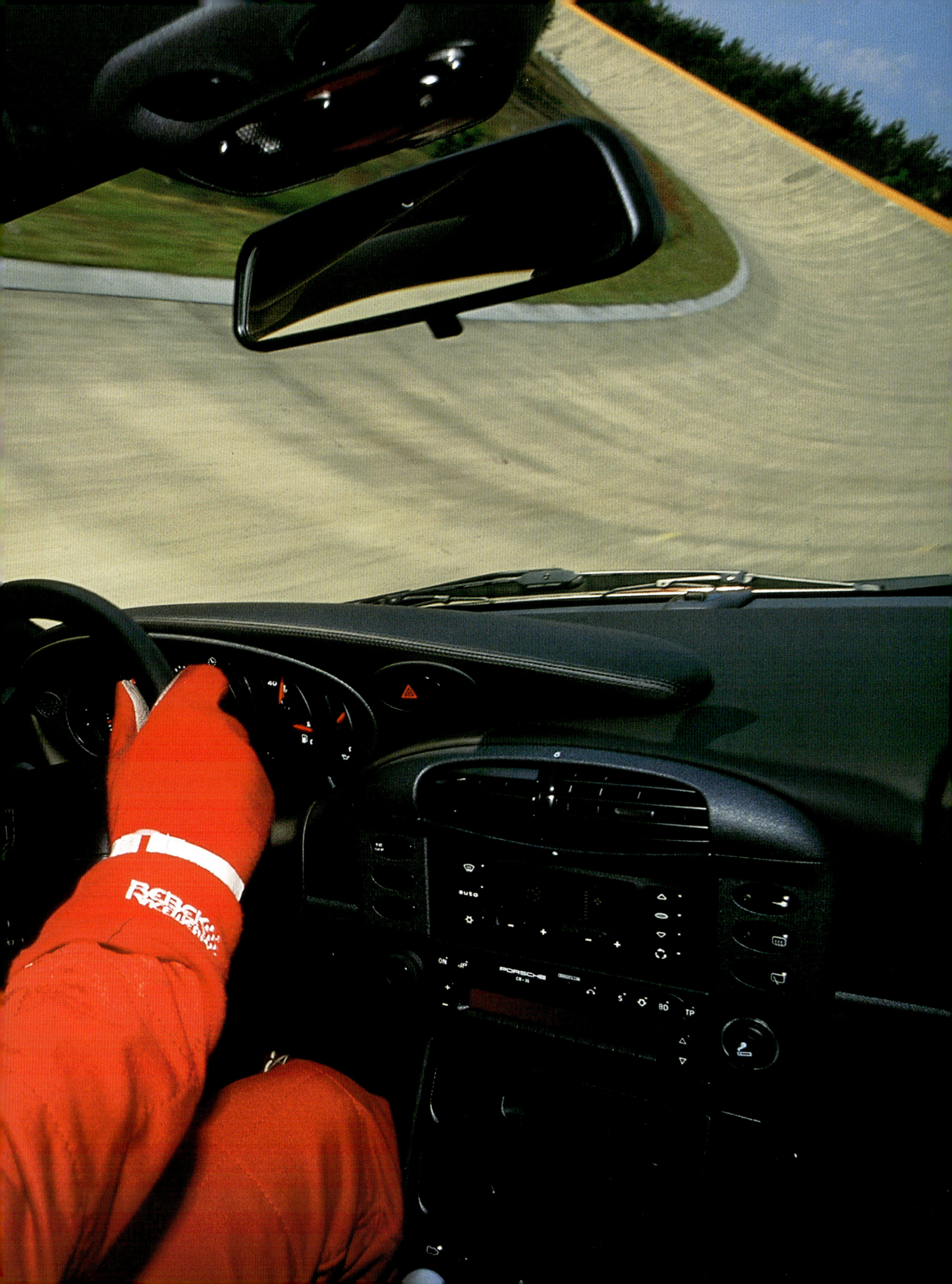
PORSCHE
auto
ON
BD
TP

The suspension of the new Carrera

The Geometry of Good Manners

With a suspension which gently reduces danger at the limit of adhesion, the Carrera sets new standards for active safety

More than one human lifetime ago, Professor Ferdinand Porsche decided that the engine of a sports car belonged behind the driver, close to the driven wheels. Yet not even convincing demonstrations of the superior traction provided by this concept altered the fact that change does not come easily – even for revolutionaries.

Indeed, it was nothing less than a revolution that began in an unassuming office building in Stuttgart's Kronenstrasse, in 1930. It was there that Porsche and his small team of engineers, working in their newly-founded design and consulting business, laid down a concept that would find its way into the race cars of a far distant future. They boldly moved the drivetrain of the Auto Union Grand Prix racer to the rear of the car.

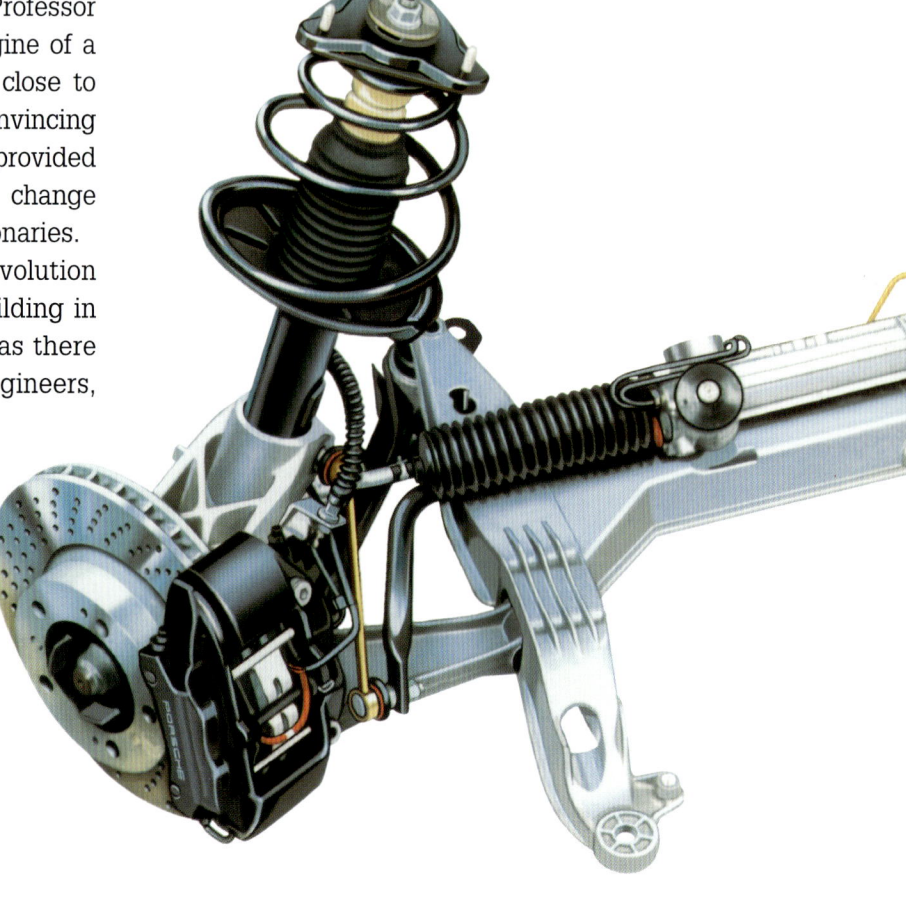

Hard lessons were learned in those early years, for the new concept transcended the existing boundaries of engineering knowledge. The racing rules of the time limited weight to a maximum of 750 kg (1650 lbs.) A supercharged 16-cylinder engine raged behind the driver; in the course of an illustrious racing career, its displacement grew from 4.4 to 6.0 liters, and output from 295 to 520 horsepower. Engineers as well as drivers had their hands full in their efforts to tame these beasts.

And so, more than 60 years ago, the groundwork was laid for a concept that would become Porsche's trademark. More than 20 million Volkswagen Beetles have spread the rear-engined gospel around the world. And for more than fifty years, Porsche engineers have cultivated the principle which they have brought to perfection in two different guises: the mid-engined Boxster and the rear-engined 911. That this unique drivetrain concept was kept alive and nurtured for decades, to the benefit of today's Boxster and Carrera, is due to more than just outstanding traction from optimally loaded drive wheels. Engineering development has reinforced the dynamic advantages inherent in the concept. These advantages are expressed in the car's steering behavior: the weight distribution of these mid- and rear-engined designs results in responsive, agile sports car handling. In addition, the payoff for extensive chassis tuning is seen in the fact that the Boxster and Carrera return lateral g and slalom test numbers well above the average of all other sports cars.

After six decades of precision engineering, Porsche's key advantage lies not in taking risks with complex technology, but rather in the disciplined development of proven components and the perfect fine-tuning of all applicable parameters. Porsche engineers learn the lessons needed for this uncompromising, goal-oriented development strategy at the toughest engineering school in the world: on the race track.

The front suspension of the Carrera provides an excellent example of the special relationship between Porsche's investment in technological development and the ensuing results. Its technical specifications read like any other spec sheet from the world of more mundane cars; even the new 911 has a strut suspension based on the decades-old designs by an American engineer, Earle S. MacPherson.

As is typical at Porsche, the key difference lies in the details, most apparent being the choice of materials. Longitudinal and transverse links, as well as the crossmember forming the basic lower pickup points to the chassis, consist of aluminum alloy. Due to the forces which they must bear, the struts themselves, with their dual-tube shock absorbers, are made of steel tubing with conically drawn strut tubes, an unusual and more costly solution. This saves 170 grams (6 oz.) per side.

The steering box is no longer located behind the front axle, as it has been for the previous

The front suspension consists almost entirely of aluminum alloy. Transverse arms and trailing links permit controlled toe-in changes. As is standard practice for race cars, the power-assisted rack-and-pinion steering is located ahead of the axle.

61

The suspension of the new Carrera attaches to the body via aluminum subframes with widely-spaced pickup points. This provides a solid basis for optimum handling characteristics.

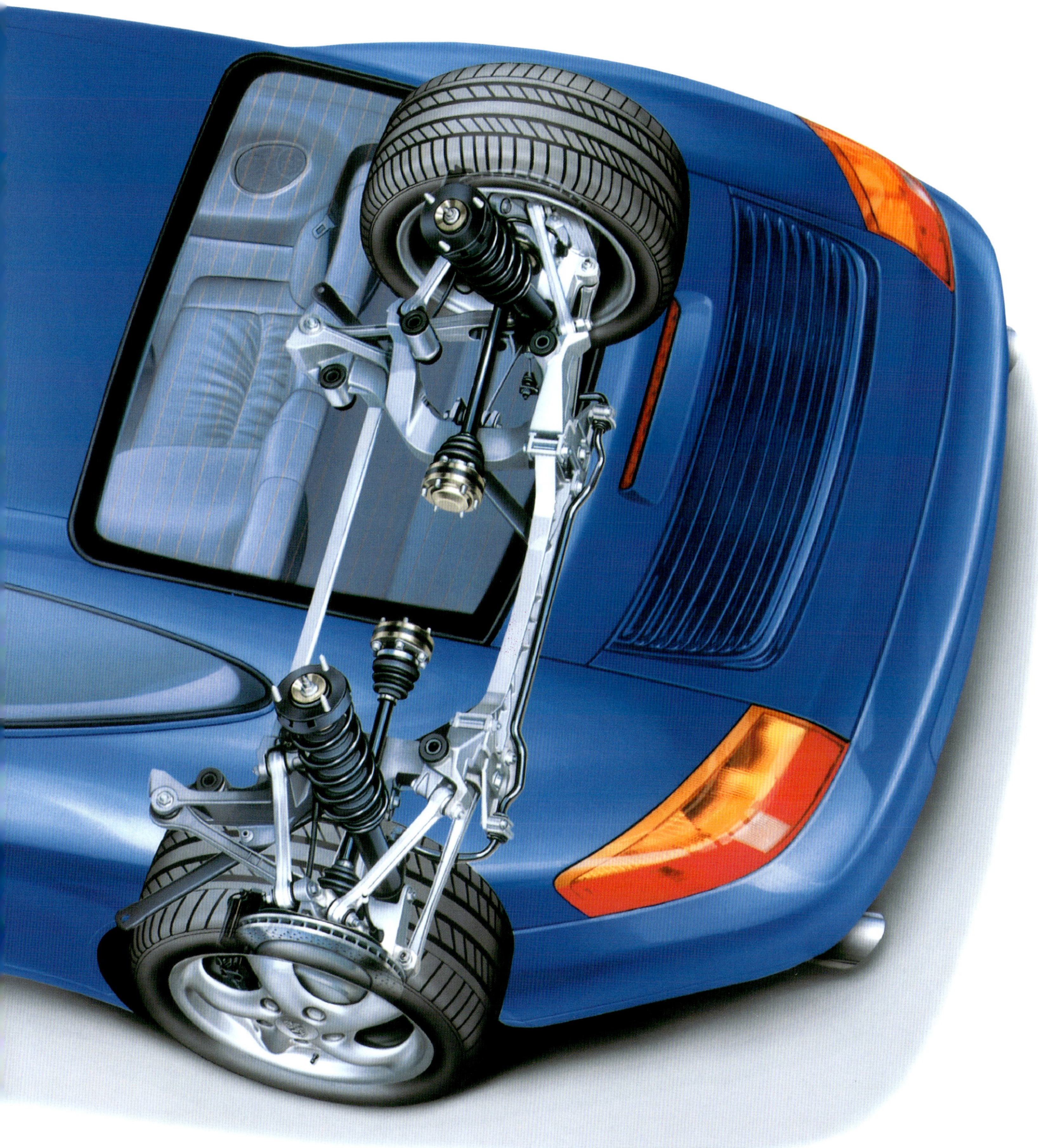

The rear suspension consists of three lateral links and one trailing link per side. As on the front suspension, cornering forces result in automatic toe correction, which effectively combats oversteer.

34 years. In the more geometrically correct style used by race cars, it is now located ahead of the wheels.

Fine tuning for perfection also can be discerned in the front coil springs. There are sound engineering reasons for offsetting the spring axis from the strut centerline, or, to put it simply, mounting them crooked. In this way, lateral forces during jounce and rebound are not transferred to the shock absorbers. Sticking of the shocks is eliminated, and the suspension remains responsive.

To pack the most spring into the least space, the coils are wound to allow extreme compression. Geometrically speaking, they are in the shape of truncated cones. But for optimum progressive-rate springing, the variation in coil diameter alone is not sufficient; the thickness of the coil wire also varies to alter the spring stiffness over its travel. Another unusual feature is the anti-roll bar, which works in partnership with the springs to provide a sporting suspension. To minimize weight, this anti-roll or stabilizer bar is made of steel tubing.

Where once a rigid steel A-arm took up lateral forces, we now find an elegant, cast-aluminum lateral member and longitudinal link, joined by an elastic element. Precisely defined flexibility is the newest grail sought by suspension designers, for softness in just the right amount can benefit ride comfort as well as braking and handling performance.

The weight bias of the rear-mounted engine is reflected in the considerably greater complexity of the rear axle. Here, as at the front, an aluminum alloy casting forms the basis for the suspension. Four transverse links and two short track control arms on each side locate the rear wheels and provide optimum camber control. As the rear shock absorbers do not double as locating members, they are not subjected to side loads, and as there is no shortage of space, the rear springs are simple cylindrical springs, located coaxially over the shocks. But even here, in the interest of a more comfortable, progressive spring rate, the springs are wound using tapered wire, and the anti-roll bar is tubular, like the front bar.

The mounts for the rear transverse links incorporate designed-in flexibility. And when the Carrera negotiates curves or decelerates under braking, a delicate interplay between forces and resilient components is developed at both axles.

At the front, with its steering box located ahead of the wheels, side forces and body roll in cornering result in changes to the suspension geometry. Toe-in is transformed to toe-out. The effect causes a subtle but perceptible reduction in cornering force, which, as the car approaches the cornering limit, produces self-limiting understeer.

At the rear, track control arms, located behind the wheel centerline and able to exert correcting forces, combined with the compliant suspension mounts, result in an appreciable increase in toe-in under cornering and braking. This permits considerably higher lateral forces, and the car's handling becomes more stable and easier for the driver to master.

For those who would prefer their 911 driving experience to be more direct, firmer, and at higher speeds, the new model is available with an optional sport suspension, a logical addition to wide tires on 18-inch rims. Shorter springs lower the body by 10 mm. Stiffer tuning of shocks and springs, as well as larger, stiffer anti-roll bars, equip the Carrera for even more spirited driving on winding roads or in club autocrosses. The increase in sporting ability comes at the cost of some comfort, a result of the laws of physics which even Porsche engineers cannot defy.

Still, the engineers push the limits of those laws. The design goals of the new 911 included several targets for the steering system:

In addition to the standard suspension tuning,
the Carrera is also available

better straight-line stability, an important consideration for a car that can now reach 280 km/h (174 mph).

In designing the new front suspension, several factors contributed to successfully realizing the engineers' goal of better handling. More freedom in the steering geometry laid open the path to improved performance. With more space under the fenders than ever, the target of a smaller turning circle was easily achieved.

To put the final touches on the front suspension, the engineers in Weissach reexamined a component which had proven itself over several decades: the power-assisted rack and pinion steering system. They inspected the system's precision and its assistance forces, and found unexpectedly high tolerances in its hydraulics. Tests showed that these had a considerable effect on the steering; even small deviations from the ideal could detract from the character of the steering and the controllability of the car. After this was reaized, every steering system installed in a Porsche is checked for precise adherence to design tolerances.

The new Carrera's elastokinematic toe correction is but the latest step on the long road to perfection. The liberal design trend toward allowing suspensions to steer themselves, within certain clearly defined limits, began twenty years ago when Porsche introduced its so-called "Weissach" rear suspension

lower steering forces, more responsive turn-in and a smaller turning circle. These three goals were to be met despite the longer wheelbase, which fundamentally opposes them. On the other hand, the 70 mm (nearly 3 inch) greater distance between the front and rear wheels assisted the engineers in giving the new Carrera on the 928. The 928's "automatic" toe correction resulted in increased cornering forces. At the time, this development was misinterpreted as a predecessor to all-wheel steering – a concept which several Japanese carmakers eagerly embraced in the early 1980s with the aim of revolutionizing handling. But the complex sy-

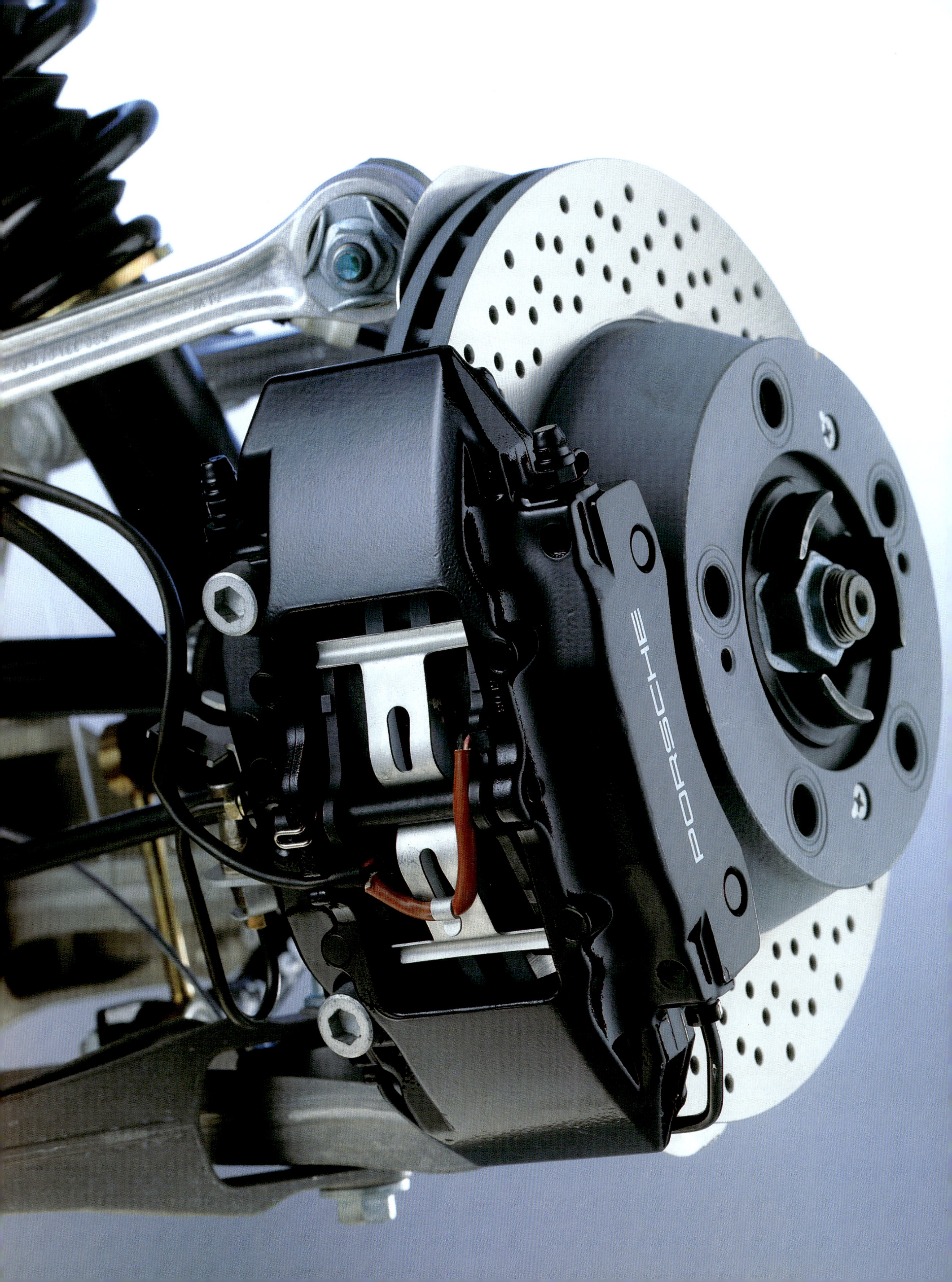
PORSCHE

The ventilated, cross-drilled disc brakes, combined with four-piston aluminum monoblock calipers, are masters of deceleration. In testing, they must withstand 25 successive maximum-effort stops from 90 percent of the car's top speed without fading.

stems required to steer all four wheels have since fallen out of fashion. Instead, suspensions with elastokinematic toe correction have established themselves as state of the art, not only at Porsche but throughout the automotive world.

To fine-tune vehicle handling, Porsche engineers call upon the drivetrain itself to make a contribution. After all, it is the drivetrain which imposes load transfer on the suspension when the throttle is suddenly closed, thereby inducing the oversteer which many drivers find objectionable. In their battle against this tendency, test drivers made two key observations: with an automatic transmission and torque converter, the changes in forces are gentler, and sudden load transfers simply do not occur. With a manual transmission, load transfer from the much more solid, immediate transmission of forces can be tamed by a limited-slip differential. Because the limited-slip function is most critical in coasting or engine braking situations, the lockup factor under these conditions has been set relatively high, at 40 percent. Under the opposite conditions, when the car is accelerating, the lockup factor remains at a more neutral 25 percent. With the excellent traction provided by the 911, lockup during acceleration is not absolutely necessary – but it is not possible to build a limited slip differential which only works in one direction.

The elastokinematic suspension permits the best of two worlds. Rolling straight ahead, the wheels are set almost parallel, with no toe-in, resulting in lower rolling resistance and reduced tire wear. Yet the suspension can instantly change toe-in to increase tire grip. This also yields benefits in the braking department. Braking, too, results in forces on the suspension which can be used to make elastokinematic corrections. Porsche was able to improve tire grip by increasing the tire slip angle under hard braking. Because the tires and road surface are interlocked, in effect are "geared together," deceleration rates well above the theoretical maximum of one g (9.81 m/sec^2, 32.2 ft/sec^2) are taken for granted in a Porsche. The brake system conforms to a longstanding Porsche tradition: if engine power is increased, the braking system must follow. Once again, Porsche has improved the braking power of its latest model.

This is apparent in the Carrera's larger brake discs, now 318 mm in diameter at the front and 299 mm at the rear. All four discs are ventilated and crossdrilled. These are matched by brake calipers which have proven themselves at Le Mans; the Italian-made four-piston Brembo monobloc calipers are virtually identical to those which stop the Porsche GT1, a racer with nearly twice the horsepower of the civilian Carrera.

Surprisingly, the procedure with which the development engineers test a production brake system is even more brutal than the Le Mans race course. The brake test conditions are unique to Porsche. Maximum-effort braking begins from 90 percent of the car's top speed (in this case about 250 km/h or 155 mph) down to 100 km/h (62 mph). So far, this is an everyday occurrence for any brake system. But at Porsche, a brake system must survive this treatment twenty-five times in rapid succession, as quickly as the car can accelerate back to its 90 percent speed, without any appreciable loss of braking effectiveness. One Weissach engineer confides that "Only the very best brakes and the toughest test drivers can do this – namely, ours."

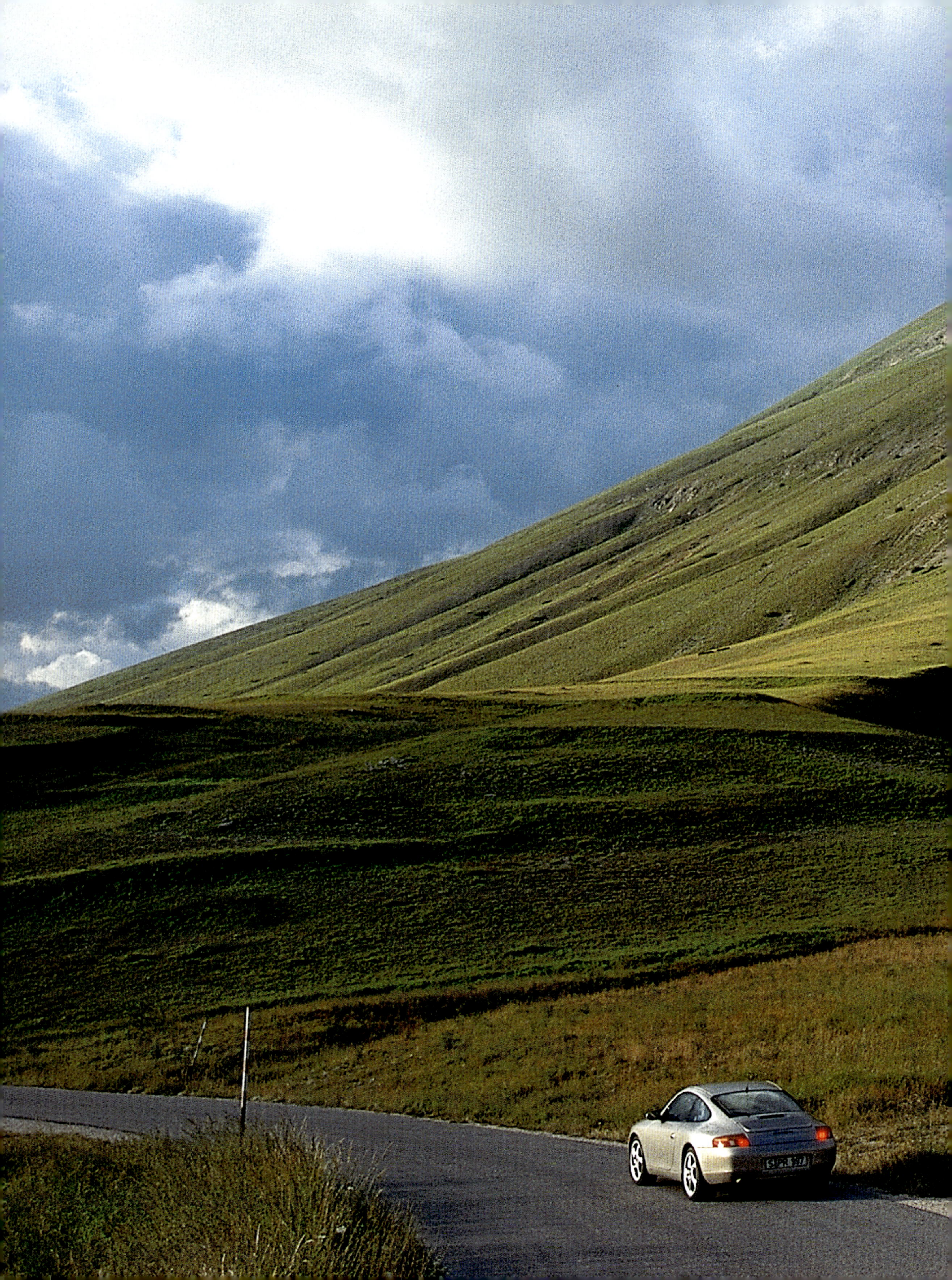

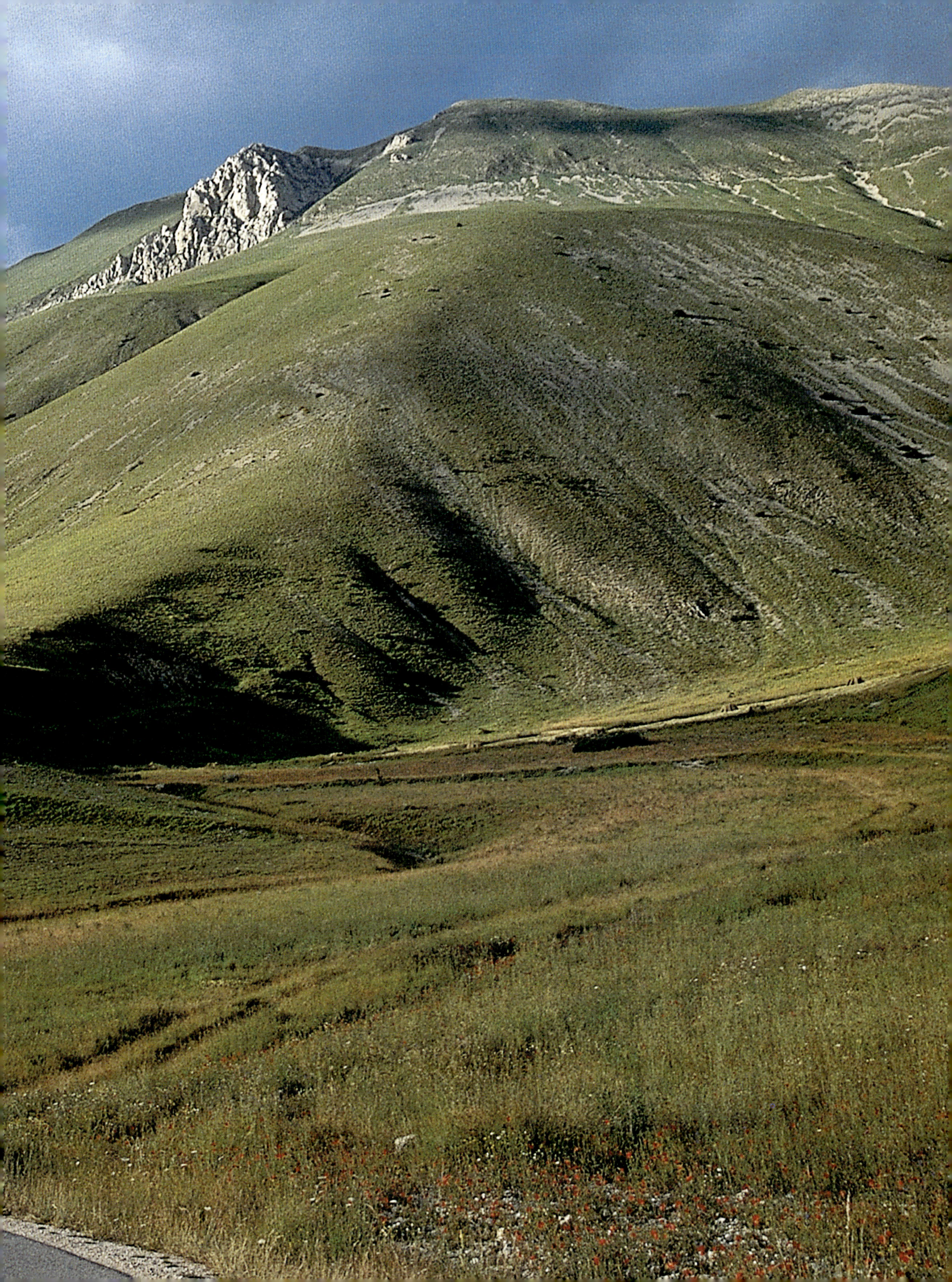

Driving the Carrera through Italy's Monti Sibillini

New Heights

The Monti Sibillini see few tourists, and are known to only a few hikers and hang gliding enthusiasts

High in the Monti Sibillini, a carpet of green extends to the horizon.

Except for the annual running of the Mille Miglia, the Monti Sibillini see few tourists, and are known to only a few hikers and hang gliding enthusiasts. A shame, really; the area around the serendipitously named Mt. Porche (2223 meters, 7293 ft.) is a veritable paradise for devotees of mountain motoring and fine cuisine.

Located in the center of Italy, the Monti Sibillini create a pleasant, green no-man's land, neatly tucked between the provinces of Umbria and the Marches. If our planet is being visited by aliens, they must surely have this area circled on their maps, in case they ever need to land unobserved within 150 kilometers (less than 100 miles) of Rome.

These hills provide a discreet paradise for clandestine excursions in heavily disguised prototype cars (such as our new Carrera) months before they are unveiled to the public. The world directs its attention to this region only a few days each year, when the Mille Miglia, a historic rally for veteran and classic cars, winds through these hills.

Even tourist guidebooks describe the green solitude of the southern Apennines with less than their usual exaggeration; they honor this beautiful emptiness with few but honest words. They emphasize the fact that there isn't much to see here, indeed, they don't even recommend any of the local hotels. And I have no reason to criticise this omission; after all, by omitting unimportant details, Michelin's trustworthy guide keeps us from languishing over bland dishes in mountain restaurants. Instead, it directs us to the valleys, where Etruscan culture still flourishes. In Foligno (a pleasant market town on the plains, according to German novelist and Nobel laureate Heinrich Böll) we find the Villa Roncalli, perfectly hidden alongside the Via Roma. Here, the Scolastico family runs an elegant hotel, a new business within ancient walls. The

The valley towns below are rich in history.

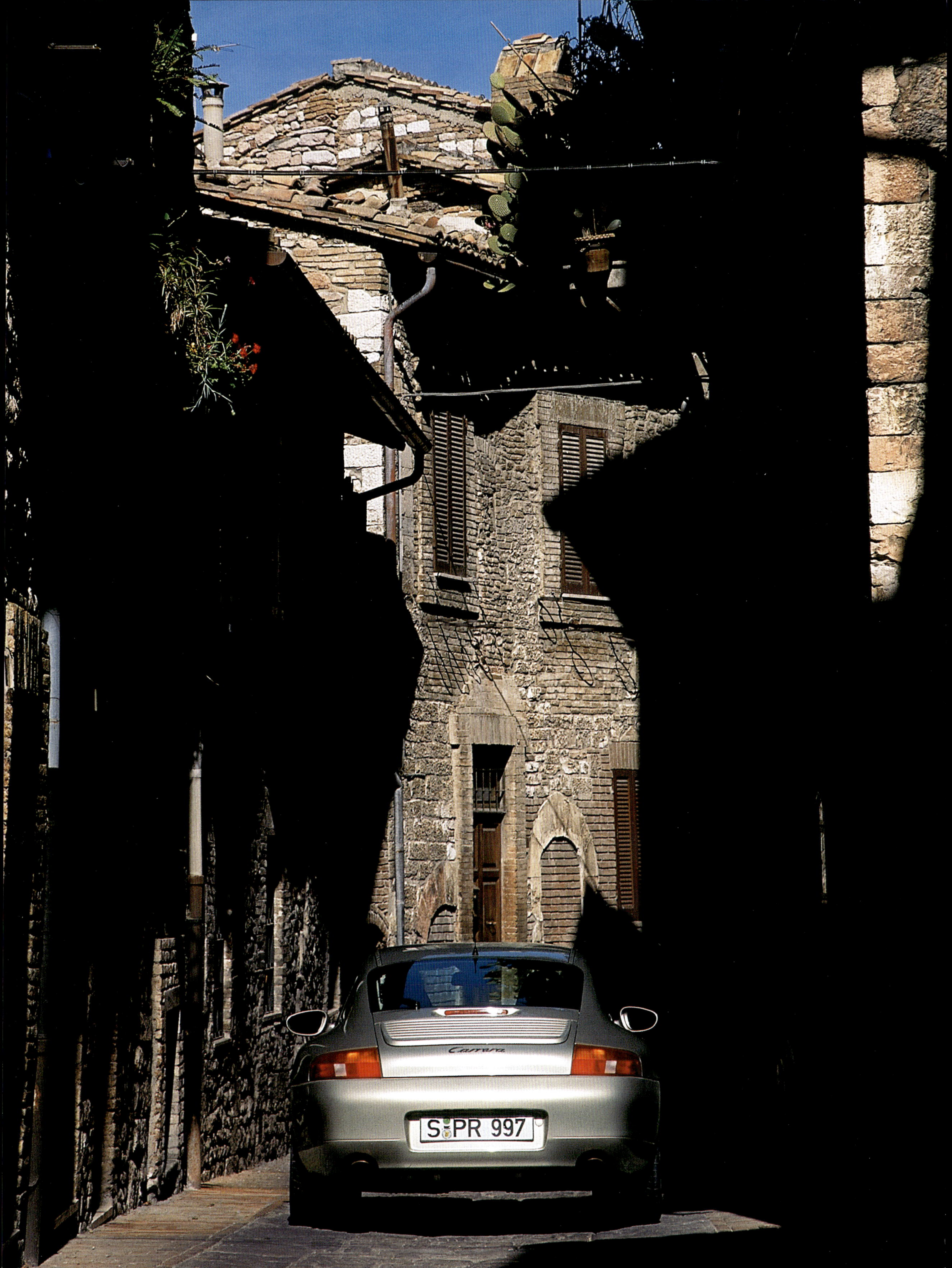
Carrera
S PR 997

The recommendation of St. Benedict of Norcia is apparent.

one-star restaurant pampers its guests with classic Umbrian cuisine, which, in the modern idiom, graces the plate in a light, slender style. Instead of choosing from the tempting handwritten menu, we cast ourselves on the mercy of the chef with the words "Faccia lei." We will let cellar and kitchen provide our meal as he sees fit. The festivities begin with a Chardonnay Riserva Lungarotti; the delicious procession of courses culminates in lamb from the endless meadows of the Monti Sibillini as the aroma of rosemary works its magic on the roast.

In Foligno, at six in the morning, we reluctantly pull our gaze away from the green hills in the magic light of dawn. We're on a different clock now, the best measure of time for a curving road: the "Carrera Hour." The connecting leg between Casenove Serrone, Cerreto di Spoleto, Norcia, and up to the pass below the Piano Grande, makes up for the rudeness of our early wakening.

Umbria still cultivates peace and quiet, the roads are empty, and, with no opposing traffic, we can take the ideal line through corners. The new Carrera happily shows us what it has learned in the course of its rapid development.

The Piano Grande in its blue period.

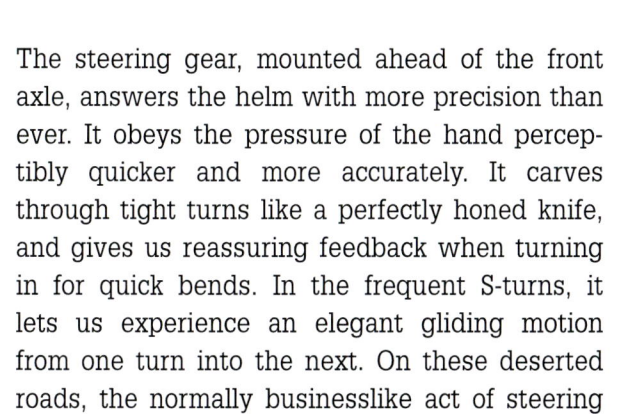

The steering gear, mounted ahead of the front axle, answers the helm with more precision than ever. It obeys the pressure of the hand perceptibly quicker and more accurately. It carves through tight turns like a perfectly honed knife, and gives us reassuring feedback when turning in for quick bends. In the frequent S-turns, it lets us experience an elegant gliding motion from one turn into the next. On these deserted roads, the normally businesslike act of steering

The Mille Miglia provides a wonderful excuse for classic cars to explore the Monti Sibillini.

75

a car begins to resemble an exercise in penmanship as we trace a flowing line across the asphalt.

The blessing of solitude allows the Carrera to flex the elastokinematic muscles of its suspension. Cornering forces gently correct the toe-in of both axles, and intentional deformation catches us on our way to oversteer with benevolent, decelerating understeer as the rear tires grip the road with determination.

This, however, is not an immutable condition. After all, there are 300 horses going into the differential, and a maximum torque of 350 Newton-meters (258 ft.-lbs.) stands ready to overcome even this extraordinary cornering grip. Select the right gear, a determined stomp on the gas pedal, and a completely different form of "power steering" takes hold of the rear end. Even before we reach the apex, the corner is history, as the steering wheel returns to center more quickly than usual to correct the throttle-induced oversteer.

On such twisting roads, the new boxer engine need not always sing its high-powered song. Its massive midrange power propels the Carrera in short, intense sprints to the next curve, punctuated by hard braking. Despite a cost of 1960 Lire per liter of super senza piombo, I happily burden my economic conscience with brief bursts beyond 7000 rpm, heights easily scaled by this engine, the familiar Porsche sound never becoming oppressive. The engine package is acoustically well-balanced or, if you will, its sound signature has been well tailored; either way, this new six-cylinder still plays the old

Albergo Castelluccio. We're guaranteed to find lenticchie here.

Green means go; curves and hills of the Italian Marches.

tunes. One could say that the sound has been sanitized in that the roar of the old engine's air cooling fan has been eliminated.

The minor Strada del Stato 319 is tailor-made for exercising the six-speed transmission, which now employs a cable shifter like the Boxster. The close-ratio box seems to contain just the right gear for any corner, and soon we come to the realization that with this powerful engine, a higher gear will serve just as well. Fifth and sixth gears are best saved for the occasional towns; after all, this early in the morning, no decent human being would blast through Italy's sleeping villages quite so fortissimo.

A second Carrera lets us experience the interplay of the five gears in the Tiptronic S transmission. With the lever in "D," the transmission and its computer interpret the driver's every wish from nothing more than the movement of his or her shoe sole. The computer infers from

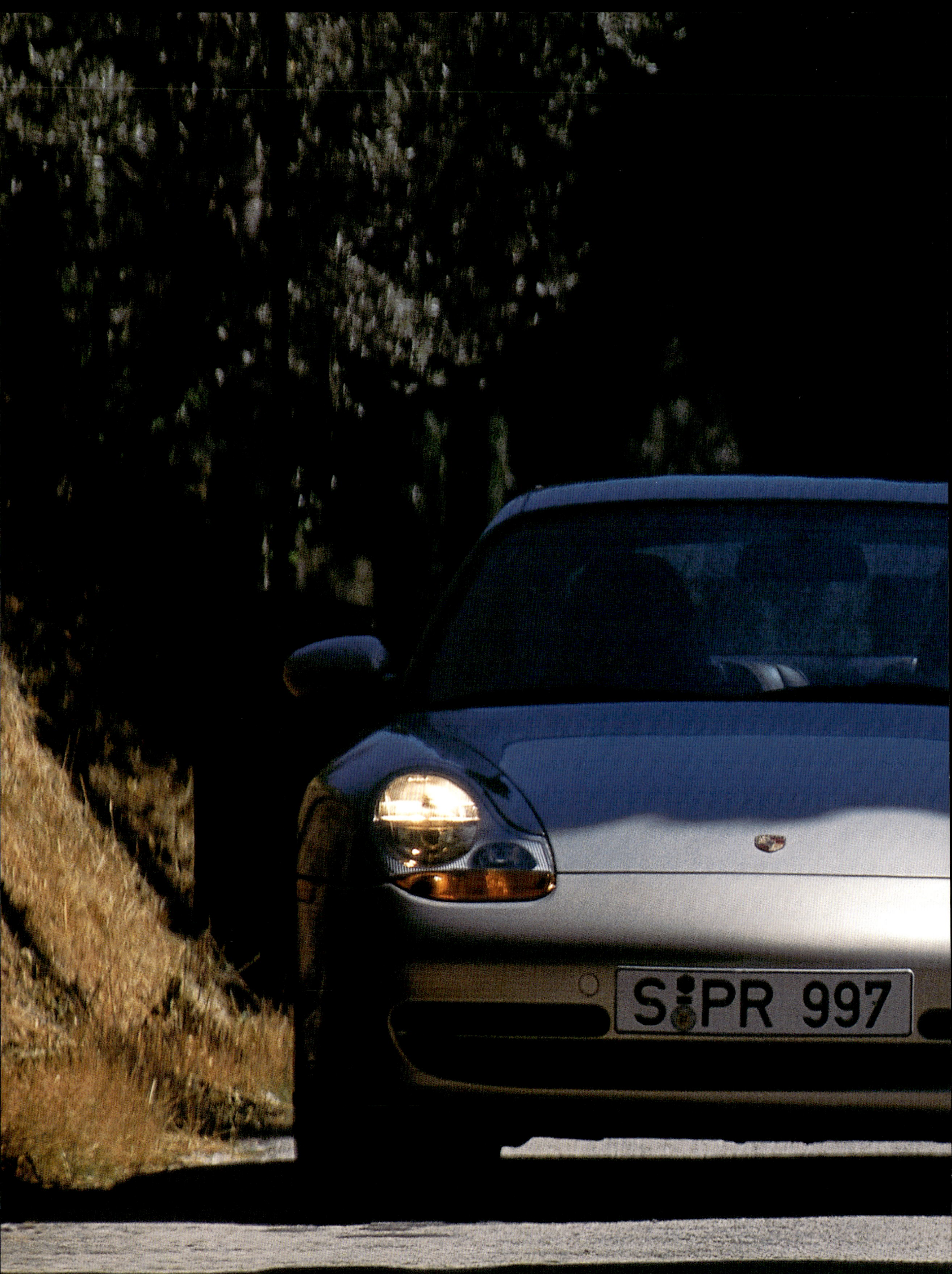
S PR 997

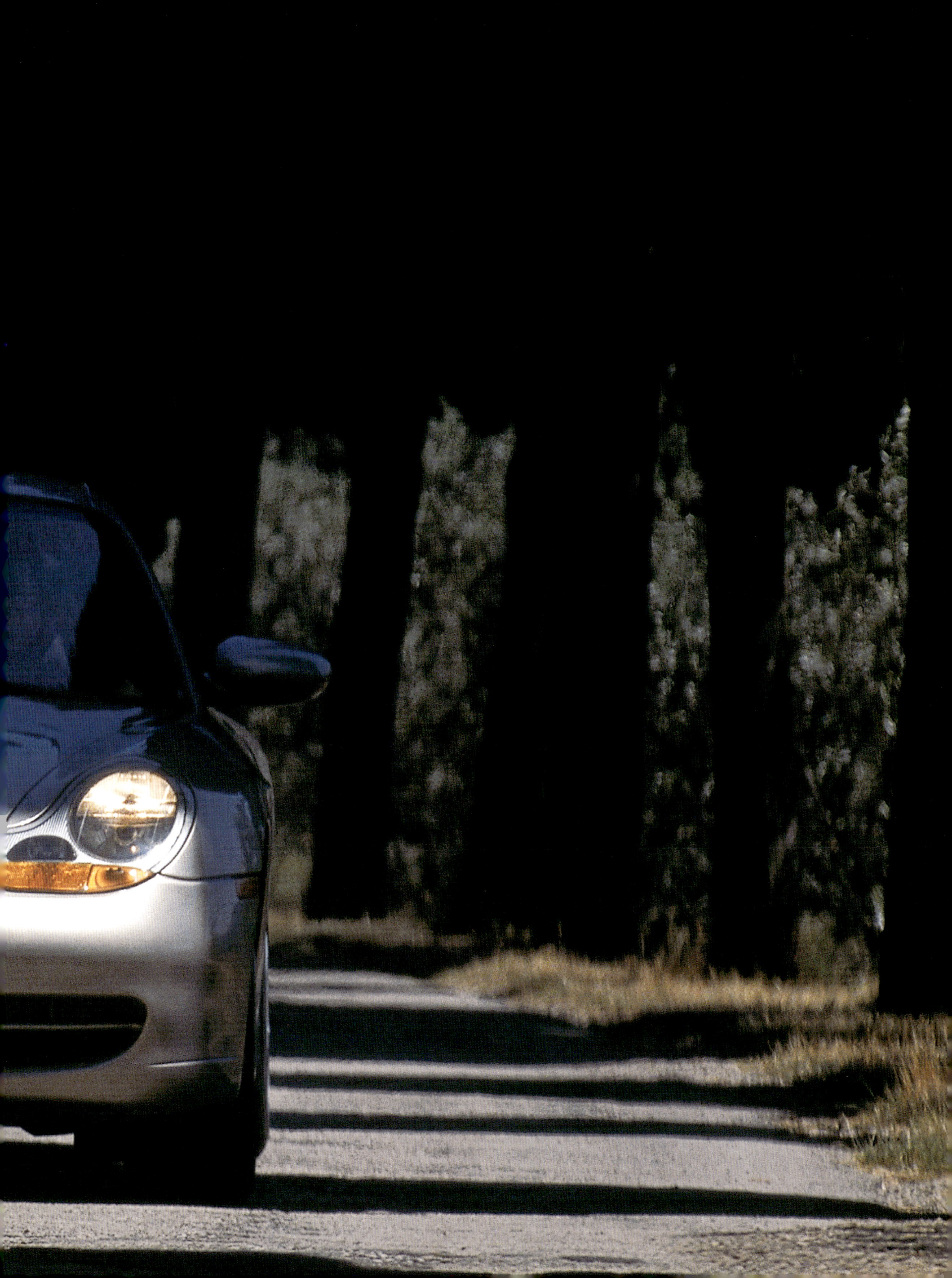

The Chiesa Santa Chiara of Assisi is 700 years older than the 911.

the gentle lifting of one's designer athletic footwear that there is no longer a need for lower gears. On the other hand, the semiconductor-packed brain deciphers rapid departure of the foot from the gas pedal as a warning: "Curve ahead, stay in this gear, we're going to need it soon." Nothing escapes the computer. Sensors tell it when we are negotiating turns, how bravely we do so, and how much lateral acceleration we are generating. The computer senses the rise and fall of hills without ever seeing them, and converts all its stored knowledge into digital commands to the transmission.

We can let the automatic transmission continue its deliberations – it does this very well, and tirelessly – but we can also move the lever to the left and put the computer into semi-hibernation. That done, we can shift for ourselves, using two paddles or keys on the steering wheel; this brings us a couple of cable lengths closer to current Formula 1 practice. There are virtuosos who perform on the keys of the Tiptronic S; one of these is Herr Klaus, who, with no more than the pressure of a thumb on a shift paddle, motivates the engine's full 350 Nm of torque to go from one gearset to another, without a trace of tremor; he can glide a Carrera through the Monti Sibillini as gently as a royal limousine. Then there are other drivers, their names only slightly different, who attempt to dispel their longing for a manual transmission with rapid shifts at the rev limit and more aggressive acceleration, without ever achieving the discreet speed of an experienced Tiptronic

Spello. Parts of the town walls date to Roman times.

The Monti Sibillini: Italy as few ever see it.

master. In the final analysis, the question of which transmission to choose is not so much a matter of cost but rather of the character of the purchaser.

Past Norcia, the road winds up a hill, through a small assortment of switchbacks, to a small, nameless pass at 1500 meters (4900 ft).

At the top, the scenery suddenly changes. Before us lie the Monti Sibillini – grass-covered, treeless hills. Between us and the hills is the broad Piano Grande, the Great Plain, a flat grassland of deepest green. A little creek, the Mergani – apparently seldom filled to overflowing – has carved a tiny canyon into the plain; its branches meet at a point with no apparent exit to the valleys beyond. The Monti Sibillini are like the Mergani: isolated, and seemingly not even part of Italy. Add a couple of yaks for decoration, and Piano Grande could just as easily be in Mongolia. Even after our return to the edges of civilization, in Castelluccio, we encounter a different, less polished Italy, whose few tourists prefer hiking boots or cross-country skis. Tiny and isolated, Castelluccio is nevertheless a metropolis. The best of all lenticchie grow here, tiny green, brown or delicate red lentils, delicious beyond words.

The small villages in the area carry long, self-important names: Castelsantángelo sul Nera in the north, Aquate del Tronto in the southwest. The roads leading to these hamlets are destinations in themselves, carved into the endless green flanks of 2000-meter mountains. Occasionally, hang gliders drift down from their heights. In the Montagna, the roads caress the contours of the landscape so affectionately that the flow of driving is never spoiled by the interruption of a straight piece of road. In Norcia, we finally return to Italy. For Italians, this town in the Piano di San Scolastico is the home of delicious pork specialties. Butcher Vittorio Ansuni is regarded as a grand master of sausage and ham, which might come either from tame or wild pigs.

The Ristorante Granaro del Monte celebrates not only the sausage and the lentil; the chef also favors the third specialty of the region, Umbria's black truffle. This delicacy is served with tagliatelle and butter. A Scacciadiavoli – Rosso di Montefalco so nicely rounds out our feast that we decide to spend the night in the Hotel Grotta Azzura.

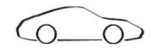

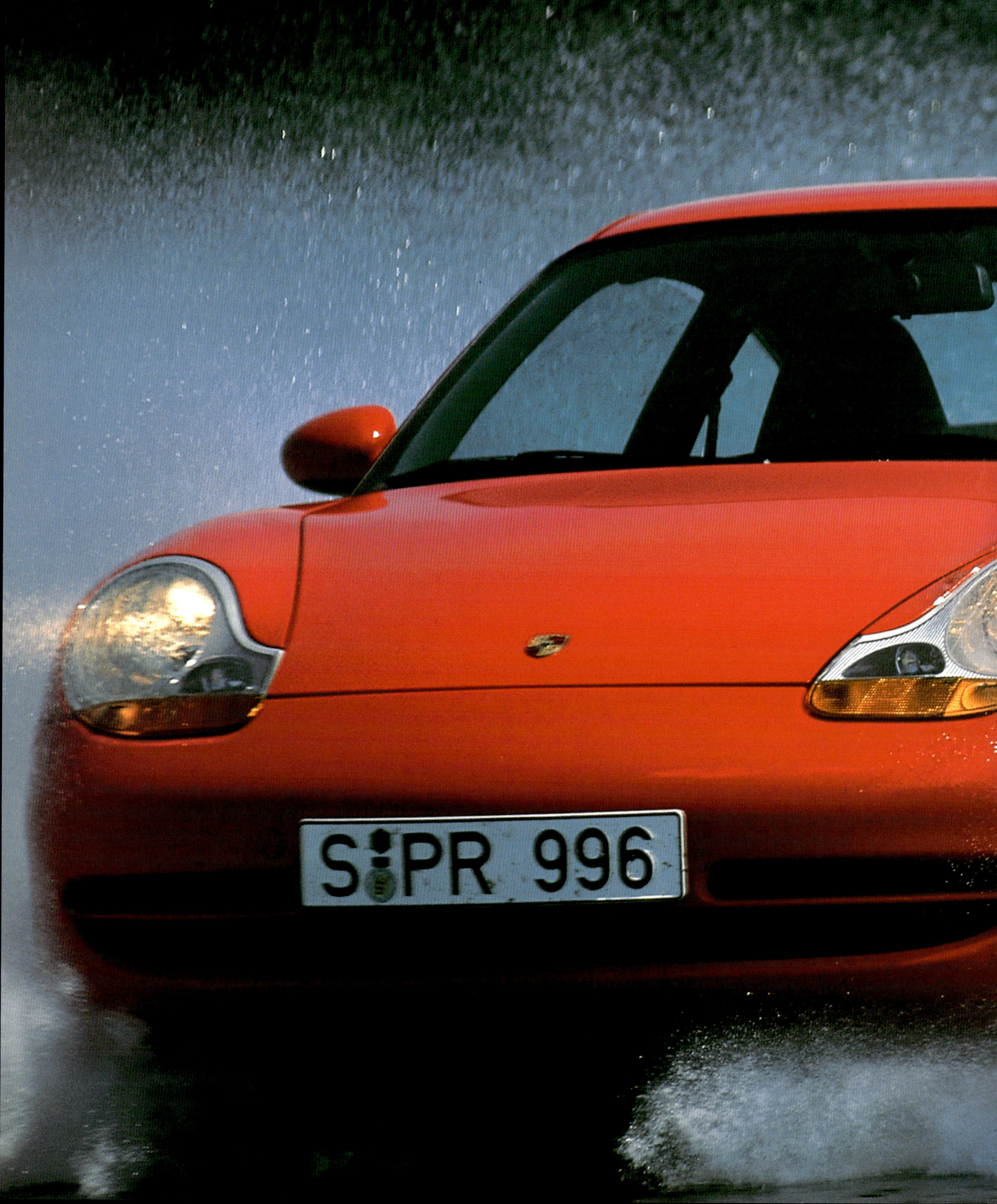
S PR 996

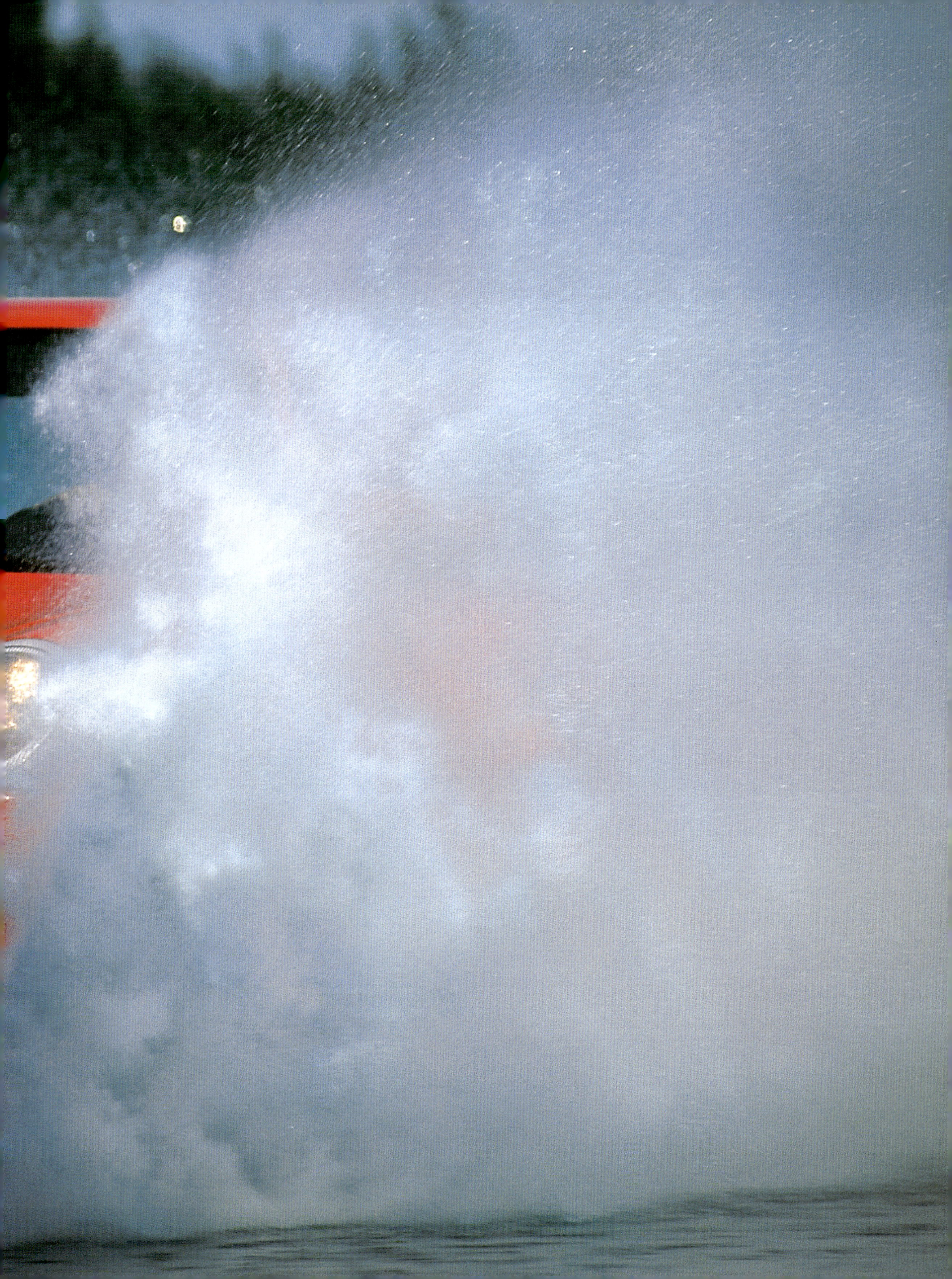

Wheels and tires of the new Carrera

Getting a Grip

If we were to attempt to quantify fifty years of progress by reciting wheel sizes, the results would at first appear rather modest

If we were to attempt to quantify fifty years of progress by reciting wheel sizes, the results would at first appear rather modest. That first Porsche of 1948 had 16-inch wheels; except for a brief excursion to 15 inches, this remained the basis for all production 911s until 1997. For the new generation, a decent amount of growth was called for; the wheel diameter increases by one inch. And because at Porsche, extra helpings always are available from the options menu, 18-inch wheels also are offered.

These steps toward progress indicate that from the very beginning, Porsche chose the right path. Fast cars need large-diameter wheels.

If we search for further signs of progress, we readily find them in wheel widths. The first rims were slim – only 3½ inches wide, while the bias-belted tires were only five inches wide.

Today, the running gear of a 911 looks quite different. Wheel width has more than doubled; while 3½ inches was standard in the early years, today's front rims start at seven inches. The widest rear wheels are measured at ten inches. The metric tire dimensions range from 205/50 ZR 17 for the slimmest front tires to 265/35 R 18 for the widest rear rubber. The road-going version of the GT1 exceeds even these dimensions: 295/35 ZR 18 at the front, 335/30 ZR 18 at the rear.

The trend to differential tire sizes – narrow at the front, wide at the rear – was born on the race track and introduced on the production Porsche Carrera RS for 1973. The difference in wheel widths reflects the rearward weight distribution of the Porsche 911; thirty-eight percent of its weight is carried by the front wheels, and 62 percent on the rears – much like a race car. The generous width of the rear wheels increases grip and indicates their dual role – they must cope with drive forces as well as cornering loads.

This increase in tire widths is remarkable. From an original width of only five inches, Carrera rubber is now more than double – and on the GT1 nearly triple – that of the original 1964 911. What is not as obvious is the growth in tire contact-patch area. A quick

The 17-inch cast-aluminum Monoblock wheel is standard equipment on the new Carrera. Its five spokes are solid.

calculation shows how essential this is, in view of the steady escalation in engine output. The first Porsche 356 had 40 horsepower; 49 years later, the Carrera develops 300 hp, or 7½ times as much power. And the GT1, with its 544 hp, brings nearly fourteen times as much power to bear. But it's not only higher engine output that places greater stress on today's tires; over the decades, Porsches have become considerably faster. Forty hp and 140 km/h (87 mph) were sufficient to crown the first Porsche 356 as king of the road in postwar Europe. By contrast, our current 300 hp will propel us twice as fast – 280 km/h (174 mph) – albeit for only a few lucky moments. Our modern Autobahn is no longer as empty as it was in 1948.

The wheels themselves also underwent a fundamental transformation. For the first twenty years, all Porsches rolled on steel rims; forged alloy wheels from Fuchs were first fitted to production cars in 1968. From the early 1970s onward, all 911s have had aluminum wheels as standard equipment.

The new Carrera offers a 17-inch "Monoblock" wheel as standard equipment, with solid cast-alloy spokes. The "Techno" wheel is available as an option, with hollow-cast spokes. What is remarkable is the small weight difference between the smaller, more affordable Monoblock wheel and the larger, more expensive high tech wheel:

Monoblock

Front wheel	7 J x 17	8.7 kg (19.07 lbs.)
Rear wheel	9 J x 17	10.1 kg (22.267 lbs.)

Techno

Front wheel	7.5 J x 18	8.6 kg (18.96 lbs.)
Rear wheel	10 J x 18	10.6 kg (23.369 lbs.)

Optional equipment for the new Carrera: the 18-inch Techno wheel. To save weight, it is cast with five hollow spokes.

By contrast, the weight difference among tires is greater, but overall, the disadvantage of increased rotational and unsprung weight for 18-inch wheels and tires is not significant. Five decades ago, the most important quality for the tires of a Porsche 356 was their ability to run at 140 km/h continuously. Over the years, the list of demands placed on a Porsche's tires has grown. For many years, it has been customary for tire manufacturers to develop special tires specifically for Porsche.

Front tires	
205/50 ZR 17	8.7 to 9.3 kg (19.14 to 20.50 lbs.)
225/40 ZR 18	9.800 kg (21.61 lbs.)

Rear tires	
255/50 ZR 17	9.6 to 11.2 kg (21.23 to 24.692 lbs.)
265/35 ZR 10	11.100 kg (24.471 lbs.)

The test program for evaluating whether or not the tire makers have done their homework is comprehensive and formidable; it encompasses more severe tests than most drivers will ever risk in an entire lifetime of driving.

The handling evaluation on dry, as well as wet, roads was established by Dr. Ing. Jürgen Rappen, head of Porsche's tire department. It encompasses more than 30 different test criteria. Beyond simply driving at the limit, many of these criteria are subjective. Questions of responsiveness, slip angle, steering precision and feedback have little to do with turning fast times on the test track; rather, they seek to establish those indices deemed critical for road manners befitting a Porsche. One of these criteria is comfort, a cornerstone of the everyday utility found in every Porsche.

Some of the standards, however, come straight from the road testers' chamber of horrors, representing situations that normal drivers may never experience. For example, with a 911 of the 1990s, fishtailing in a corner is possible only if the driver abandons all vestiges of responsibility for his actions at the wheel.

Similarly, the test for hydroplaning in turns steps over the boundaries of sensible driving in the everyday world. Travelling at 65 to 100 km/h (40 to 60 mph), the test driver cranks the car around a 200 meter (650 ft.) skidpad. At one point on the pad, a special surprise lies in wait: a section of flowing water, 20 meters long and five meters wide (66 x 16 ft.), which, at speeds above 80 km/h (50 mph), will throw a car out of its perfectly circular orbit.

The most difficult test of all is nearly as old as the Porsche company itself. Ever since sports cars have rolled out of the Zuffenhausen factory, Porsche has conducted tests on the Nürburgring North Circuit. Porsche's senior tire tester, Günther Steckkönig, recently retired, has driven through the "Green Hell" in the Eifel Mountains for more than thirty years. He is convinced that even today, the 'Ring is irreplaceable as a test track. "No other race track in the world is able to challenge tires as thoroughly as the North Circuit."

His description of a single lap gives us brief glimpses into a career specialty which is anything but relaxing.

"Turning in for the fast Hatzenbach righthander, you know what's coming. Here you'll find out whether the steering remains precise even at high speeds, and whether the front tires can translate the steering input into cornering forces. And at the rear, there shouldn't be anything unusual happening, otherwise the next twenty kilometers are going to be an adventure. The next key section is at the Flugplatz; the car flies over a hump, gets light, and drops into a right-hand sweeper. The car has to stay precisely on course. Although the section between Schwedenkreuz and Aremberg is anything but straight, this is the fastest section of the Nürburgring, demanding steering precision and, at the end, stable braking behavior. Suspension compression in the Fuchsröhre jolts the entire car. If you show up here with mushy tires, you can expect the worst. If you drive through the Adenauer Forst on exactly the right line, you'll get your first good impression of how the car will behave in S-turns. The descent between Kallenhard and Breitscheid is dangerous; if you risk too much here, you'll go hard against the edge of the envelope, but in the process you'll learn about how forgiving the tires and suspension are. The section between Hohe Acht and Brünnchen is wonderful; a perfect combination of curves taken at medium speeds. Here we notice above all whether we have the right amount of grip at the front end. After Brünnchen, the murderously fast corners past Pflanzgarten to the Schwalbenschwanz are highly selective; the suspension is put to the test, and the car itself is literally twisted. And the hump adds yet another complication. Here, the rear axle has to remain stable. If a tire doesn't have this under control, and the rear end starts to fishtail, the tires get a penalty flag. Even on the main straight, test drivers can't take a rest; there, we check high-speed lane changes."

Porsche test drivers take about 8½ minutes to lap the North Circuit. Anyone who would like to duplicate this feat should be prepared for tire wear about ten times as great as in spirited driving on normal roads, to say nothing of the other risks and side effects involved.

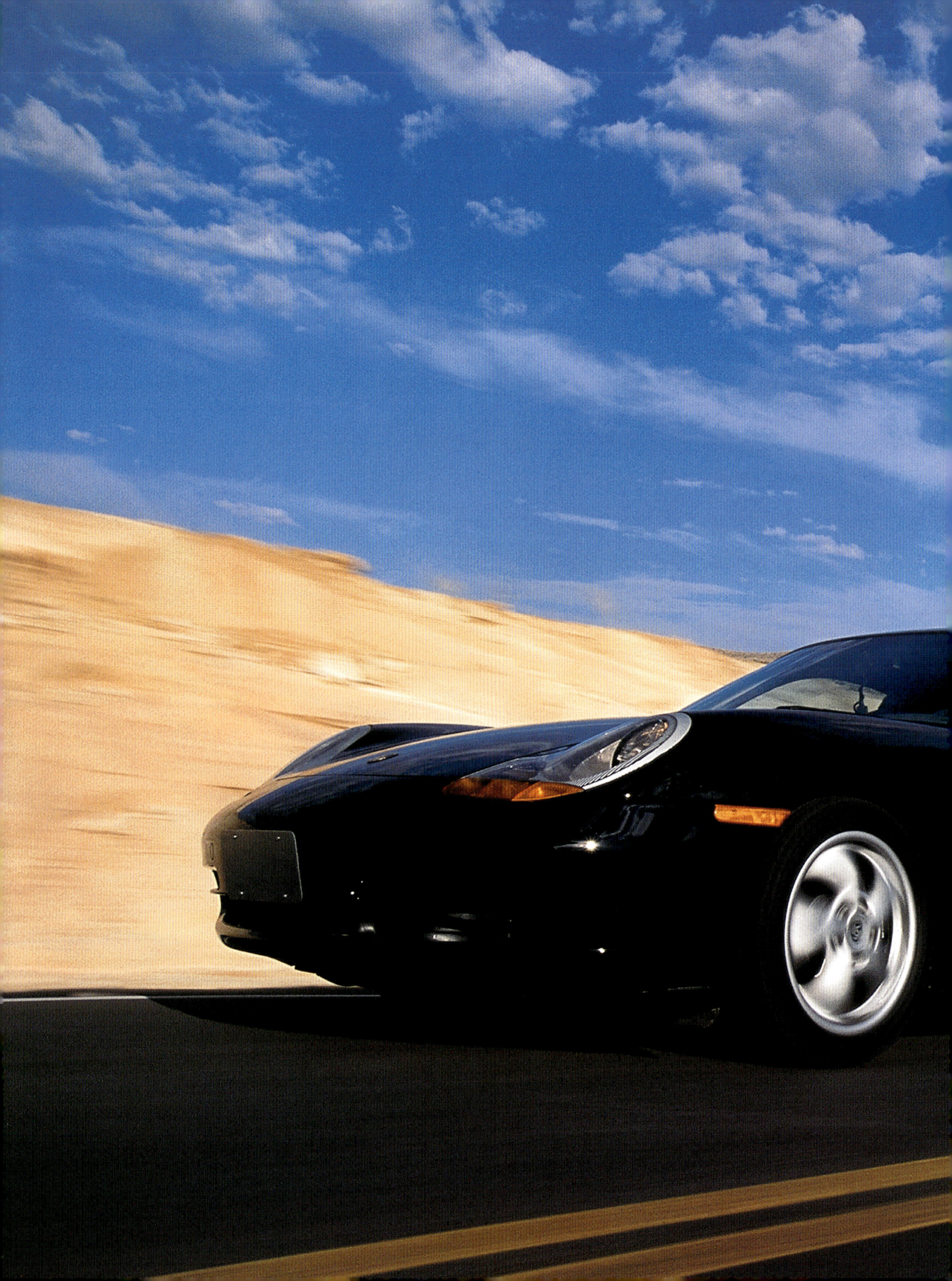

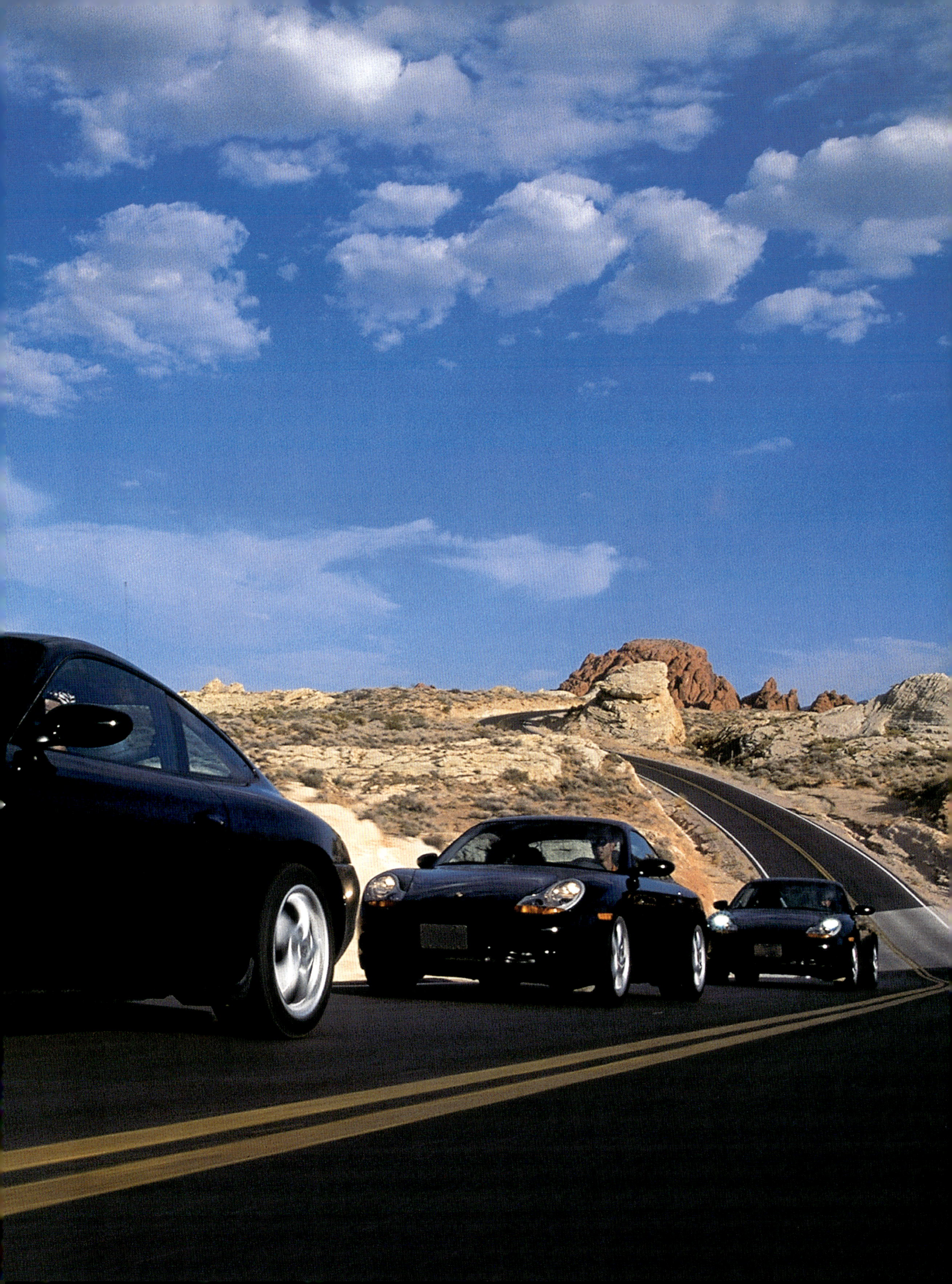

Test driving the new Carrera in the American Southwest

Once Upon a Time in the West

Summers are hot in Death Valley; let's find out how 21 liters of engine coolant feel about it

A visit to Tombstone and the immortal legend of Wyatt Earp.

Somehow, the details of this rendezvous seemed familiar. A secret meeting had been arranged on a crossroads somewhere in the United States. We had seen it all before in Hitchcock's thriller North by Northwest. In that classic film, it was Cary Grant who appeared precisely on time, and awaited the unknown amidst the corn fields; the unknown soon materialized as he was attacked by a hired killer flying a crop duster.

Dawn fades at the end of a long journey as we approach our appointed crossroads – the intersection of Interstate 10 and Highway 191, in southern Arizona. We are precisely on time, 8 A.M., but we are disturbingly alone. Other than that, everything is the exact opposite of Hitchcock's vision. The road runs south by southwest, there are no cornfields – indeed nothing at all to hide a fugitive. No airplanes, no homicidal pilot, but most important, no Porsche caravan conducting hot weather testing. And, because we are in the middle of the desert, no breakfast for miles around.

Our solitude lasts for 45 minutes, until a column of black prototypes appears out of the shimmering heat of late morning. The test crew is in a good mood; they've just had breakfast!

Three new 911s in the furnace of Death Valley.

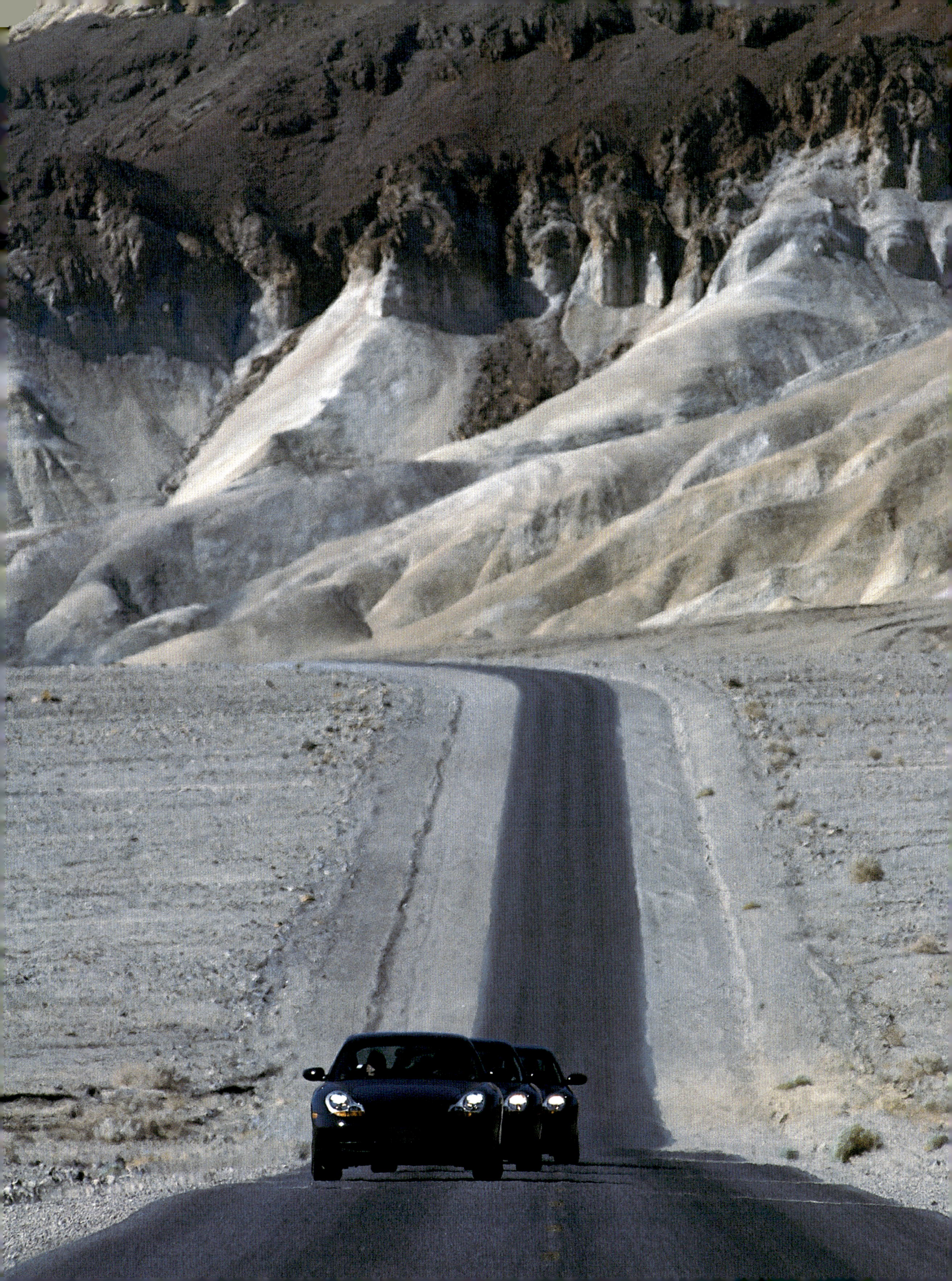

Highway 191 leads through a desolate little town named Cochise, in a Western landscape that you won't ever see in any Western movie: flat, arid farmland, dotted with Arizona's trademark saguaro cactus. But by the time we reach Tombstone, it becomes obvious that only a century ago, the legends of a young America were being written in this land. Wyatt Earp lived here, with his brothers James and Virgil, all principals in the Gunfight at the O.K. Corral on October 26, 1881. Today, Tombstone's Western celebration runs 365 days a year. The locals favor the clothes and look of the last century, for the fun of it – and to avoid looking like tourists.

Emanuel Eckardt, from the German magazine Stern and I acquire a special souvenir from Tombstone, which we experience on a bench in front of the saloon, during a brief rest period while the test crews load data into their notebook computers. Unfortunately, our pose is not in keeping with the local style. We enjoy huge servings of frozen yoghurt, which happily fills our bellies.

The Wild West on either side of the highway gradually becomes more appropriate for the big screen. We drive through the Papago Indian Reservation. Until now, town names recalled the old days; Gunsight is fairly obvious, but as to a town called Why, we just don't know...

On the Mountain Road in Organ Pipe Cactus National Monument, the test convoy combines the challenge of a steep ascent and air temperatures of 40°C (104°F) in the shade, with a suitably Wild Western backdrop for photography and video. Kathrin Speck and Jens Thering von der Osten begin filming their Porsche

Organ Pipe Cactus National Monument has all the gravel one could ever want.

horse opera. Jörg Wischmann attaches a tobacco-colored filter – what he calls his "Marlboro filter" – to the lens of his Canon.

Our quarters for this night are in Gila Bend. The Gila River has apparently gone on summer vacation. Our accommodations are more noteworthy than this dried-out riverbed; it is the Space Hotel, built and decorated during the early, heady days of space flight. It perfectly embodies the concept of "spaced out." Here lies an undiscovered point of interest, but Emanuel, who writes and dines for the gourmet magazine Feinschmecker, advises us to steer well clear of its restaurant.

In Gila Bend, the routine of the test program begins, as it does every day, at 6 A.M. But today, driving is not uppermost on the agenda; intercontinental data transfer is the first order of the day. Porsche's engine test team is working in hot weather too, but nine time zones away in the mountains of Andalusia. The connection to distant colleagues is carried out not only via a voice on a mobile telephone; megabytes of Motronic data travel from a notebook computer in Andalusia to a German "Handy" phone, to a satellite above

Following pages: Valley of Fire.

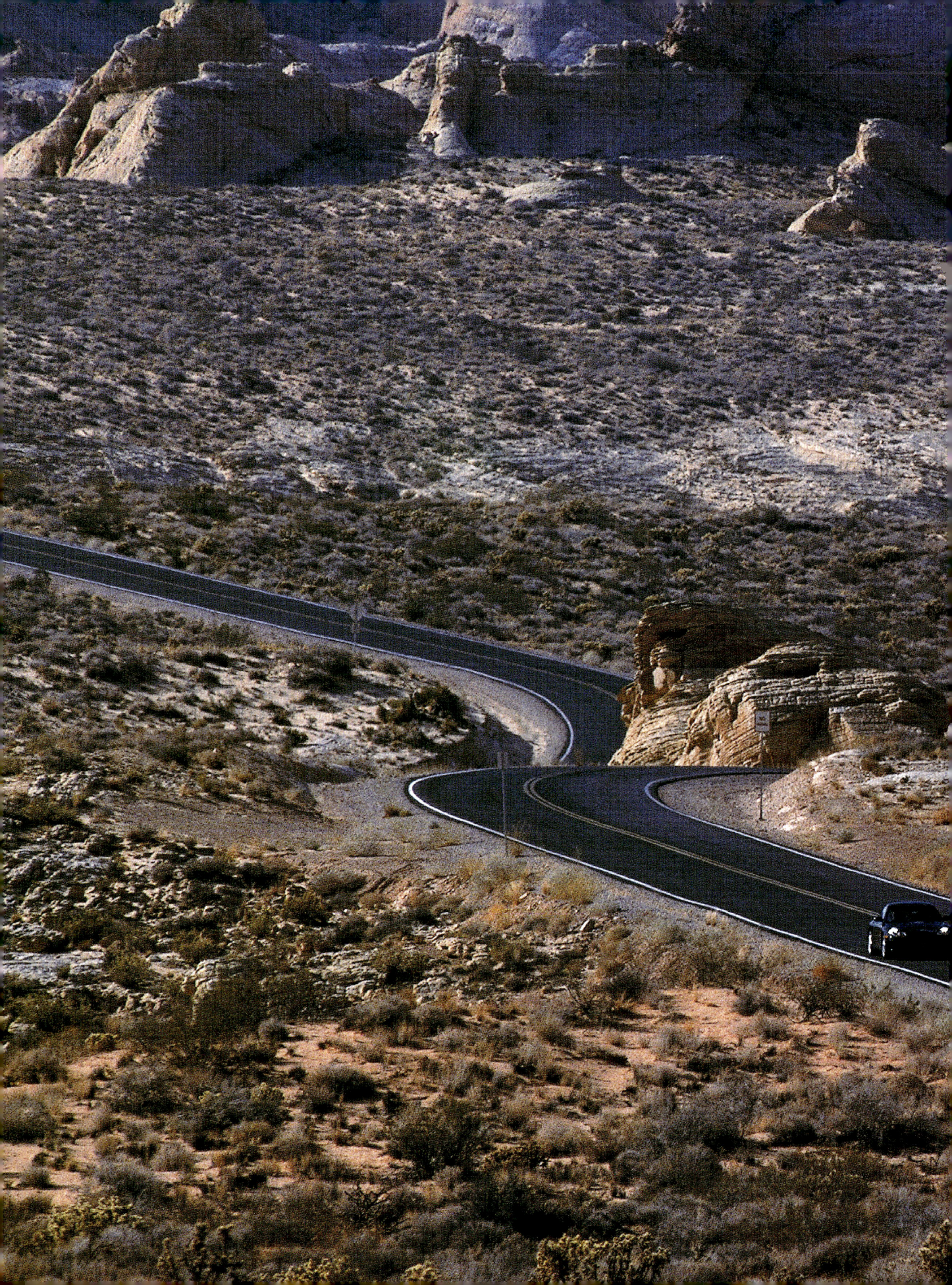

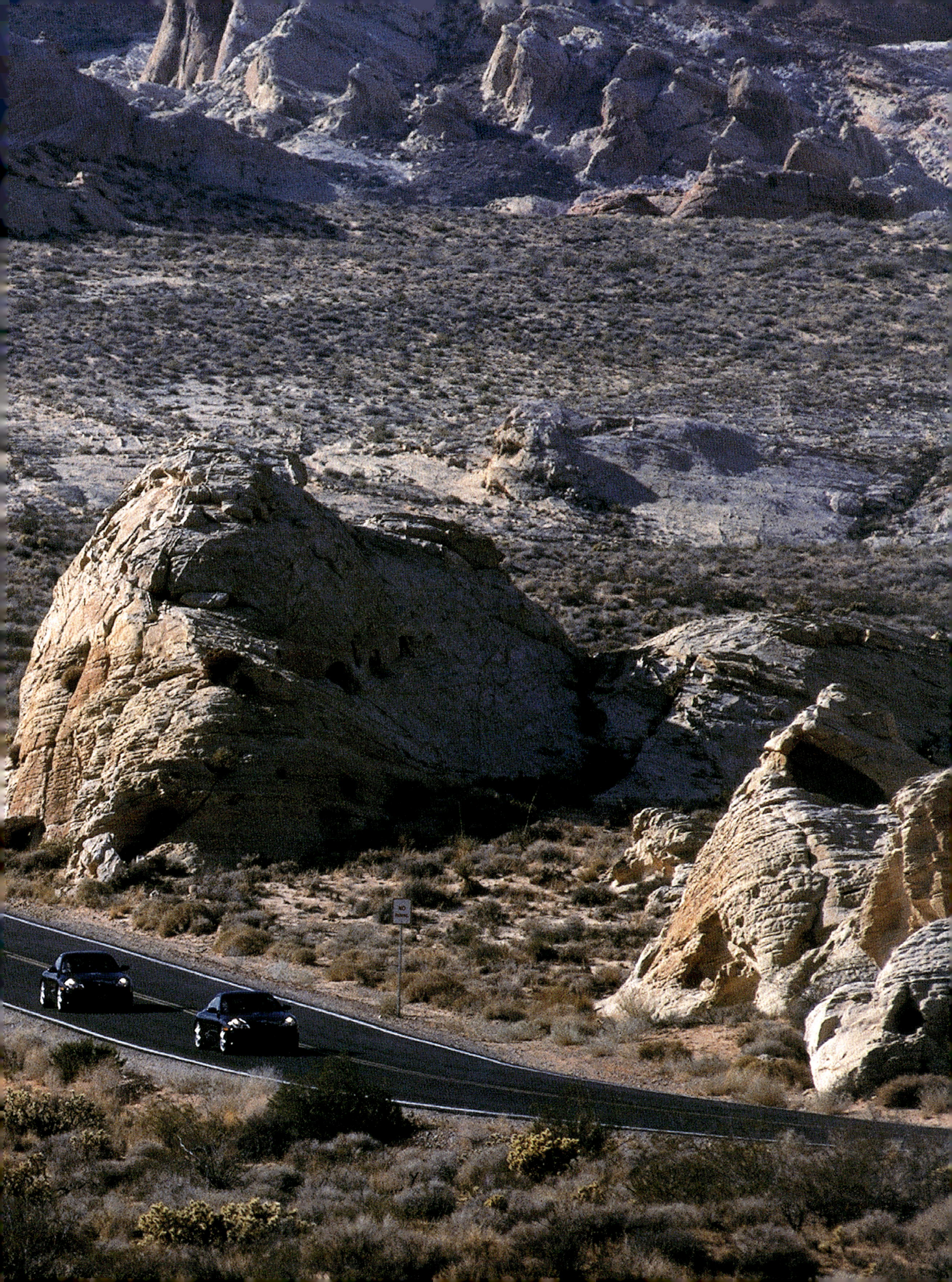

The test caravan consists of a mixture of Boxsters and Carreras.

the Atlantic, to an American cell phone and finally to a notebook in Arizona.

Next, the tiny computer passes the new data to the Motronic units in the test cars. Thereafter, the engine may run a bit better; if not, the engineers can confer with their opposite numbers in Andalusia at the same time tomorrow morning.

Test data reaches the Porsche development center in Weissach in the same way. Equipped with the appropriate software, a notebook computer can store all the data acquired by the a test car's on-board electronics: how high the engine revved, its peak oil and coolant temperatures, how much fuel was pumped by its injection system, and whether this fuel was of acceptable quality or whether it demanded the attention of the knock control system. The team regards the computer as a genial colleague, one who happily handles the tedious task of recording test data. And requires no breakfast.

The remainder of the day is dedicated to long endurance runs through the blistering landscape. Daily operation in the heat of the American Southwest is a major part of the program. South of Las Vegas, the mercury climbs to 46°C (115°F). Heinz Bernhard, leader of the test team, explains that "We successfully completed the high-temperature, high-speed test program last winter, in Australia's Northern Territory."

We continue in desert heat to the Valley of Fire, east of the gambling metropolis of Las Vegas. This day's test program finished, the "magic light" of sunset belongs to Christoph Bauer, whose photographs lend their color to this book.

A long evening of shooting under the lights of Vegas is followed by a very short night; after an eighteen-hour workday, the twenty men of the test team and the eight members of the media are too tired to try their luck in the casinos.

The next day: Death Valley, and pure unadulterated heat. The Furnace Creek Inn is the usual headquarters for test drivers seeking the ultimate in high temperatures. Since Death Valley has become a national park, heat is no longer free; the tariff for subjecting a vehicle to this torture is now $35 per car.

The obligatory tour of the local hot spots (it is now 48°C, 118°F) runs from Furnace Creek to Badwater, to nearly the lowest spot in the valley at 86 meters (282 ft.) below sea level. The local lake has dried out in the scorching summer heat; its surface now is brilliant, blinding white salt, as hard as ice.

On the mostly straight roads of the region, we could drive from Furnace Creek to Badwater at a good 250 km/h (155 mph). But American speed limits won't allow such excesses; we are restricted to 55 mph. And whenever the test teams appear, there is almost certainly a nearby police officer, complete with radar gun in eager anticipation of writing an expensive

Touring the local hot spots.

ticket. At about 90 km/h, the Porsches handle these temperatures with ease. At steady speed and light throttle, the cooling system readily copes with these desert conditions.

The test program encounters a greater challenge in the hill test, which extends from Furnace Creek Wash at 920 meters (3018 ft.) to Dante's View at 1669 m (5476 ft.) The cockpit temperature readout agrees well with reality, indicating an outside temperature of 45°C (113°F). Ahead of the test cars lie twenty miles of up- and downgrades. A sign at the western entrance to Death Valley recommends turning

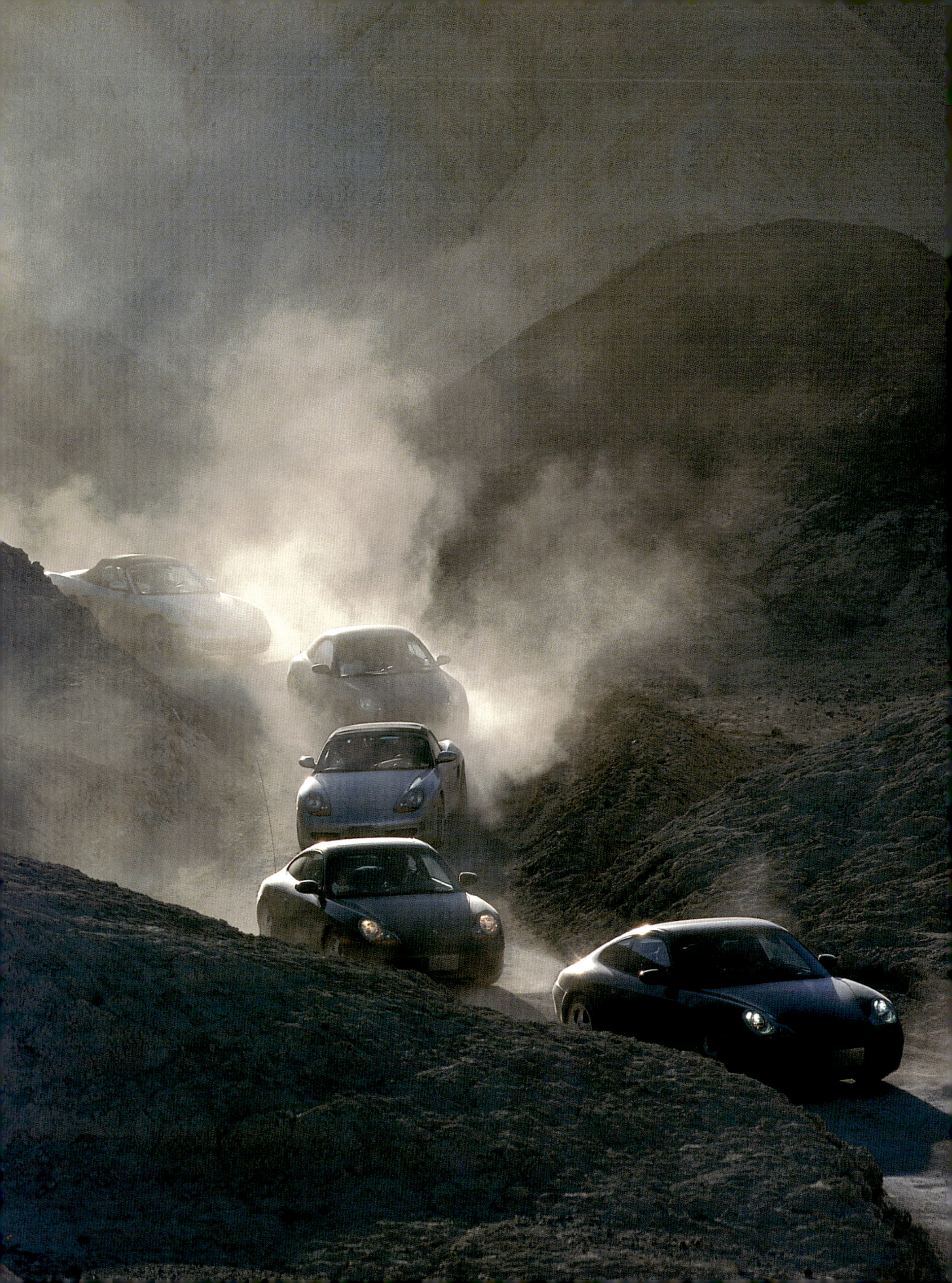

off the air conditioning to prevent overheating engines. I don't know of anybody who actually does this. Certainly not the tourists, who reach the heights of Dante's View in the air-conditioned comfort of their rental cars.

Porsche test drivers keep the air conditioning turned on for professional reasons. For the benefit of future customers, in addition to healthy temperatures in the coolant and oil sump, they are interested in how well the air leaving the air conditioning ducts is cooled.

On the last, steep 16 percent ascent, there are a few furrowed brows as the cabin cooling air briefly climbs from its normal stagnation temperature of 16°C (61°F), to a bit over 20°C (68°F). Horst Petri acknowledges that "This temperature is just barely inside our tolerance; after all, we don't want to completely isolate the driver from reality."

Engine man Johann-Georg Ulrich is happy with the numbers coming out of the data recorder. At 116°C (241°F), the pressurized coolant retains a healthy margin of safety to its boiling point. The temperature warning light would have first alerted the driver at 125°C (257°F). For the engineers, the oil temperature, kept at nearly the same level by the oil-water heat exchanger, is of almost no consequence, even though the conditions at Dante's View are almost as hard on the cars as Dante's Peak was on filmgoers.

"High ambient temperatures, relatively low speeds, and high rpms are the most difficult test of an engine cooling system," explains Johann-Georg Ulrich, "but stop-and-go traffic can be equally demanding."

Porsche test drivers perform this test when

Dusty stop-and-go traffic in Twenty Mule Team Canyon.

On the 20 Mule Team Trail.

the heat of the day has gathered its full strength on a deserted gravel road. In the previous century, this desert trail was laid down for the famed Twenty-Mule Teams, which used a gigantic wagon drawn by said animals to haul borax from the mines of Death Valley to the washtubs of the West Coast. This booming bleach trade ended when borax was discovered only half as far from Los Angeles. Since then, Twenty Mule Team Canyon, created by man and beast, has existed alongside the main road. Adventuresome tourists ex-

101

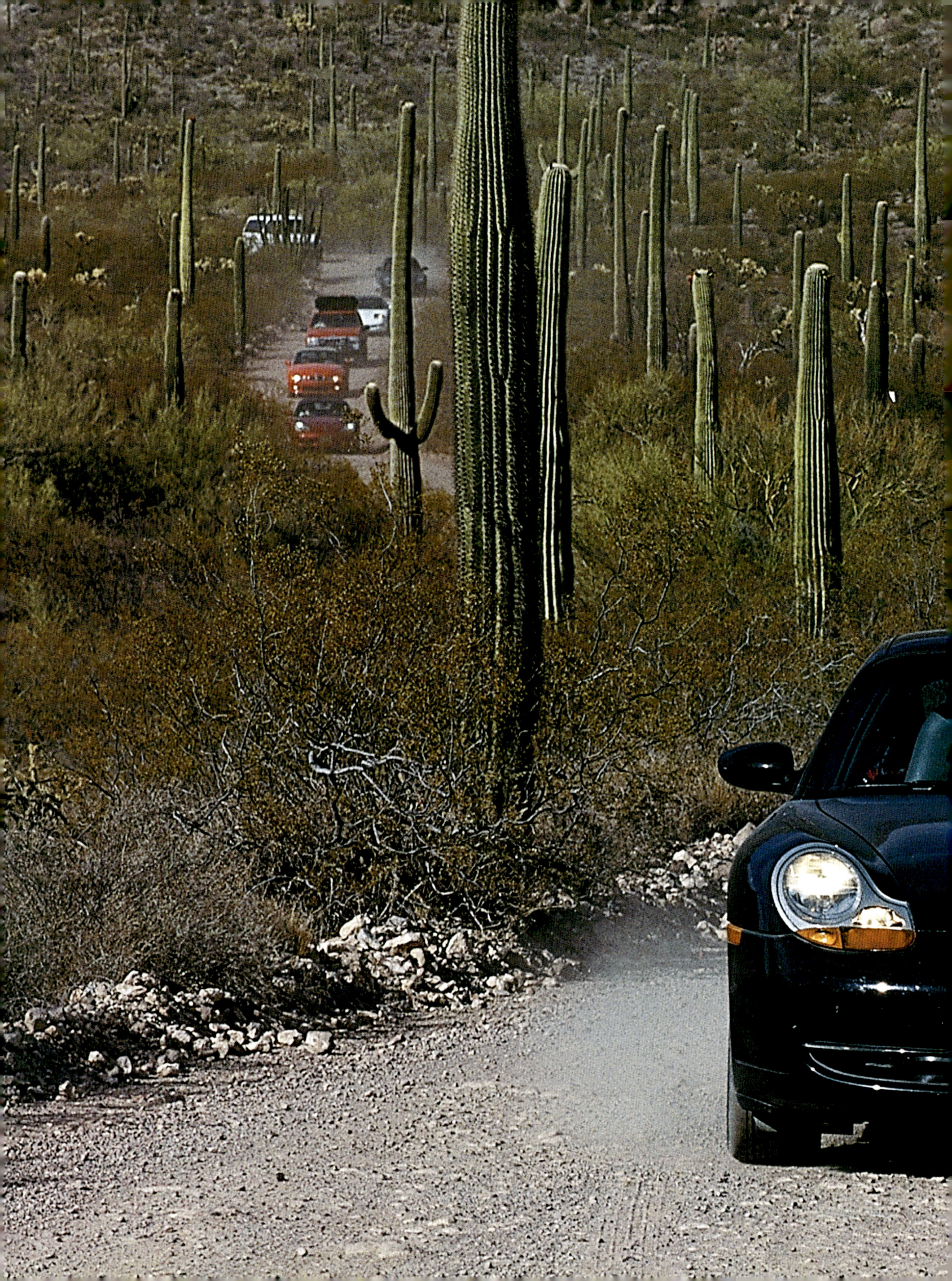

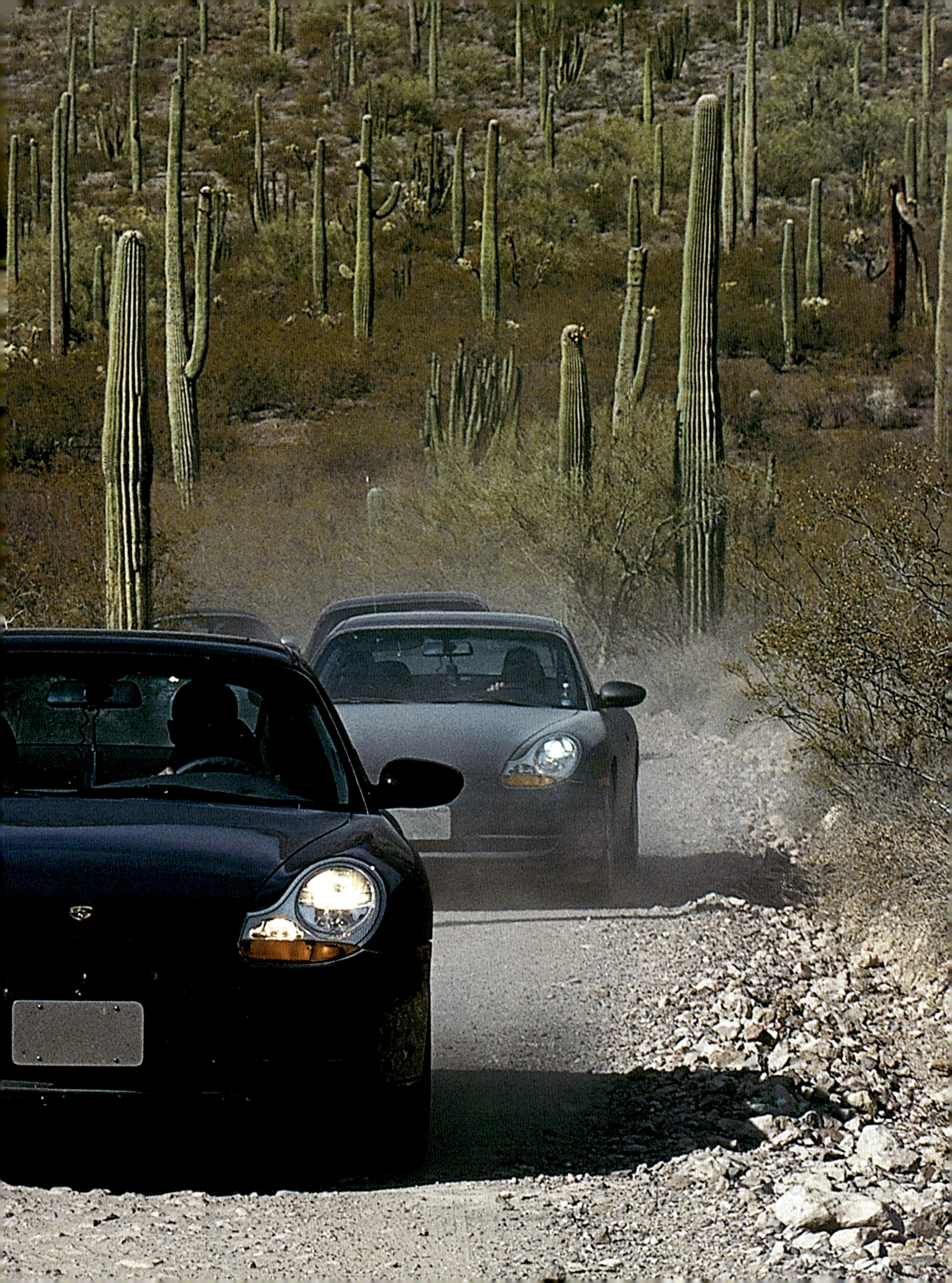

Las Vegas night life

plore its winding reaches, photographers seek out its vistas and its backlit dust columns. The Porsche Carreras seem bored by the deliberate stop-and-go routine, with unremarkable water temperatures. Only the normally unfaltering support vehicle, a Jeep Grand Cherokee, is breathing a bit hard, thanks to vapor lock in its fuel system.

Evenings in Death Valley are dressed in pink, like an elderly American grand dame. As we stand in front of the Furnace Creek Inn and look toward Badwater, the apparent desolation we see is more fertile and friendlier than the surface of Mars, which at this very moment is being explored by the Mars Pathfinder lander and its six-wheeled "Sojourner" vehicle.

Our road back to more habitable regions swings eastward out of Death Valley, to link up with one of the finest roads between Nevada and California. From Chocolate Mountain, Highway 168 drops from an altitude of nearly 2000 meters (6560 ft.) through dense forests and a rugged gorge to the small town of Big Pine, behind which the Sierra Nevada Range rises to the sky.

This is the start of our final leg to Reno: Highway 395, cherished by knowledgeable tourists for its beauty and proximity to so many parks and lakes. North of Death Valley, it passes Yosemite National Park, the string of jewels known as Mammoth Lakes, in their mountain setting, Mono Lake with its bizarre tuff forma-

Not all highways in the western United States are straight and boring.

105

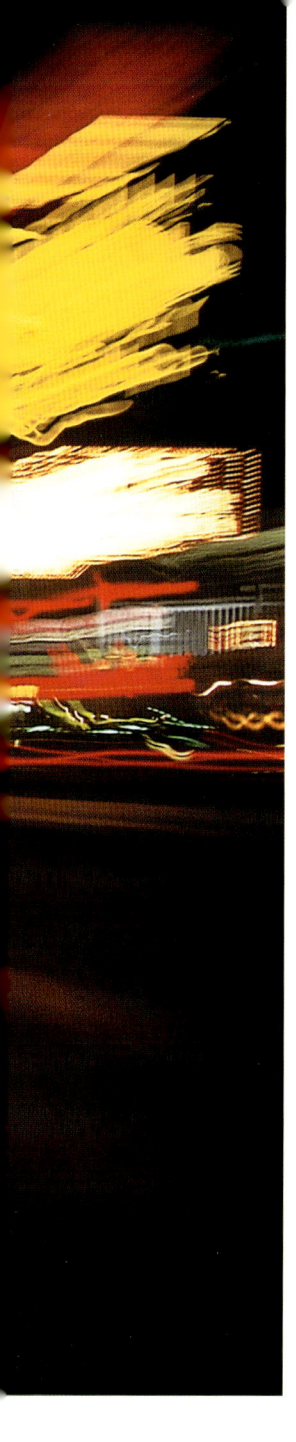

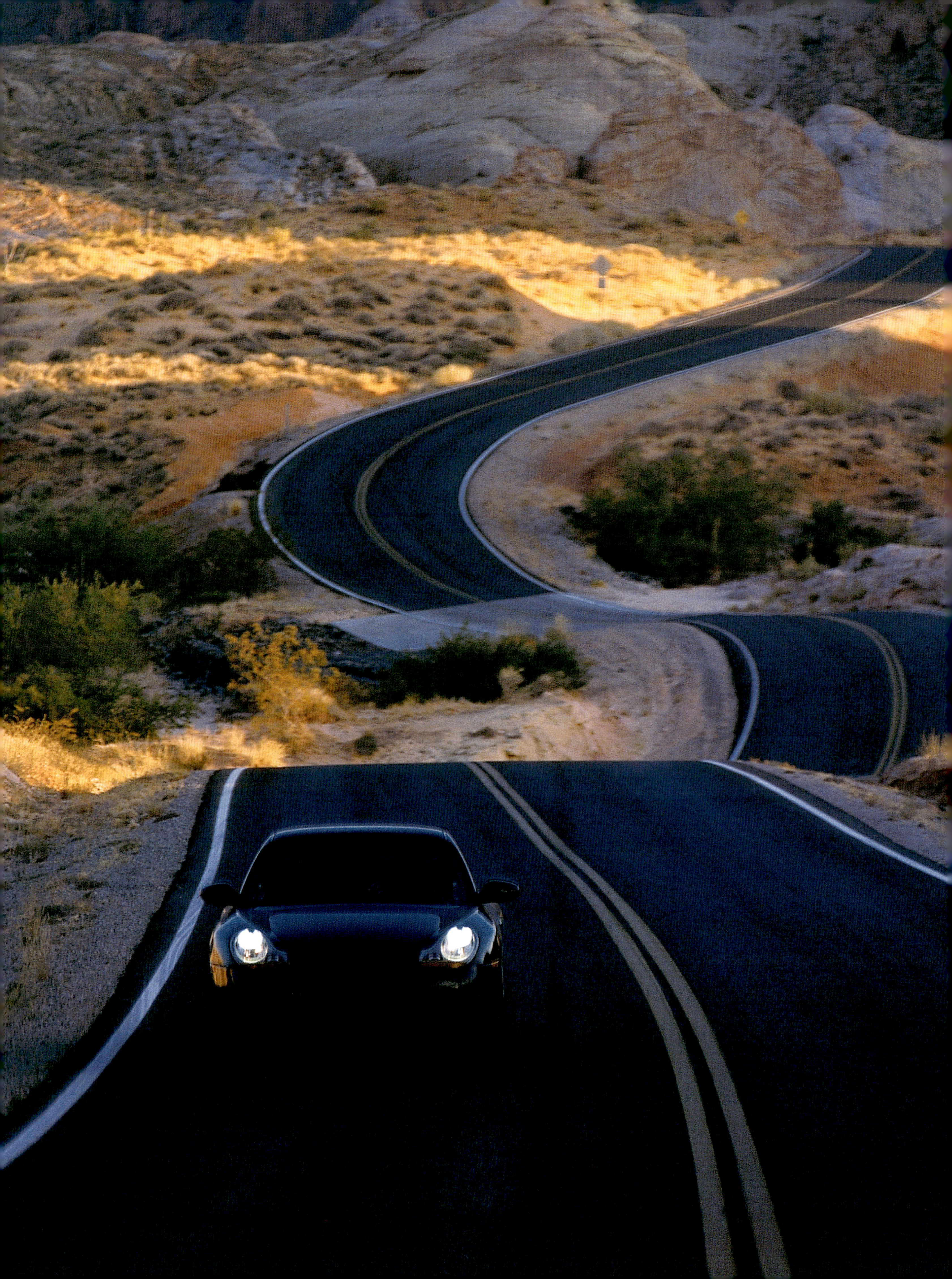

tions, the historic ghost town of Bodie, and, farther north, Lake Tahoe at its cool, refreshing altitude of 2000 meters (6560 ft.) The Porsche procession has to leave these pleasant destinations to the tourists; we are heading for a routine service appointment at Porsche's own shops in Reno.

This great highway gives the new Carrera an early, cautious public appearance. Californians on their way to the cooler summer air of the north are excited about the new car. At every refueling stop, one of the first questions is its price. And the announcement of a 175 mph top speed seems as incredible as a message from another planet.

At our journey's end in Reno, filled order books at Porsche's North American office confirms this car's enthusiastic reception. Over dinner, Fred Schwab, CEO of Porsche Cars North America – a man with Swabian ancestors, as his name indicates – declares that

"The old Carrera was a fantastic seller, and evidently the new one will go it one better. Our only concern for the future is getting enough cars to satisfy the American market."

Double yellow: in the U.S., this represents an impenetrable barrier (the ideal line through a corner notwithstanding).

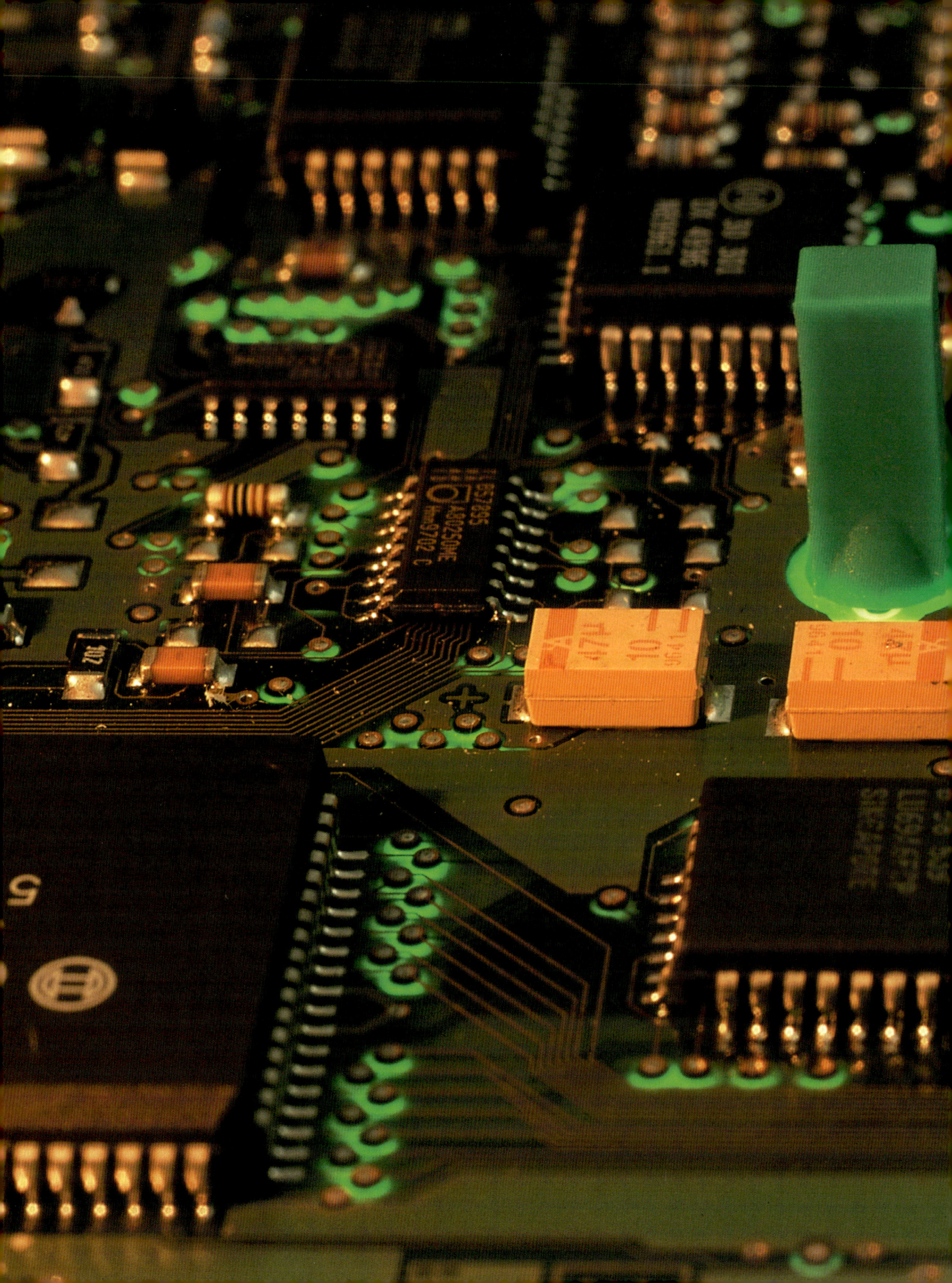

447NDK6Y

TL B57562
HA
AM A72650ME
ID   Hnn9702 B

100
4
PH
HNK

The electronic systems of the New Carrera

Just a Bit More

The electronic systems of a modern, high-quality automobile overshadow anything we might find in our homes.

The electronic systems of a modern, high-quality automobile overshadow anything we might find in our homes. Within the relatively small space occupied by the new Carrera – 4.43 meters long and 1.77 meters wide (about 84 sq. ft.) – we find a harness whose wires, if laid end to end, would stretch up to four kilometers (2½ miles) if all available options are ordered. Like the rest of the car, the wiring harnesses of today's Porsches are precision engineered. To cut weight and costs, no wires are installed unless they actually are needed.

The electrical system incorporates no less than 60 electrical motors, which in their various capacities make the life of a Carrera driver more comfortable. The most powerful of these is the starter, with an output of 1.2 kilowatts (1.6 hp). It has enough power to ensure starting even at 40 degrees below zero. Given proper gearing, the starter would be capable of moving the 911 at 30 km/h × nearly 20 mph. Most of the other electrical motors operate items such as the windshield wipers, sunroof, seat adjustment, and ventilation blowers. Much less obvious are tiny motors which adjust flaps in the climate control system, or load a compact disc into the CD player.

Even though the system voltage is nominally listed as 12 Volts, the 911, like any other modern car, uses both higher and lower voltages in its various systems. The ignition system puts out up to 100,000 Volts in the short wires between the ignition coil and the spark plugs. By contrast, the complex data processing system operates at only 5 Volts, in keeping with standard computer practice.

Indeed, digital processing is employed in virtually every nook and cranny of the modern Porsche. Without all these bits and bytes of data, nothing would operate. Even while the car is parked, the electronic system is hard at work, as the alarm system maintains its vigil.

As we approach the car press the remote button on the ignition key, our electronic servants become more active. A receiver inside the car, waiting patiently for just such a signal, checks to see if the key transmitter is using the same password as they had agreed upon when the car was locked. The electronic sentry "hears" the awaited "password," and stands at ease.

Now, the electronic security sequence begins. The central locking system unlocks, the alarm system's interior monitoring is turned off, the turn signals flash in verification. In hot weather the side windows may be opened if the button on the ignition key is pressed for two seconds.

We get in and press the "memory" button. The seat "knows" what we want and moves to our favorite position as six microchip-based control units spring into action, ensuring our comfort. The ignition key is located to the left of the

The instrument cluster has long since parted company from the old-fashioned speedometer cable. It now consists of an integrated electronic system which processes digital signals from the Motronic and ABS computers. The needles are moved by servomotors.

steering column, as it has been in every Porsche ever built. Turn it to the first position, and the 911 runs through its checklist. All warning lights come on momentarily to indicate that they are functioning properly. The fuel level is immediately readable, the engine oil level is evaluated by a microprocessor which delivers its findings mere seconds later.

When the ignition is activated, the remaining electronic systems become operational. Air bag igniters are armed; radio, on-board computer and navigation system stand at the ready; all control elements are functional; and, depending on options, a further 15 to 20 intelligent electronic systems are activated.

When the ignition key is turned to the "start" position, a brief dialog takes place between the transponder in the key and its counterpart in the ignition lock. One asks "are we on the same wavelength?" If the answer is affirmative, the computer responds with "drive lockout deactivated, ready to roll."

Now the real calculations start, as the Motronic engine control system goes about its business of managing fuel mixture and ignition timing. This electronic system is in command of an efficient operation, with a minimum of managerial overhead; recently, there has been a radical downsizing of staff. The ignition distributor was fired, so to speak, as were ignition timing, the centrifugal advance mechanism, and even the vacuum advance. The staff remaining in the fuel supply department consists of six injection nozzles, a fuel pump and a supervisory board of sensors.

Nearly every function once carried out by mechanical devices is now accomplished by electronics and microprocessors. They carry out their jobs in an effective and timely manner, performing their calculations once every crankshaft revolution. This may amount to as many as 100 per second. A multitude of information must be processed: crankshaft rpm, the mass of inducted air, throttle position, engine temperature and the oxygen content of the exhaust stream. This formidable math assignment must be solved in a fraction of a second,

111

Visitor's Guide to Motronic City

Relay output section. This controls the function of external relays for fuel pump, cooling fans, and other engine-specific electrical devices

Office of Optimum Thermodynamics. Central monitoring station for knock sensors.

Technical Review Board for Ecologically Correct Combustion. This office monitors the resistance of oxygen sensors in the exhaust system.

Central Monument. No electrical function; serves to insulate a mounting screw.

Flash Memory. The working archives. Programs which may be updated to improve operation during the service life of the car are maintained here.

EPROM – Erasable Programmable Read-Only Memory. The City Records Office. All permanent programs, which may not be changed, are stored here.

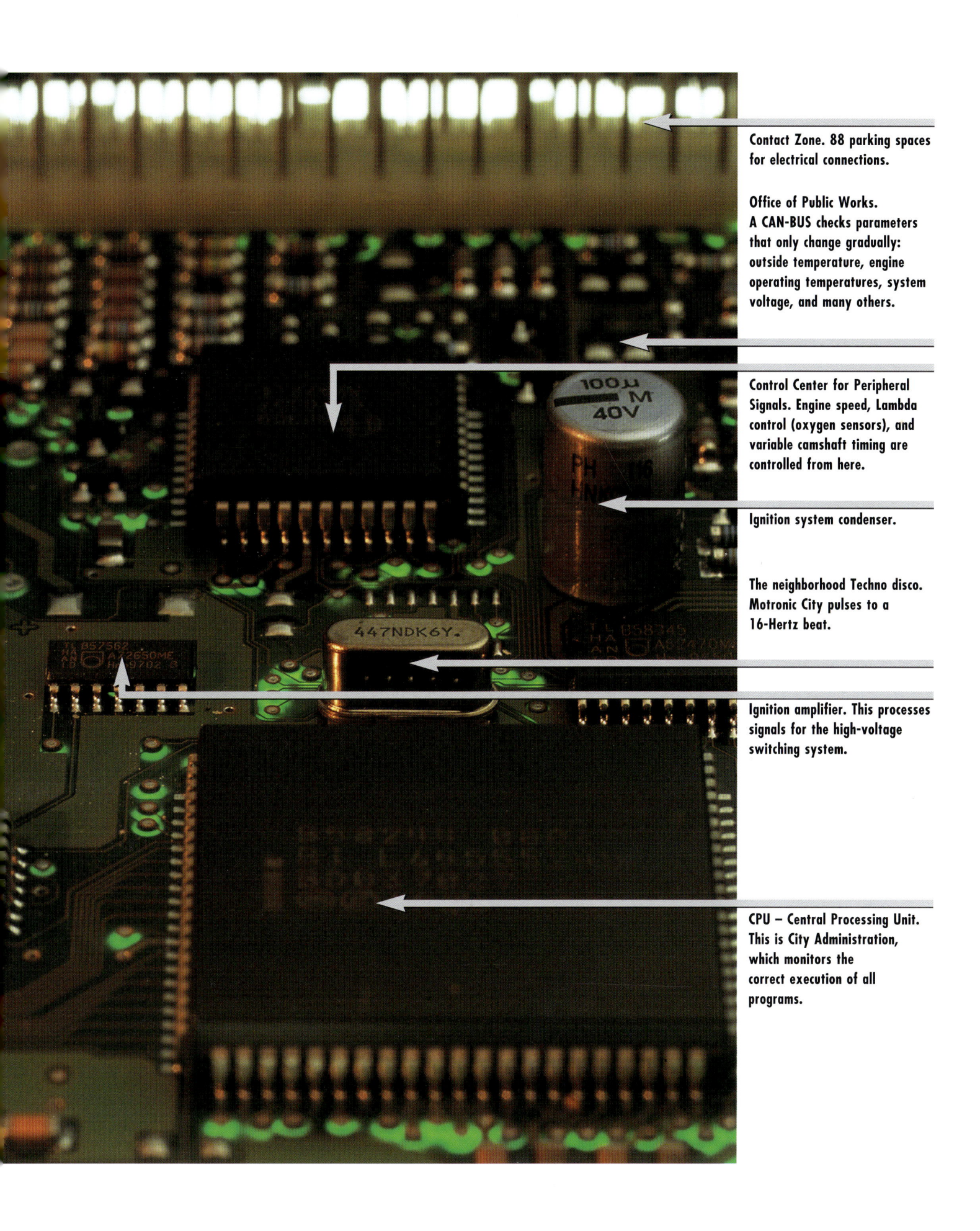

Contact Zone. 88 parking spaces for electrical connections.

Office of Public Works. A CAN-BUS checks parameters that only change gradually: outside temperature, engine operating temperatures, system voltage, and many others.

Control Center for Peripheral Signals. Engine speed, Lambda control (oxygen sensors), and variable camshaft timing are controlled from here.

Ignition system condenser.

The neighborhood Techno disco. Motronic City pulses to a 16-Hertz beat.

Ignition amplifier. This processes signals for the high-voltage switching system.

CPU – Central Processing Unit. This is City Administration, which monitors the correct execution of all programs.

113

with any grade lower than a perfect "A" unacceptable. The ability of electronics to make rapid decisions is less critical in the initial warmup phase, but all the more so at full throttle and high rpm operation. When the six-cylinder engine develops its 300 horsepower at 6800 rpm, the injection system must meter 340 charges of fuel every second, at precisely the right instant, through the injector nozzle to the correct combustion chamber. But that's not all; to actually burn this fuel, a further 340 ignition impulses must be delivered with microsecond accuracy.

These rapid-fire calculations are all in a day's work for a Motronic unit. Its true brilliance, however, is demonstrated by other functions. For example, cylinder-specific knock control may report that somewhere along the line, the combustion process is not proceeding as planned. The Motronic then uses its sensors to "listen" and determine which cylinder is not doing its job, then dials back the ignition timing for that cylinder only.

On-board electronics permit smooth interaction between the engine and the optional automatic transmission.

▪ All shifts are controlled by data stored in on-board computers, using road speed, engine rpm and throttle position as parameters.

▪ During every gear shift, the control unit briefly reduces engine output to ensure smoother shifts.

▪ By means of a throttle position sensor, the control unit recognizes if the driver has moved his foot quickly, and therefore presumably wants to drive in a more spirited manner. The unit then chooses a "sportier" shift program.

▪ Sudden closing of the throttle is recognized as a need for deceleration, and in such cases the transmission will not shift up.

The anti-lock brake system already is a classic among automotive electronic systems, but its sensors are used for more than just braking situations.

▪ Precise speed measurement at the individual wheels enables the computers to determine whether the car is moving straight ahead or through curves. ABS is but one system to make use of this information; electronic traction control systems use it as well.

▪ Extreme wheel-speed differences are interpreted as spinning of the drive wheels. The Automatic Brake Differential counters with application of the brake on the non-conforming wheel.

▪ The many impulses sent by the ABS sensors allow precise measurement of speed and distance. This provides data not only to the speedometer and odometer, but also the navigation system.

Which brings us to the biggest leap into the future yet undertaken by Porsche electronics. Ever-increasing interconnection of on-board electronics has prompted Porsche, together with Siemens, to develop the highly integrated Porsche Communications Management (PCM) system. This system allows the computer, via a user interface, to communicate directly with the car's occupants.

The following functions are arrayed around a color monitor in the center of the instrument panel:

▪ audio system with CD changer

▪ on-board computer with readouts for fuel consumption, driving time, average speed, etc.

▪ automatic air conditioning, heating and ventilation

▪ "hands-free" cellular phone

▪ satellite navigation system with maps stored on CD-ROM

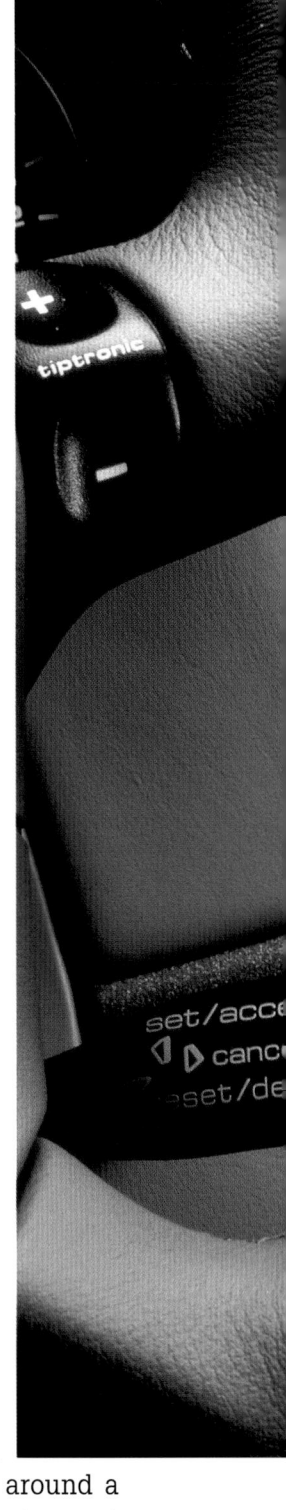

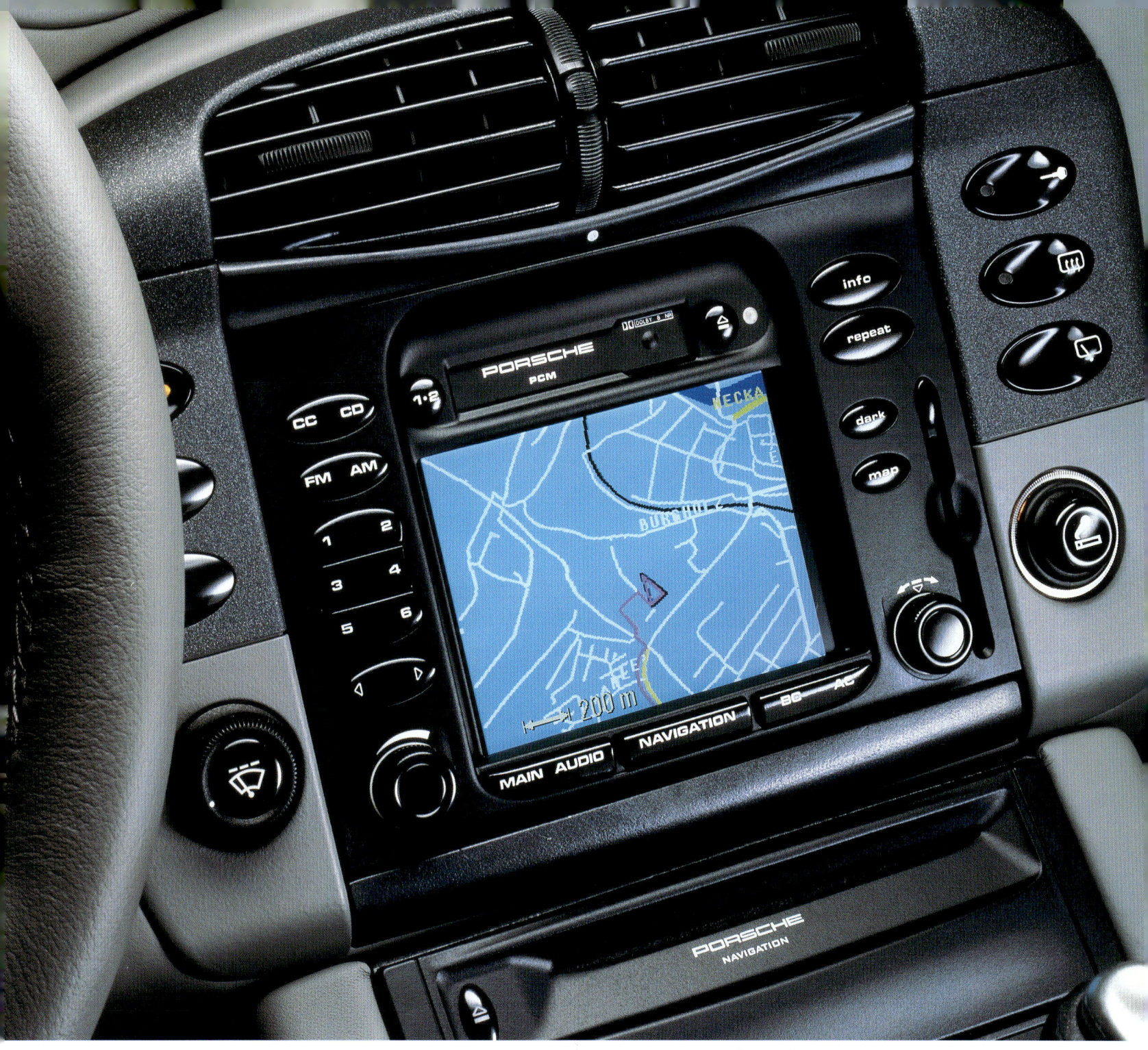

The Porsche Communication Management System: the map display can zoom in to 50 meters per side, or out to 50 km views.

The monitor becomes a perfect window on the outside world. The car no longer is an isolated island in traffic; rather, at the touch of a button, it becomes a vehicle for information and communication.

Moreover, electronic systems ensure that there are times when the car deliberately does not work as planned. The alarm system recognizes when the locks are being tampered with, detects motion and intrusions into the car's interior. The immediate response is a warning issued by an old-fashioned electromechanical device of rather limited intelligence – the car's horn. At the same time, a drive lockout system ensures that any attempt at theft goes no farther, by cutting off current to the starter, the Motronic engine management system, and the fuel pump. None of these will work until the correct ignition key is inserted into the lock.

All in one – the Porsche Communication Management System

Combination Display
The monitor screen can also display other information, including audio selection, outside air temperature, time, and compass heading.

The Porsche Communication Management System turns the center console of the new Carrera into a master control panel for five separate electronic systems. Here, a city map is displayed by the navigation system. The screen can display map sections from 50 meters (164 ft.) to 50 kilometers (30 miles) per side. Audible directions guide the driver to his destination.

On-board Computer

While under way, it is possible to display information on the screen, including trip duration, average speed, fuel economy, and, if the original distance to destination is entered manually, the remaining travel time and distance.

Audio System

The monitor shows which radio stations can be received with acceptable signal strength. Selection and tuning is done via buttons. Traffic reports may be stored automatically.

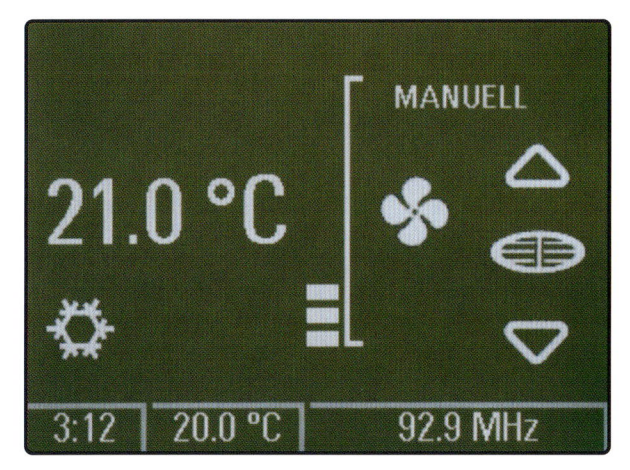

Climate Control System

All heating, ventilation and air conditioning functions can be accessed through the central control panel. In this mode, the monitor displays all relevant climate control data.

Satellite Navigation System

The PCM includes a satellite navigation system, which combines signals from Global Positioning System satellites with country-specific CD-ROMs to guide the Carrera driver to his destination. The simplified representation, using optical and acoustic directions instead of a visible map, is less likely to distract a driver's attention from the road.

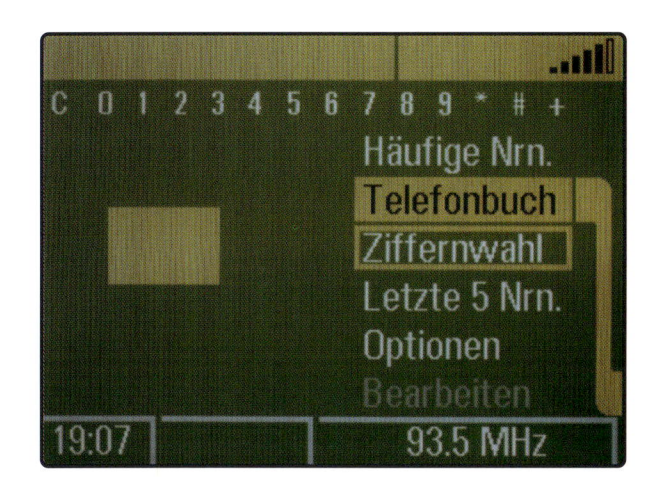

Mobile Telephone

The hands-free GSM telephone integrated in the PCM is operated via buttons on the center console. Several numbers may be preprogrammed Caller ID and pager messages may be displayed on the monitor.

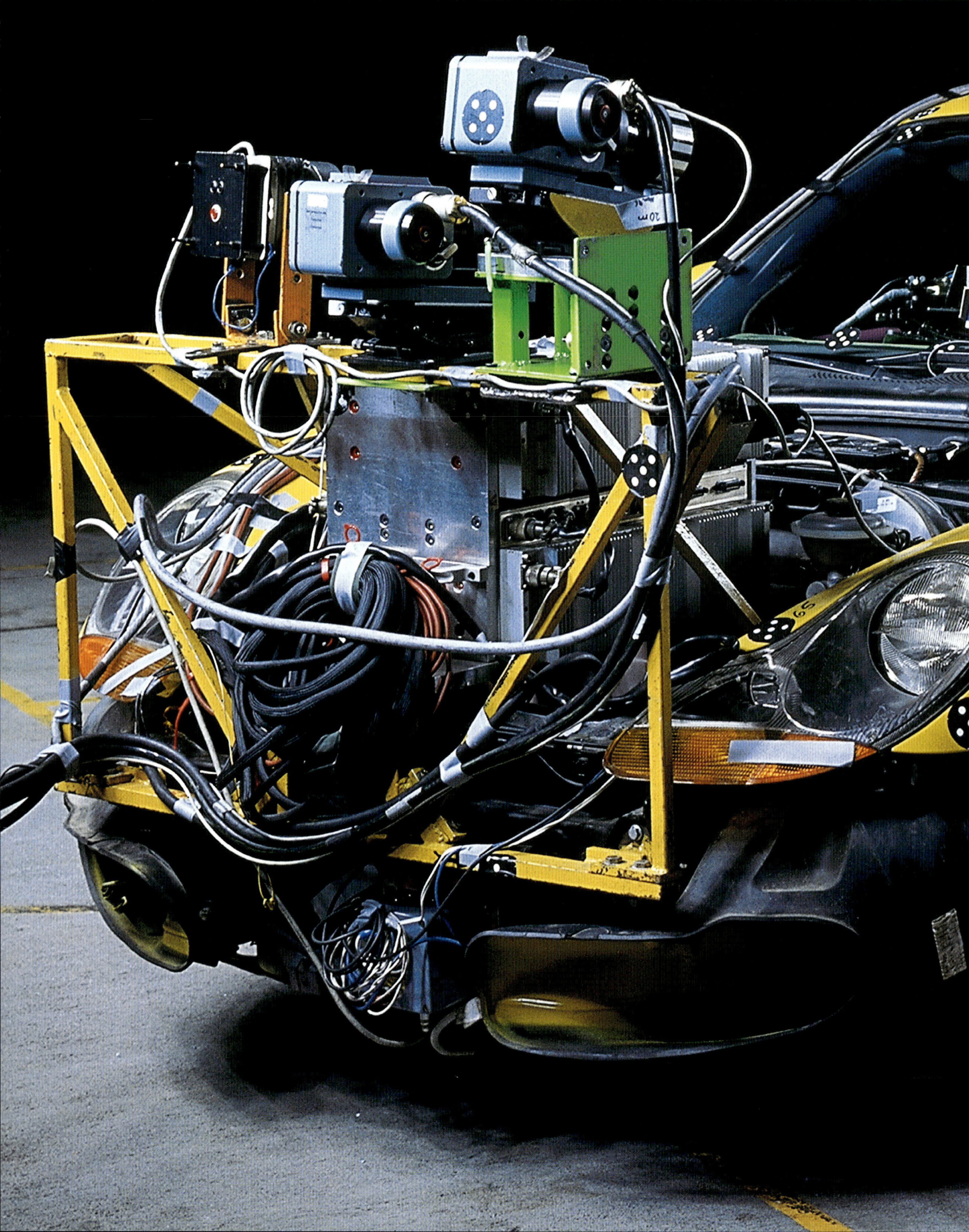

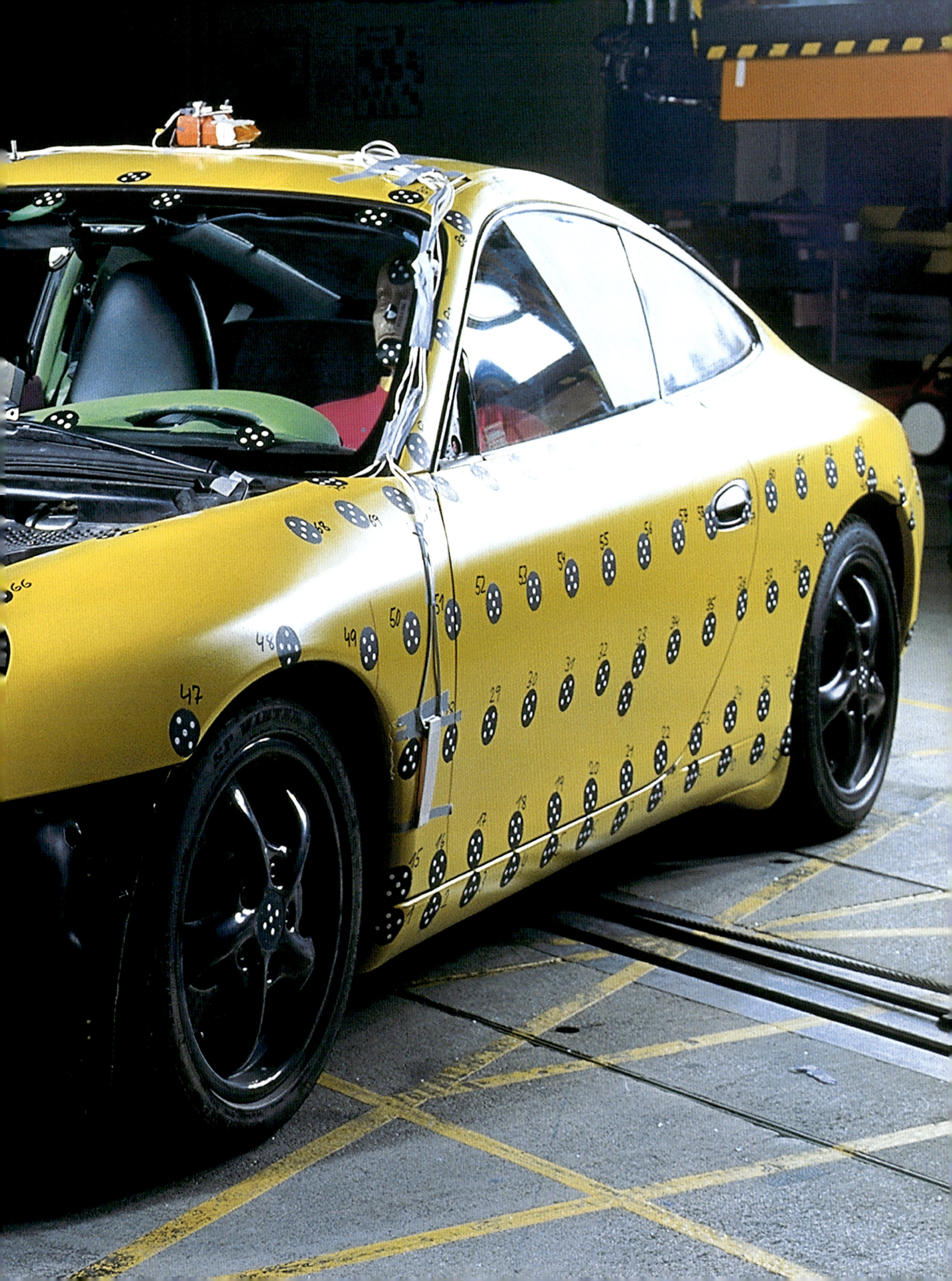
66
47
48
49
50
52
53
54
55
29
30
31

Passive Safety Features of the new 911

Safety First

It was a lofty goal. The engineers at Porsche's Weissach Development Center had challenged themselves to set new standards of passive safety for sports cars. And, of course, they succeeded

The new Carrera experienced its first crash in the summer of 1993. Although it looked like the new 911, in fact it was an entirely virtual creation, existing only as several gigabytes inside a computer's memory. This binary prototype left its parking space on a mainframe computer's hard disk only for short excursions on a monitor, where it regularly drove into disaster. This marvelous creation of ones and zeroes headed straight into a wall.

This was no short, sharp shock, with a damage estimate falling somewhere between a fender bender and a total writeoff; rather, it was a slow, informative process of almost complete destruction, taking place on the monitor without the usual accompaniment of screeching, shattering, crashing sounds of a real impact. Yet the engineers stared at this gruesome video in utter fascination, because long before the car even existed, they could see whether their passive safety strategy obeyed the laws of physics as expected.

The means by which today's engineers represent the design conditions that will make a serious accident survivable are reminiscent of the maps and diagrams of ancient battles, dimly recalled from our history lessons.

Just as generals depict their troops as a bundle of broad arrows, poised to attack, engineers display the defensive posture of their cars by so-called "load paths," formed by discrete structures within the body. They calculate the stiffness of the structure in order to ensure that the body will be stable and torsionally rigid for many hundreds of thousands of miles, but more important, their complex analysis takes into consideration deliberate deformation in the event of a really good wreck.

Long before actual prototype cars are made, these computer simulations depict nearly every crease that would be pounded into the body during an actual collision. In the event that these virtual accidents indicate a certain certain structure is too weak – or possibly too strong – the problem can be corrected with the light pen without ever cutting metal, quickly and at virtually no cost. The most fascinating aspect of these computer crashes is the repair process; simply press the "Reset" key and a brand-new car appears on the screen, unblemished by the lifelong stigma of a repaired accident. It is as if the accident were only a bad dream, and upon waking, we discover that our flawless 911 is safe and sound in the garage.

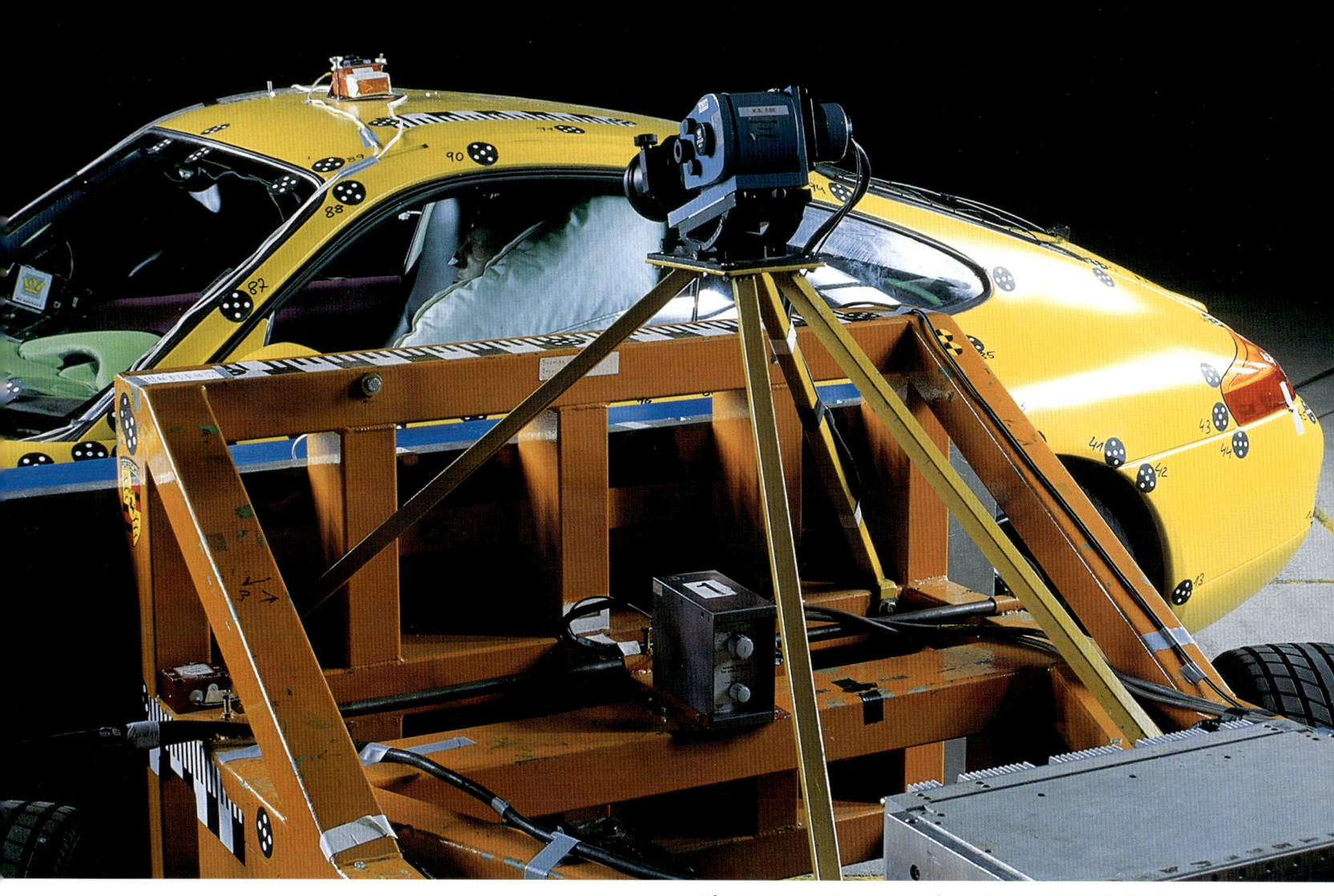

Side-impact protection was a vital consideration during the development of the new Carrera. This photo of a side impact crash test shows the side air bag, visible only as a blur during its deployment.

Even if we never call on the crashworthiness built into our cars, such computer simulations and their transformation into actual sheet metal yield significant benefits. Today's computer-modelled cars are simply better and more solidly built than the cars of yesterday, created as they were by pen and ink on the drawing board.

Not that the classic 911 of more than three decades ago was less than a truly outstanding design. For its time, it represented a rock-solid example of the finest workmanship to proudly bear the stamp "Made in Germany." But the new 911 surpasses its ancestor; its torsional stiffness has been increased by 45 percent, and stiffness in bending is as much as 50 percent higher.

These impressive gains were achieved despite a body that is significantly larger and roomier, but hardly any heavier. In the stamping plant, as in the kitchen, the secret of any lightweight confection lies in the quality of the ingredients. Among connoisseurs, the body of the new Carrera may be considered a delicacy in modern steel: 63.2 percent of the new 911's body consists of conventional deep-drawing sheet steel; high-strength steels make up 29.1 percent; 6.4 percent consists of so-called "tailored blanks;" and 1.3 percent of the structure is made of extremely strong boron steel.

The degree of refinement incorporated in these body components is exemplified by the 6.4 percent represented by "tailored blanks." As the name suggests, these are custom-tailored steel panels. They consist of pieces of varying thicknesses, which are joined by laser beam welding to form a single part. This produces structural components capable of handling extreme load variations in service, or which are intended to absorb energy progressively in a collision. Tailored-blank longitudinal members are the logical choice for this heroic, self-sacrificing role.

All load-carrying structures are optimized to one another in terms of rigidity and deformability, combining to create an integrated net-

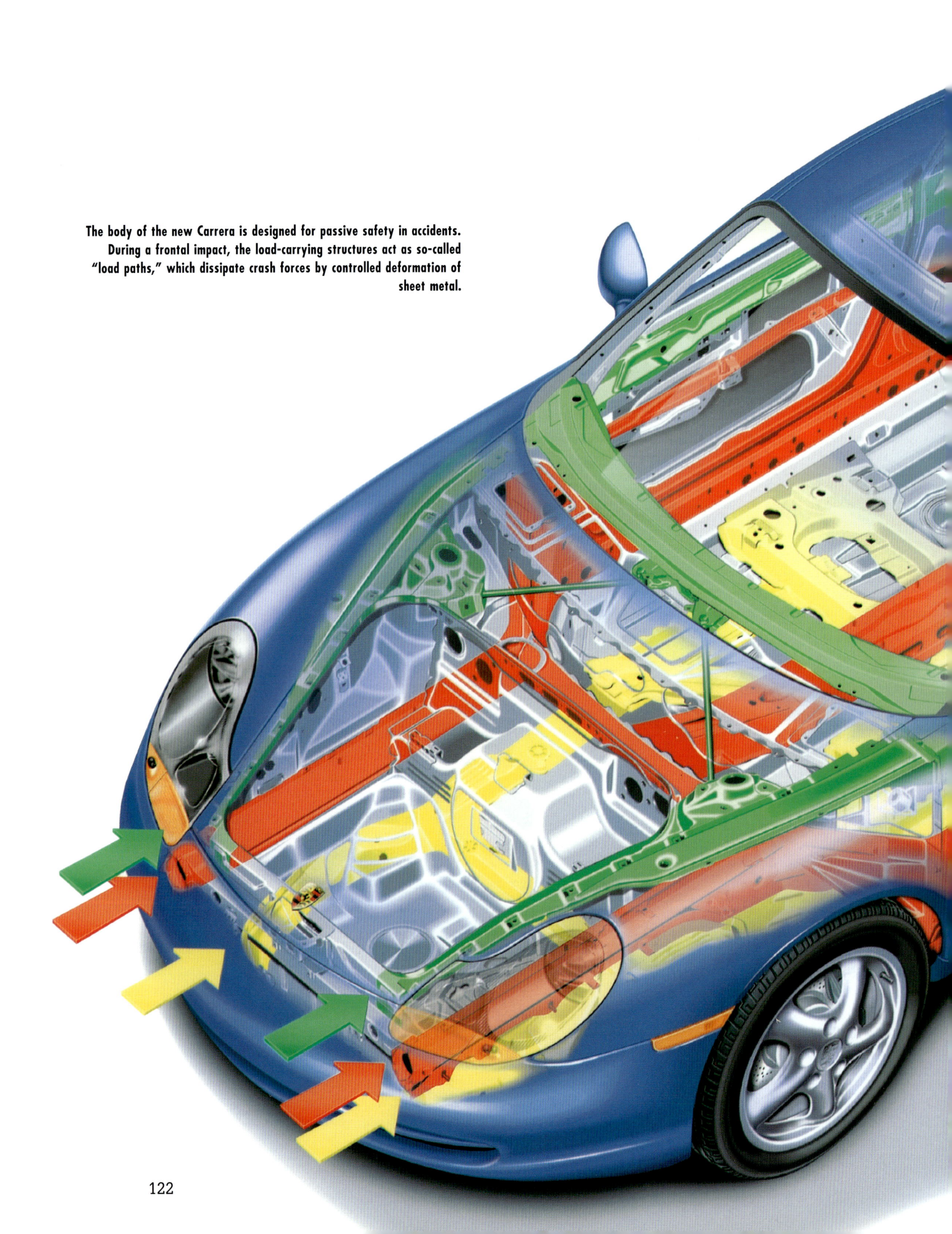

The body of the new Carrera is designed for passive safety in accidents. During a frontal impact, the load-carrying structures act as so-called "load paths," which dissipate crash forces by controlled deformation of sheet metal.

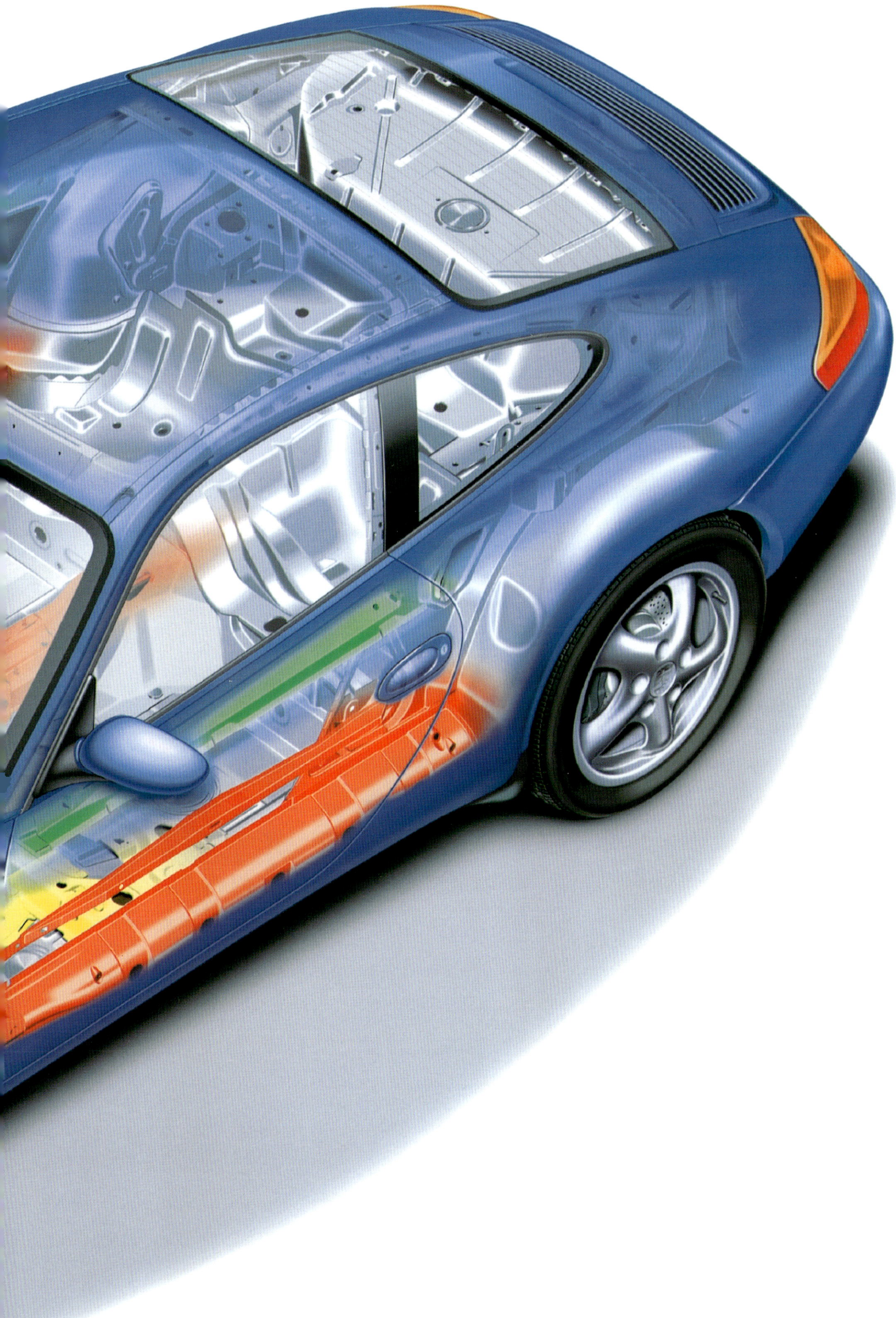

Sheet Steel
63.18%

High-Strenght Steel
29.14%

Boron Steel
1.32%

Tailored Blanks
6.36%

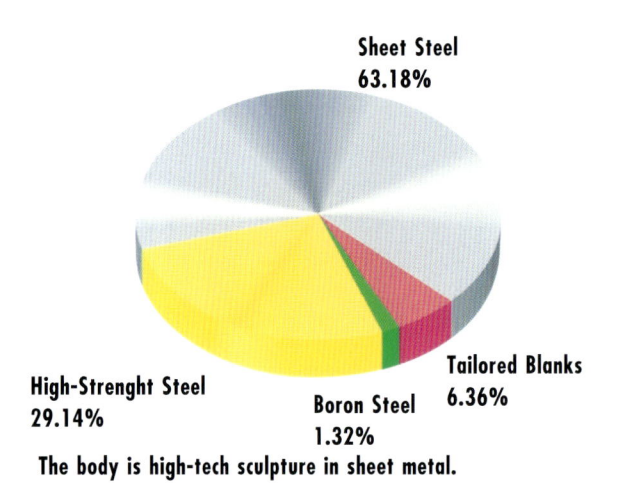

The body is high-tech sculpture in sheet metal.

work of stability during good times, and deformability under less pleasant circumstances. During a crash, forces are transmitted from one component to another through the aforementioned load paths: from the front suspension to the longitudinal members, from the longitudinals to the door frames and sills. Many parts serve a dual purpose. For example, the side impact beams can also absorb energy in a frontal collision, ensuring that the doors remain operable.

A different survival strategy is represented by the choice of steel instead of aluminum as the load-carrying material for the body. First, after Porsche's 20 years of experience with double-side galvanized steel, the engineers in Weissach are firmly convinced that they have found the most durable of all affordable materials. Second, steel has a great advantage in global terms: it can be repaired anywhere in the world. After all, Porsches are sold in 74 countries.

A second aspect of safety lies in a few readily visible systems. Safety belts continue to make the most important contribution to occupant protection; without belts, any airbags would be of little use or perhaps downright dangerous. Three-point automatic belts, including belts for the rear jump seats, have been a matter of course at Porsche for generations. The front harnesses are now adjustable for height. Moreover, they employ pyrotechnic belt tensioners, but these do not require a tension limiter. The reason: computer simulations as well as real world experiments show that during a collision, the energy absorption of the body is so progressive, and the loads on occupants so moderate, that a belt tension limiter would not improve crash safety. If anything, it might make matters worse.

Porsche was the first auto manufacturer to equip all of its cars with dual airbags as standard equipment, and has continued to refine its passive restraint systems. This new model includes a further development toward perfect optimization of a system which one hopes will never be called upon to do its task.

In an example of precise detail design, driver and passenger benefit from two different airbag concepts. The somewhat smaller volume of the full-size airbag on the driver's side employs an organic propellant gas generator, completely free of sodium azide. The advantage of this technology, appearing for the first time in any automobile, is that the propellant is less hazardous during the manufacturing process, and later when the car is recycled – even though, in the case of a Porsche, that may lie in the far distant future. Engineers also appreciate the smaller dimensions of the sodium azide-free gas generator, and its lower weight. The larger airbag on the passenger side is inflated by a hybrid gas generator, most of its volume supplied by a pressure tank filled with argon, an inert, harmless gas. Here, too, Porsche takes a decisive step toward environmental responsibility and recycling; deployment of the passenger airbag does not damage the instrument panel. After minor impacts, cost-effective replacement of the airbag is possible. Child seats, available from Porsche's accessory program, also have successfully undergone crash testing. These seats employ an electrical contact which deactivates the passenger airbag to ensure the safety of the next generation of Porsche drivers.

One added item on the new Carrera, which is likely to be taken for granted, is known as POSIP – for Porsche Side Impact Protection System. This consists of two side airbags and

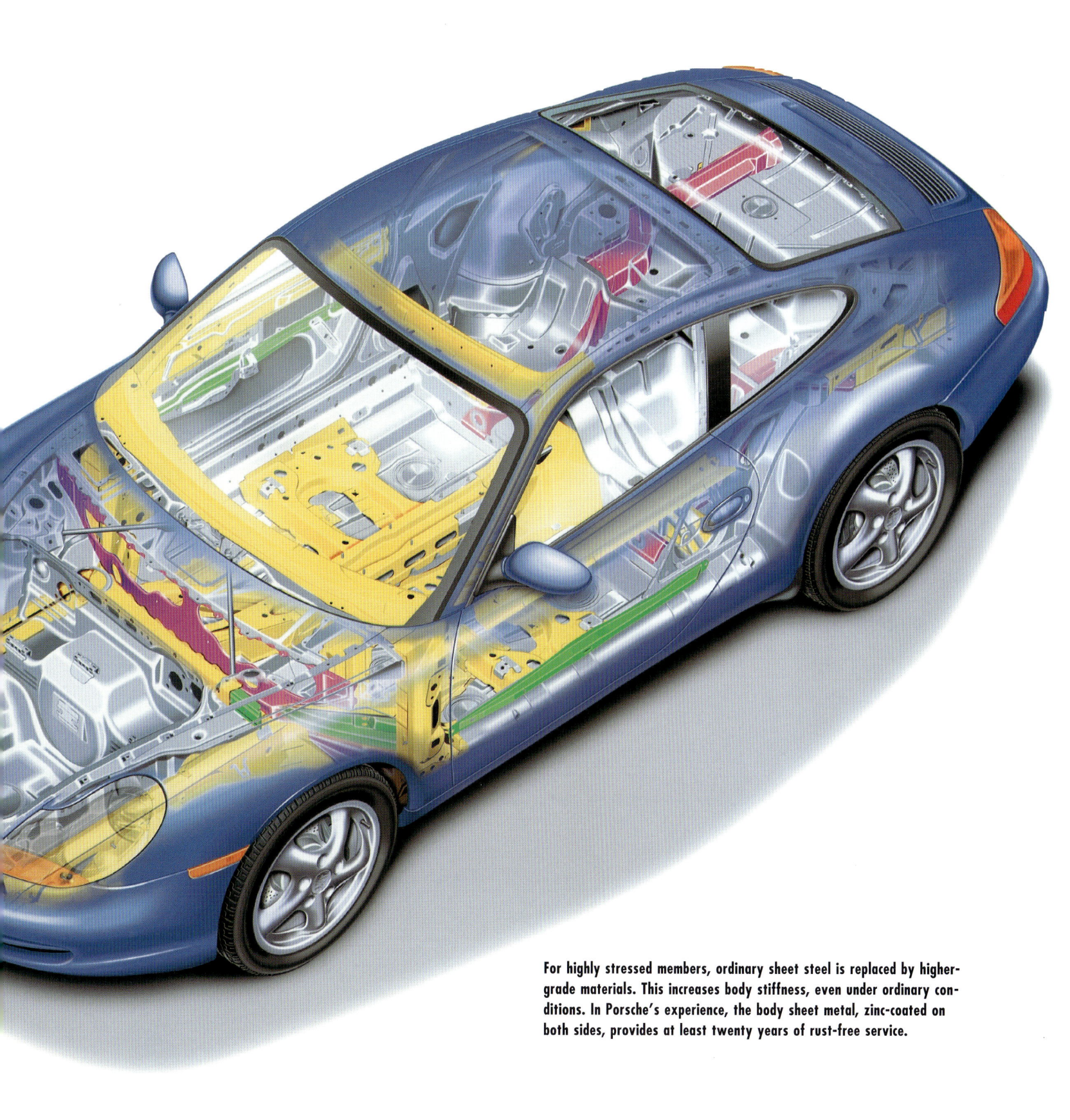

For highly stressed members, ordinary sheet steel is replaced by higher-grade materials. This increases body stiffness, even under ordinary conditions. In Porsche's experience, the body sheet metal, zinc-coated on both sides, provides at least twenty years of rust-free service.

energy-absorbing interior door panels. The side airbags have a relatively large volume of 30 liters (more than one cu. ft.) and are effective throughout the entire range of seat adjustment. POSIP improves head, chest, arm and pelvic protection in any type of side impact.

Horst Marchart, vice president of Porsche research and development, explains: "We set ourselves the goal of building the safest high-performance sports car in the world. Our preliminary calculations indicated that the extended front body structure and the rear-mounted engine should result in lower impact loads on the occupants in frontal collisions. Since then, all of our tests on actual cars confirm it – mission accomplished."

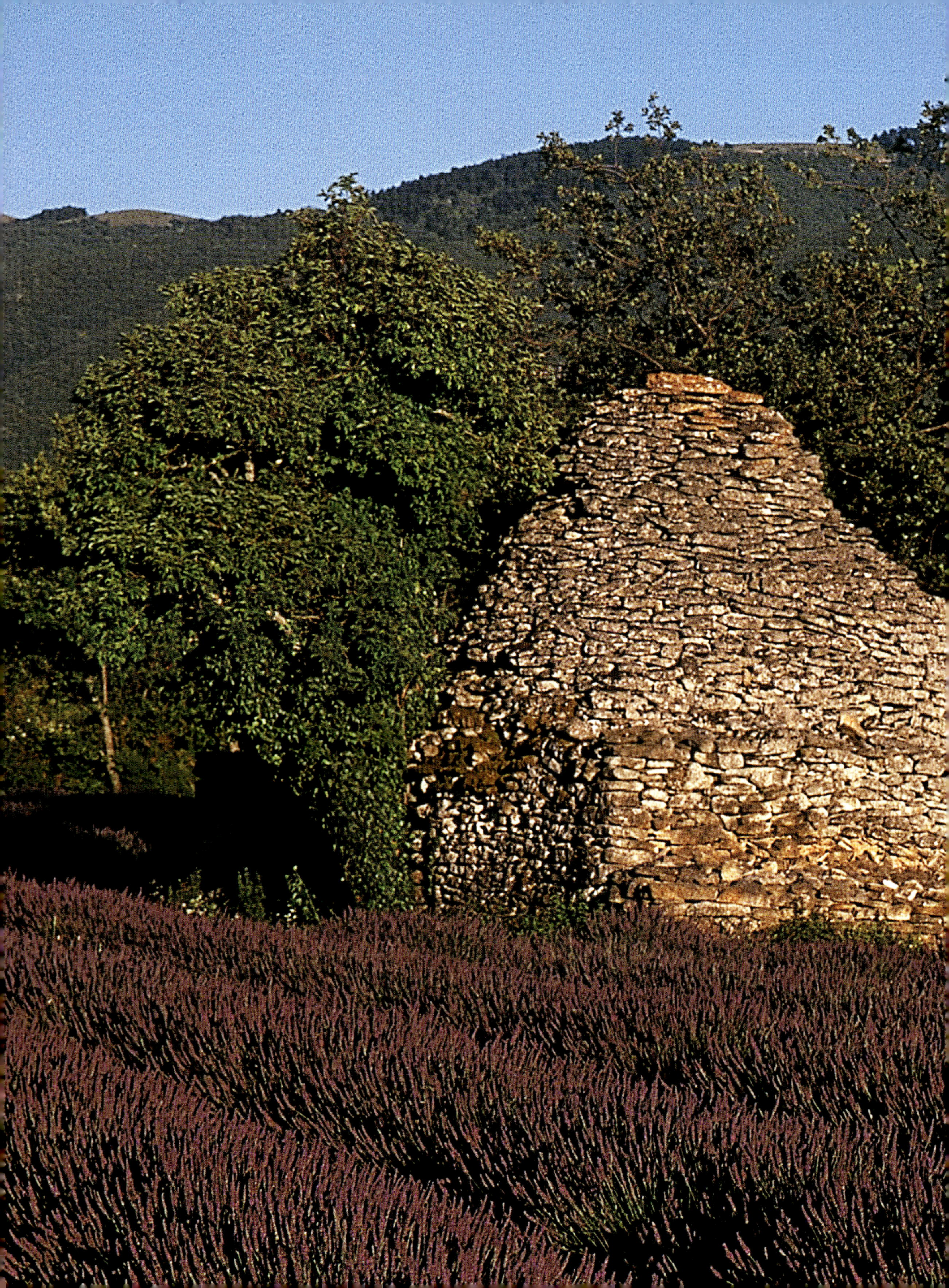

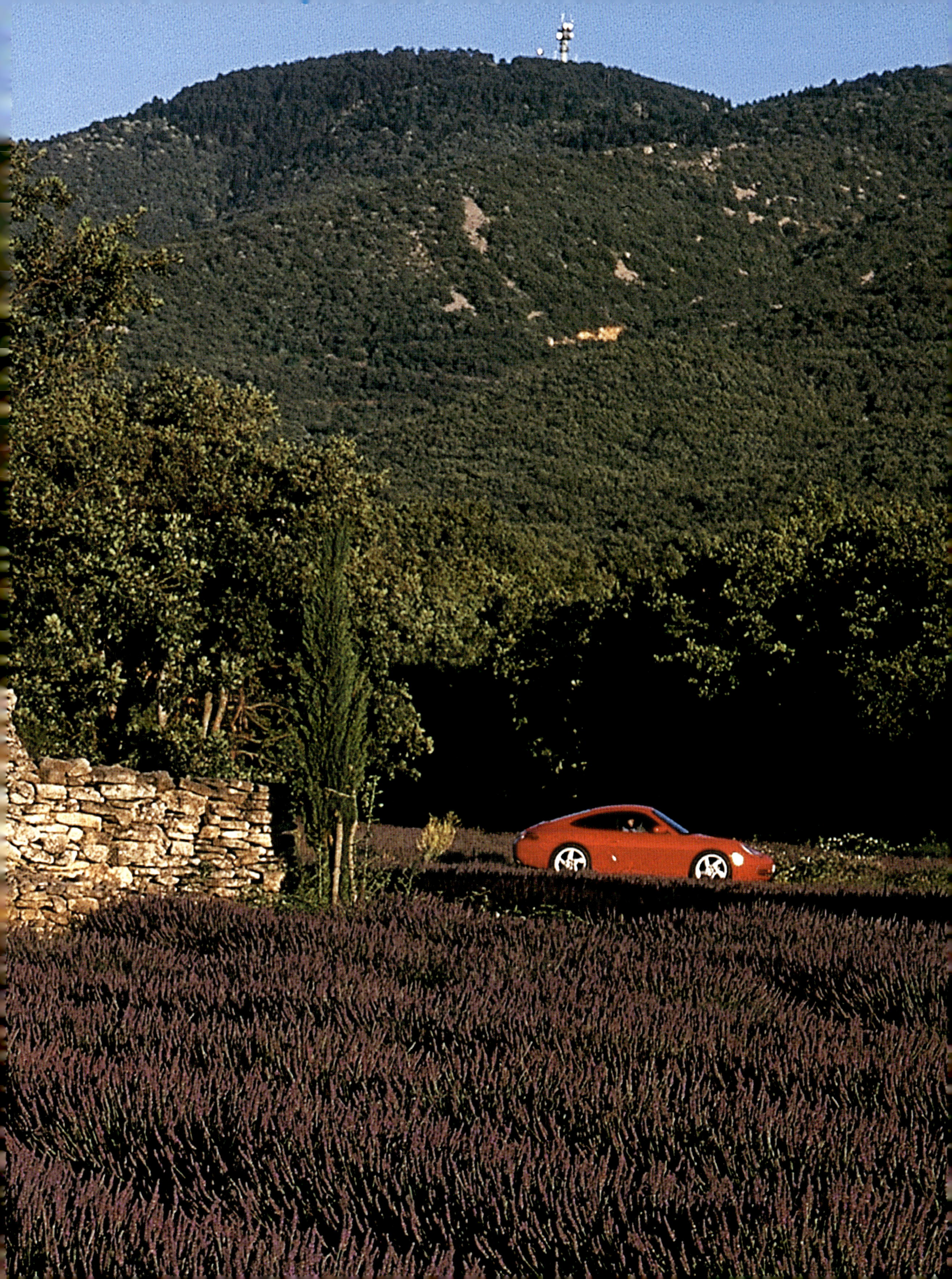

First sortie to southern France: a red Carrera in search of lavender.

Porsche Provençal

From late June to early July, Provence puts on its finest perfume as lavender comes into bloom. This is the ideal time for sunny drives through a landscape rich with winding roads

In Provence, it's a good bet that an establishment calling itself "La Forge" is a bistro.

Provence, in the south of France, is always being rediscovered. Even in antiquity, the Greeks favored the region. Long before the start of our own calendar reckoning, they founded the trading center of Arelate (Arles), the city in the swamp. In their search for a perfect climate, our own ancestors came to Provence at the end of the second century BC. But the military campaigns of the Cimbri and the Teutons were broken by Marius' Roman legions. Thereafter, the Romans provided law and order in the region. A hundred years before Christ, they made Arles their own, equipping it, as was their style, with an amphitheater. Then they sat back and enjoyed the warm sun of southern Gaul. In the ninth century, the Moorish conquest pushed north as far as this land of lavender. Later in the middle ages, the hospitable climate of Provence provided an ideal setting for the castle-building activities of the Christian nobility. Devout monks, too, built solid monasteries early on, perhaps because on this pleasant land, one was a bit closer to heaven. In the 14th century, Provence even had its own popes, at Avignon. The Impressionists arrived a few hundred wine harvests later, to paint the flaming colors of a glowing summer; tourists followed the lure of

In southern France, the fine arts are ever present.

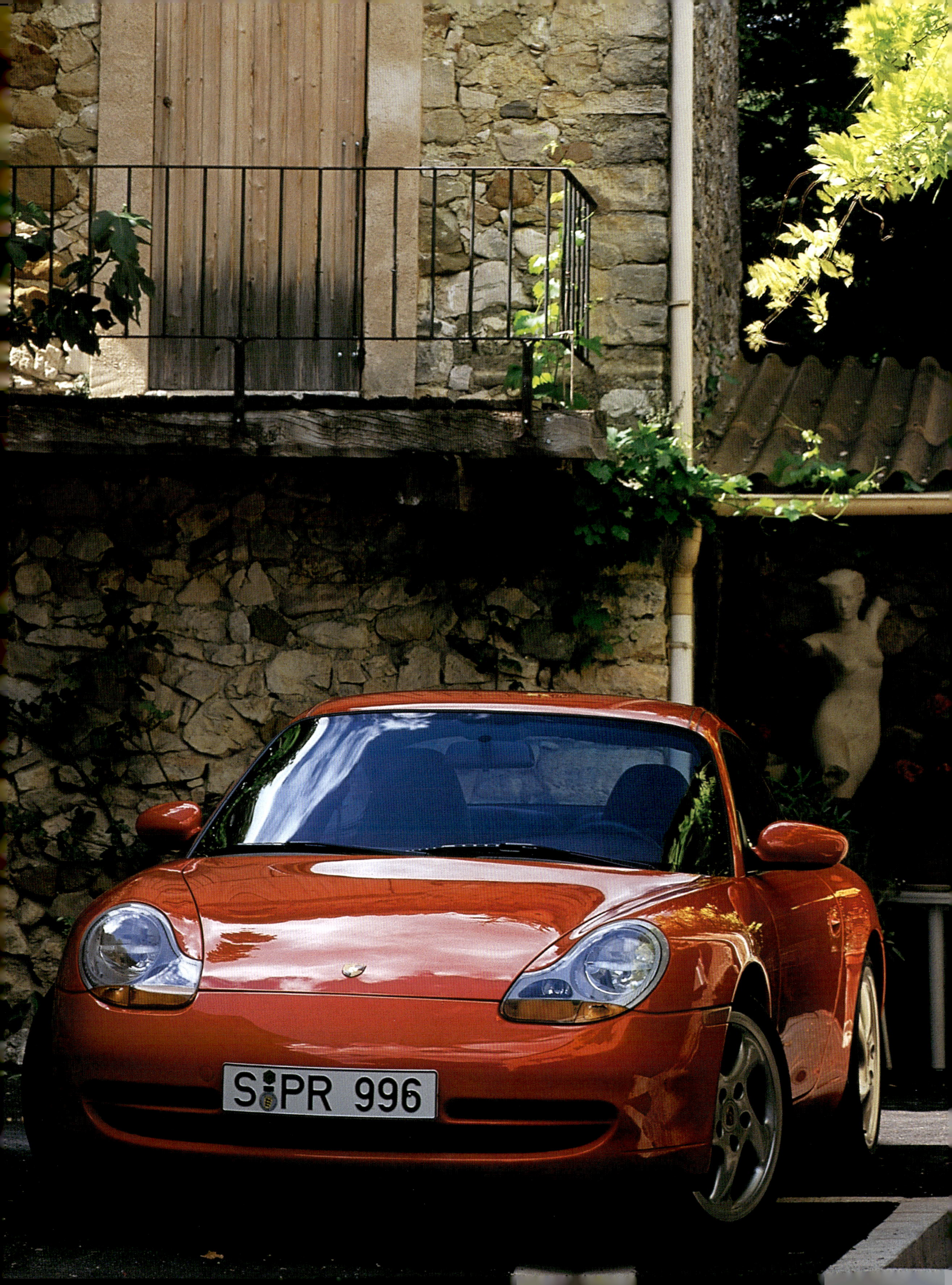
S PR 996

Les Vieilles Tourettes, a winery near Apt, is a fine hostel offering a paradise-like setting for a romantic getaway.

their paintings, and found in Provence an open history book. But it was not the ruins of antiquity, rather the magic of the region that caused many of them, like the Greeks and Romans two millennia before, to put down their own roots in Provence, in old farmhouses, stout city walls, or lonely watchtowers in deserted fields.

Provence took all who came, enfolding them in its hills. The interior, with all its castles and monasteries, holds sacred the tranquility that is lacking in the colorful towns along the coast. One may travel through history with relaxed studiousness, or – as is much more tempting in any Porsche – drive through a countryside whose curving roads gently caress the land.

The roads of Provence provide a veritable menu gastronomique of interesting twists and turns. Generations of rally drivers devoted their pace notes to these virages, neatly cataloging every curve. At some time in the past, each of these byways has borne witness to the Monte Carlo Rallye or some local competition, perhaps waiting hours for a good driver. In Provence, the road itself is the destination.

In principle, such roads can be found anywhere in this vast land between Languedoc and the Alps, but particularly fine driving may be found on either side of the Route Nationale 100 east of Avignon. The Romans laid their road, the Via Domitia, from Nimes to Brigantium (Briançon) by way of Apta Julia (Apt) and Segustero (Sisteron). A section of the Pont Ju-

A typical driveway to a Provençal mansion.

lien, eight kilometers west of Apt, dates back to Roman times. Julius Caesar must have crossed the river Coulon here, probably drawn by six horses. We, on the other hand, have a team of three hundred pulling our Carrera.

Over the past two millennia, the citizens of Apt have, in diverse ways, provided for the comfort of travelers. Every tourist guidebook praises the small town for its Romanesque cathedral, Sainte Anne, whose crypt is presumed to be nearly a thousand years old. The inhabitants of Apt were also quite industrious in developing the Luberon, a hill south of town. No fewer than five roads wind up to the 1100 meter (3600 ft.) summit. There is, for example, the slim, sinuous, asphalt-paved D 943, which, in its quiet moments, is quite Carreralike. A bit over a kilometer farther east, the narrow, tight D 113 snakes its way to the top, only to plunge into a gorge as it continues to Buoux.

All five ascents of the Luberon cross at the D 232. Its eastern reaches are worth a visit, because here we find a mystery which has not yet been fully explained: the bories. These are small, cone-shaped houses, built of stone slabs without benefit of mortar. Here, south of Apt, visitors are likely to come upon these Stone

Goats and sheep are as common in the hills of Provence as they are on the local menus.

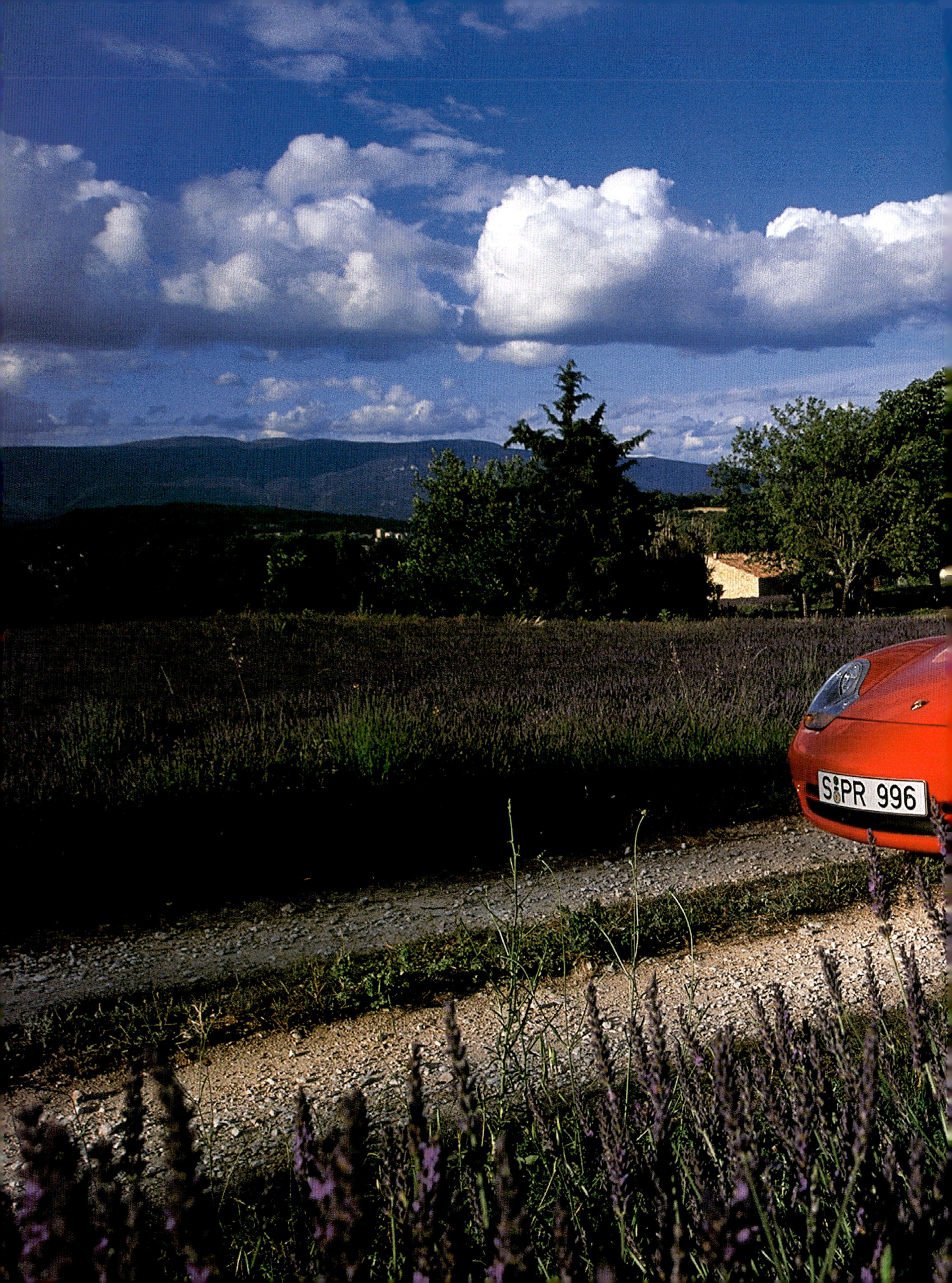
S PR 996

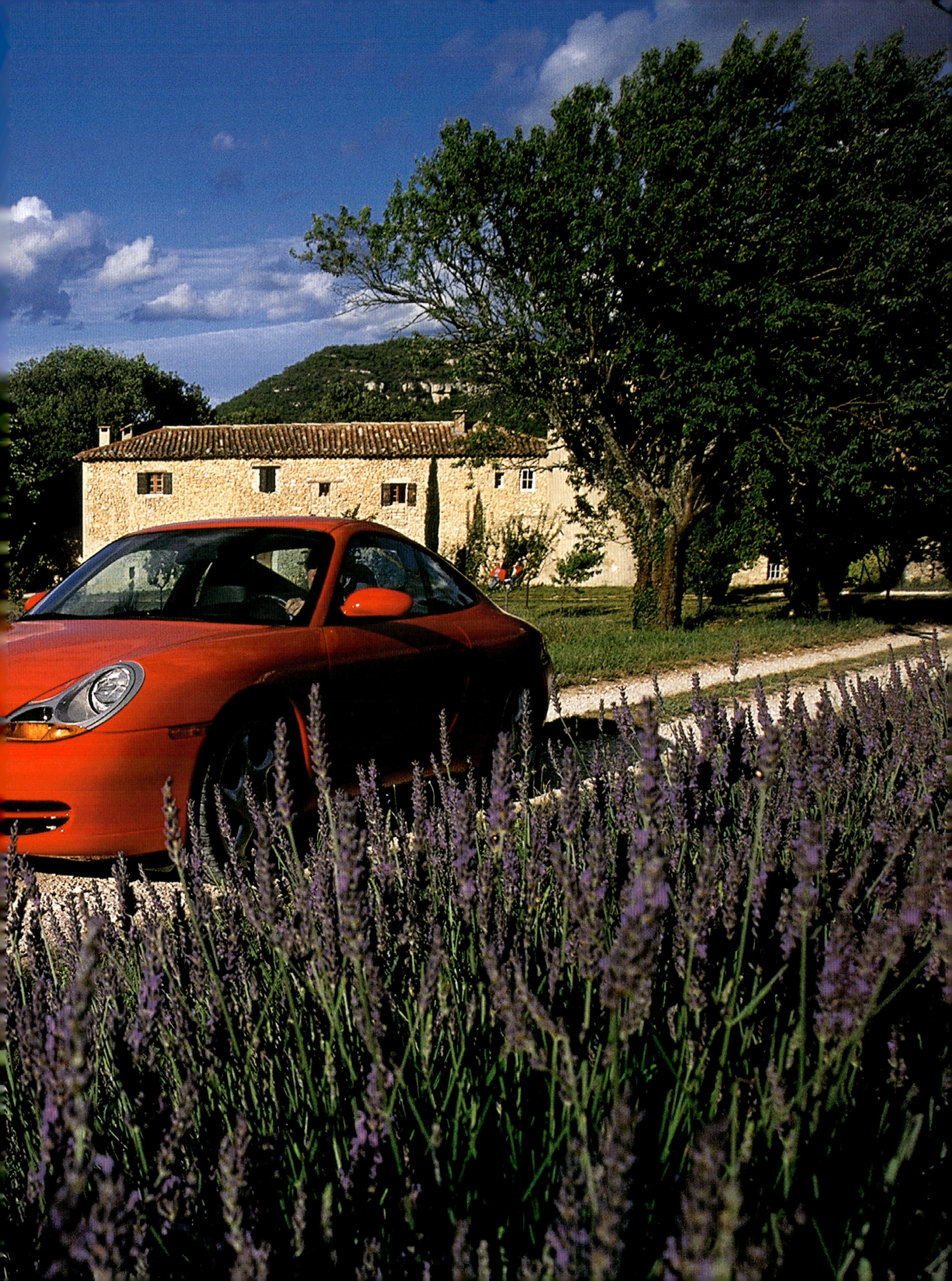

Holding fast to tradition: a newsstand in Forcalquier.

Age dwellings purely by chance. They simply dot the countryside, unchanged from when they were abandoned long ago. West of here, at Gordes, the bories village appears much better organized. Here, we may see living quarters, sheep pens, and barns. But again, there is no evidence of when they were built. Presumably, they were inhabited from Medieval times, well into the previous century. From late June to early July, the glowing purple and sweet fragrance of lavender in bloom surround the shepherd huts, as it does everything else in the region.

On a quiet workday, continuing in our Carrera to Bonnieux and Lourmarin is a wonderful experience as we savor the cornering forces on this cliff-lined, curving road. At the top of second gear, the magnificent echo of the water-cooled boxer engine wafts in through the open windows. Bonnieux, with its bars and antique shops, is perfectly equipped for the tourist trade, nestled high on a hillside. Loumarin, on the other hand, is in a valley on the south slopes of the Luberon. The sign posted beside the city limits marker leaves no doubt about its status as one of the most attractive villages in France. A Renaissance chateau, winding paths in the city center, the restaurant La Fenière – graced by its one Michelin star – and the apparently well-developed business sense of the locals have made Lourmarin a veritable treasure, one which could easily be transplanted into the Fantasyland section of any Disney theme park. North of Apt, the scenery is not quite so picture-postcard perfect. The hills roll a bit more gently, the roads are more tranquil; curves abound, perfectly matched to our car's first five gears. The region below the Vaucluse Plateau almost invites one to take a wrong turn; each of the many new, unexpected roads, leading to places unknown, develops into a journey of discovery. The D 209, for example, exists in self-indulgent seclusion parallel to the heavily travelled Route Nationale connecting Apt and the hill town of Viens, almost ignored by traffic. In the manner of the Nürburgring north circuit, it loops around villages without touching them.

For tourists, the alternative is the D 22. Just after the turnoff for Rustel, it amazes us with signs for "Colorado Provençal." Follow the signs and you will discover that here, indeed, everything is quite colorful. The ridge that extends from Roussilion glows in a multitude of warm colors, ranging from bright yellow to deep brown, with an underlying intense ochre. These ochre sandstone cliffs, which really do impart the feel of the Wild West, are the source of color pigments to this day. The

Weathered history: the ruins of a church steeple high above Reillanne.

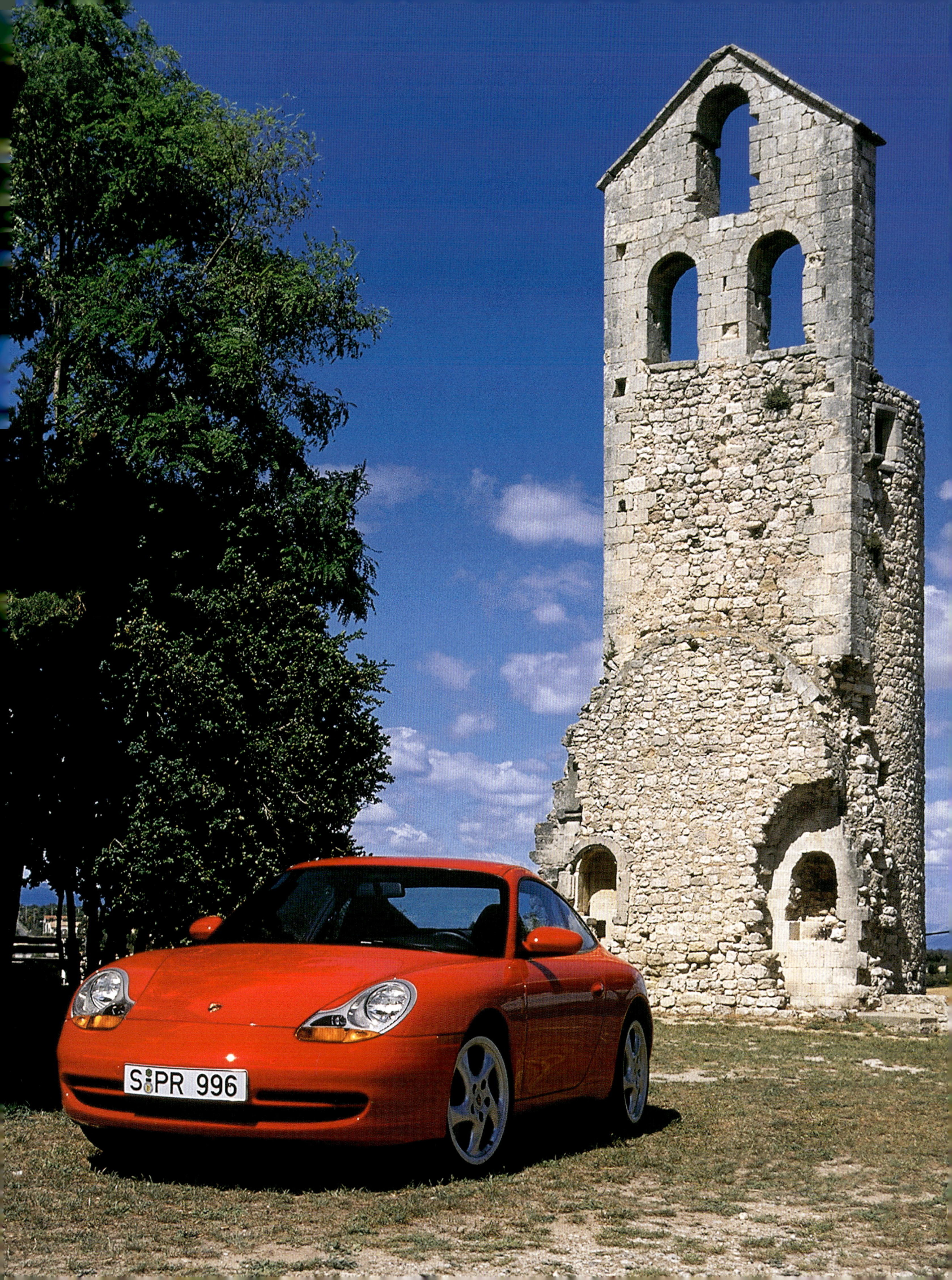
S PR 996

Lavender as far as the eye can see.

days when Colorado Provençal was a mining region, complete with archaic smelters, are long past.

Giniac, just off the small Route Départementale 22, is one of many thousands of examples of Provençal villages as we find them in the late twentieth century. The local language is no longer French, nor even Provençal. In these homes, we would hear English – either the mother tongue of that island nation, or American English, with an occasional sprinkling of German or a dash of Dutch. The French license plates hereabouts do not always carry the "84" of Vaucluse, but seem to prefer the "75" of Paris. And if we look down from the village heights onto the fields and forests, we are challenged in our belief that in this day of hotels, it is no longer necessary to own a personal vacation home; that renovated watchtower, standing guard in the meadow below, is a temptation to put down roots of our own.

The old villages of Vaucluse and Haute Provence prefer to cluster around the crests of small hills. Their founders must have been concerned about early detection of marauders. This consideration has provided visitors and resi-

Shady rest in Cereste.

A busy lunch hour in Forcalquier. The open-air market has been cleared away, and the restaurants are open.

136

J. BREMOND
RESTAURANT
RESTAURANT
RESTAURANT
BAR
Kodak
PHOTO MONNIER

dents alike with a double blessing: we cannot only peer into the wonderful, angular architecture of these villages, but also look out upon the expanse of the surrounding countryside. Viens, Vachère and Reillanne provide us with wonderful vistas. Simiane la Rotonde, with its thick-walled old tower, the remains of a 12th century castle, includes an airy chamber with an unobstructed view of a broad lavender-covered expanse.

Reillanne, built of fieldstone.

Here, every self-respecting hostelry has its own fashionable castle walls. Hôtel St. Paul, just below Viens, clearly belongs to this category. It occupies primarily old restored buildings, done in a rustic Provençal style. Perhaps the wooden beams carrying the ceiling are not quite as old or as structurally functional as they pretend, but they contribute to the illusion of actually living in a dwelling of a bygone age.

Apparently, the hill country between Mont Ventoux in the north, and the Luberon in the south, is not the home of France's greatest cuisine; the Michelin Guide has scattered only a few of its coveted stars in this region. But the rustic local delicacies are based on solid traditions, for in the villages of Provence, old-fashioned markets still compete successfully with modern supermarkets. Here, our table is likely to be graced by fresh foods from a farmer whom we know personally. And all the herbes de Provence, which waft their aromas so enticingly from our plates, grow in abundance right at our doorstep.

The Route Nationale 100, the old Via Domitia, becomes less travelled the farther east we go. The small town of Céreste bears its Provençal character unfiltered and without attempting to ingratiate itself to tourists. The town maintains a fully-grown symbol of southern France: the Route Nationale leaves Céreste for Forcalquier through an avenue of huge plane trees.

The same scene greets us just before Forcalquier, where, in the center of town, Provençal life is reenacted in the form of a play. Mornings, the town square is occupied by an open-air market, with all the fresh herbs of the region, fresh-picked fruits and vegetables as well as fresh fish from the nearby Mediterranean coast. Around noon, the set for this first act is cleared, revealing a picture-perfect promenade complete with bistros, bars and restaurants, where we may sit in the shade of an umbrella. The well-known aperitif Pastis comes from the local distillery, right around the corner.

The dominating Montagne de Lure towers nearly 1300 meters (4265 ft.) above Forcalquier. Michelin map number 245 invites us to the top, with its promise of a fine twisting road. On the first stage of our route to St. Etienne des Orgues, we discover that both the Carrera and its crew are drawn to these mountains. The D 12 is nearly deserted. The switchback road up to the Signal de Lure winds through a lonely, exotic land-

Montagne de Lure: broad vistas of paradise.

scape of cedars. Far above the tree line, the ascent reaches the summit and the France Telecom radio transmitter, 1826 meters (5990 ft.) above sea level. A 360-degree panorama presents both aspects of Provence: not far to the north we see the snow-covered Alps; in the south a broad, green land of rolling hills extending to the Mediterranean beyond the horizon. To our west, Mont Ventoux seems close enough to touch, and to the east it's not far to the Grand Canyon du Verdon. Provence has more roads to offer a Carrera than this chapter has words to describe them.

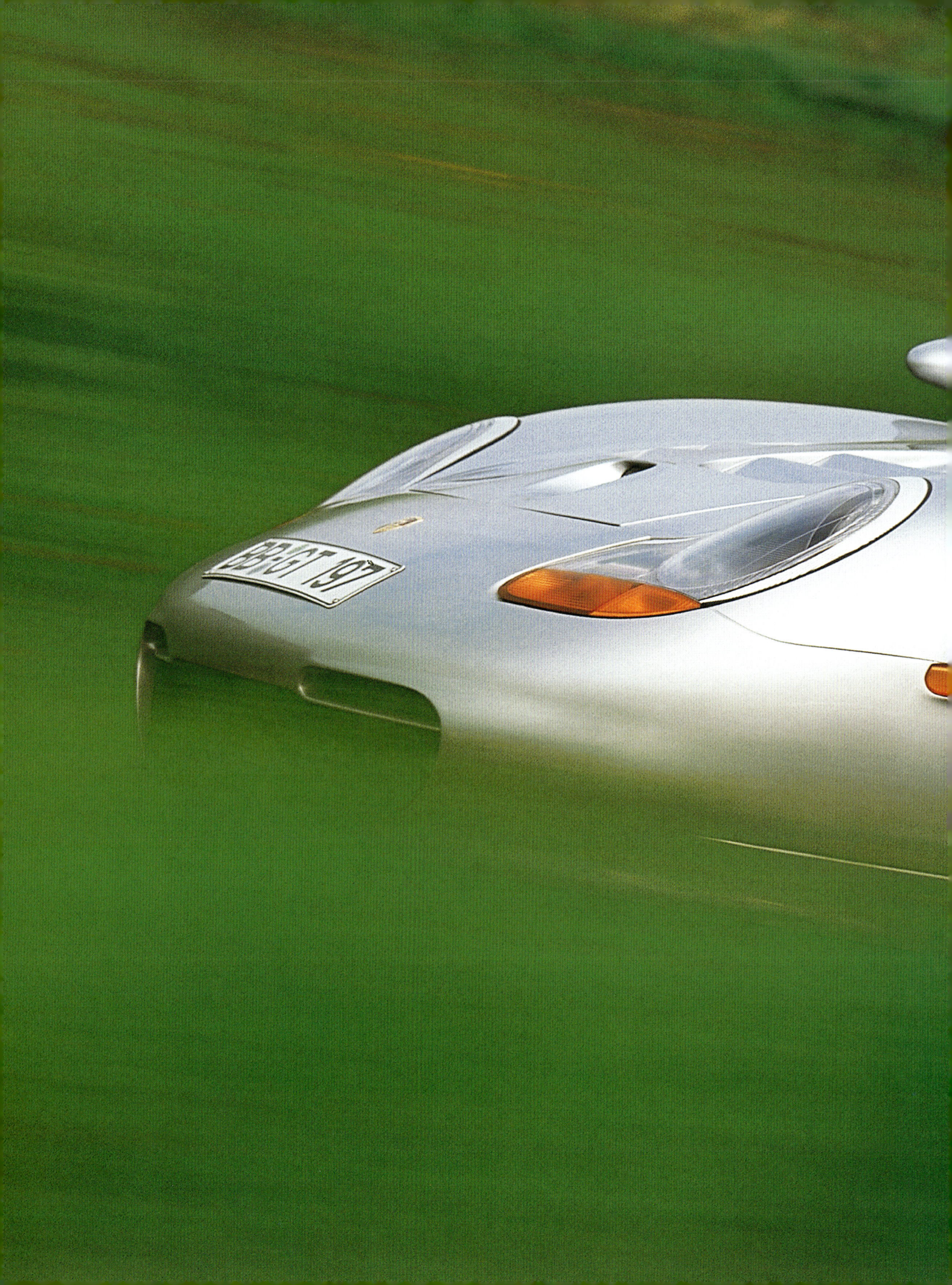

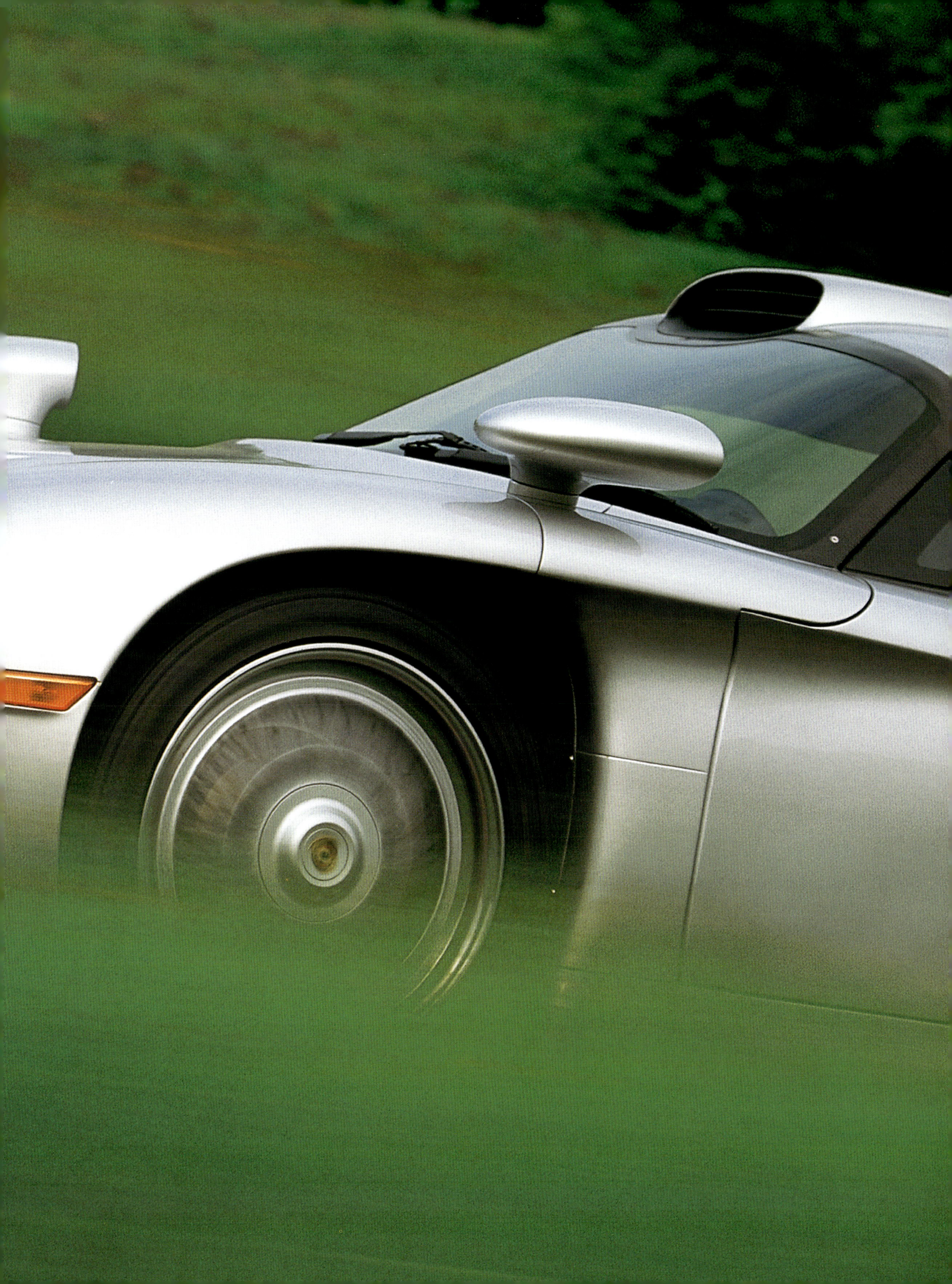

Porsche GT1: the ultimate 911

Super plus

Its technical specifications eclipse those of every previous 911: 544 horsepower, 433 ft.-lbs. of torque – 1.5 million Deutschmarks

The second version of the GT1 has a wider front section, exhibiting the headlight units of the latest Porsche generation.

Mathematicians may have their doubts, but the GT1 is approximately equal to the third power of the prime number 911. Besides which, the GT1 is rolling proof of what Porsche's racing department can do with the basic 911 concept.

And because the clocks run a bit faster for Herbert Ampferer and his team, this Porsche GT1 has already reached the second development stage. The first stage was recognizably the offspring of the latest production Carrera, known internally as the Type 993. It was essentially the current chisel-nosed GT1, but with a smaller front track and narrower front suspension. While the prototype still carried the trademark round headlights of the classic production model, the new GT1, with its integrated headlight units, adopts the Boxster styling idiom. (This theme continues in the new Carrera, the Type 996). The front track is now 100 mm wider, and the bodywork has filled out accordingly.

High downforce was a priority in the aerodynamic design of the new body. But it is not only spoilers and wings which increase the car's adhesion; the underside of the car, with its limited ground clearance and prominent door sills, is perfectly smooth, rising gently at the rear to produce an area of low pressure which literally sucks the car onto the pavement.

In terms of styling, the GT1 clearly shows its kinship to the production car – even if it is 18,5 centimeters wider and 28 centimeters longer. The major technical difference is the midships engine location, which improves weight distribution as well as the aerodynamic shape of the undertray. Solid middle-class virtues, such as decent rearward vision, did not concern the creators of the GT1 in the least; there is no rear window, and therefore no inside rear view mirror. Two large exterior mirrors must suffice. The GT racing rules required this superlative Porsche to have a proper trunk, with a capacity of at least 150 liters (5.3 cubic feet); this small bin, for heat-resistant travel gear, may be found at the rear, aft of the transmission. It is advisable to carry along a can of tire inflator, as there is neither a spare tire nor space for one.

With its huge rear wing and air tunnels, the body itself generates aerodynamic downforce.

The water-cooled boxer engine has a displacement of 3163 cc, because when the design was first laid out, this size had certain advantages within the structure of the racing rules. Larger displacement engines, particularly turbocharged powerplants, are hobbled by air restrictor plates in the induction system. Although the engine layout is similar to that of the new 911, it is not directly related to the production powerplant.

The GT1 engine is based on the crankcase of the old air-cooled boxer. The case is flanked left and right by water-cooled cylinder banks, each with a separate coolant system. The assemblage is completed by two water-cooled cylinder heads, each with two overhead cams and four valves per cylinder. The cams are driven from the front of the engine by a pair of duplex chains that loop over sprockets on the cams. Cognoscenti will recognize that this engine description may be reduced to three digits; this same engine design powered the Porsche 962 racers to victory.

Twin turbochargers and intercoolers raise the power output to 544 hp (300 kW) at 7200 rpm. Engine-speed-dependent boost pressure regulation, varying between 0.95 and 1.05 bar, provides a relatively smooth power curve. As is typical of turbo motors, the torque curve is generously proportioned: its peak of 600 Newton-meters (432 ft.-lbs.) arrives sooner than on the production engine, at only 4250 rpm. Of course, power and performance have their price. Driven briskly, it is nearly impossible to keep fuel consumption under 15 liters per 100 km (16 mpg), and rapid progress demands more than 20 liters/100 km (12 mpg). If it's any consolation, the burnt remains of these liquid hydrocarbons are processed in a politically correct manner by two large three-way catalysts and oxygen sensors.

The abundant power is handled by a rugged racing gearbox appropriate for the 600 Nm torque. As is typical racing-box practice, it has straight-cut gears, dog clutches, and no synchromesh. Despite these daunting specifications, close gear ratios make shifting a relatively simple affair. The differential is equipped with mechanical limited slip, but it would be too much to expect this most powerful Porsche to have electronic anti-slip control.

The load-carrying structure of the chassis is partially based on production components. The front half, up to the B-pillars, has been transplanted from the previous 911, the Type 993. This has advantages for a limited-production model as it eliminates the necessity of again crash-testing the design. Aft of the B-pillars, a structure of steel tubes sprouts from the roll cage and extends back to the rear axles, with the engine acting in a supporting role as a stressed member. The suspension of the GT1 is pure racing technology; all four wheels are located by upper and lower A-arms. The front spring/shock units are directly actuated by the lower transverse arms. At the rear, the suspension follows Formula 1 practice with pushrods actuating the springs and shocks, which lie transversely above the transmission. The adjustable front and rear anti-roll bars are of lightweight steel tubing.

The GT1's abundant power calls for large brakes. Racers and road cars have identically-dimensioned brakes. The cast-iron discs, 380 mm in diameter, are ventilated and cross-drilled. At the front, the monoblock aluminum brake calipers have eight pistons between them, the rear calipers total a mere four pistons. ABS is available only on the street version; in racing, this safety feature is no longer allowed by the rules.

The Michelin Pilot tires on three-piece BBS modular wheels are huge: 235/35 ZR 18 at the front, 335/30 ZR 18 at the rear. A set of these giant doughnuts will set the owner back a mere 5500 DM, which, in addition to the fuel consumption, adds an additional perspective to operating the GT1. If it's any consolation, service intervals are generously spaced every 10,000 km (6000 miles).

Brace for Impact

The GT1 Driving Experience

"It's really just like a normal 911," says Gerhard Heid reassuringly as be begins the oral briefing. This rocket sled, this treasure in silver-gray metallic, is not just another Porsche GT1 of the civilian variety, intended for general use on public roads – not just another ordinary million-dollar road machine. No, the car before us is the progenitor of all street GT1s, a prototype whose real price tag is a closely guarded secret of the racing department.

Heid continues: "The sintered-metal clutch engages a bit quickly. It's no disgrace if you stall the car." But I don't believe any of his three muffed starts are genuine; they're just an act, another way to calm new drivers, routinely administered before they are turned loose in the GT1.

A more serious note enters Gerhard's voice as he covers the car's dimensions. "You have to

The GT1 is 28 cm (nearly 12 in.) longer and 18.5 cm (over 7 in.) wider than a new Carrera.

realize that the GT1 is much wider than a 911, even if everything looks just like a 911," he cautions, adding that "On the other hand, the GT1 is not all that much wider than a 928."

As I fearlessly begin the procedure of inserting myself into this projectile, I hear one more bit of advice: "In any case, you should know that the car is relatively loud inside. The design goals didn't say anything about interior noise levels."

Although the door does a convincing imitation of the production item, this effect quickly evaporates when I reach for the handle. My hand encounters not a massive, solid steel door, but rather something closer to a gauze curtain, which pulls back to reveal its secret: carbon fiber. The policy of eliminating heavy luxury items, including power windows – or for that matter mechanical window lifts – has a significant impact on vehicle weight. Even the lack of door pockets fits into a concept aimed at elimi-nating any excess ballast, even that which might be carried aboard by the driver. When closing, the featherweight doors do not immediately fall into their latches; they must be firmly pulled shut.

Entering – or better said threading one's way into the car – it becomes obvious that the GT1 favors a slim, agile physique. To achieve reasonable credibility as a GT1 pilot and sporting multimillionaire, one must master the graceful execution of a gymnastic maneuver, find one's way past the crossed side-impact beams and into the tight embrace of the racing seats. Once ensconced, the GT1 rewards us with the familiar environment of the 911: the seating position is of the deep, upright variety which Porsche has cultivated for the past fifty years, the gauges are those of the old, now classic 911 generation, and the ignition key is, as always, on the left. The steering wheel rim remains true to the tradition of covering a significant portion of the speedometer. In several details, the GT1 makes convenient use of existing production hardware. For example, I am amazed to find a switch for the electric side mirrors, which otherwise would be unadjustable without outside help. The car has a cabin

145

The twin-turbo boxer engine is topped by a huge intercooler.

heater, which becomes effective once all 20 liters of engine coolant have been warmed up. Air conditioning will be available as an option, but on this spring day in 1997, it is not an issue. There also will be a mounting location for a radio, but as we will realize shortly, such an option is superfluous in this car.

The seat grips me like a leather-covered vise, and in its authoritarian way ends any discussion of seating position. It tells me all I need to know about this virtually untamed racing machine. The seats are so confident of their infallibility with regard to backrest angle that they do not even allow any adjustments. At least the GT1 lets me move a bit closer to the steering wheel. A lever between thigh and floorpan releases the seat, and one's own muscles effortlessly do the work normally accomplished by electric motors in the production 911. Despite electric seats, the search for the proper distance isn't that much easier in the production car. The result of this minor effort is that I'm sitting comfortably; after all, I'm in a Porsche.

A twist of the ignition key with the left hand instantly awakens the race-bred engine, located just inches behind my back. There is absolutely no doubt that here we have a six-cylinder symphony in 4/4 time – accompanied by a rhythm section of twenty-four valves, soon to be joined by the wind section blowing through a pair of turbochargers. This close to the music, a racing driver's proper dress code normally prescribes ear plugs and helmet, but here I sit with unprotected eardrums.

Behind me is not the discreet, well-mannered powerplant of a production car, but rather a tumultuous powerhouse. Every mechanical component makes its presence known, the firing of every cylinder is announced to the world. What I hear at idle is the acoustic signature of a racing engine capable of wringing 170 horses out of each liter of displacement.

The boxer engine responds readily to the right foot, signalling its willingness to go. Between

Porsche Number 1 of 1948, with its 40 horsepower, and the 544 horsepower of 1997, there is little difference in the procedure for getting underway. The parking brake handle, however, has moved to the left, and disappears in a canyon between door and roll cage. A stab at the clutch, which comfortably handles 600 Newton-meters at 4250 rpm and maximum boost pressure, provides a pleasant surprise: its travel is short, and requires far less effort than I had feared. Whatever comes next, be it a traffic jam or the 24 hours of Le Mans, clutch effort will be bearable.

The shifter is a no-nonsense mechanism which makes no attempt to conceal its fascinatingly simple function; the bare-aluminum lever is topped by a map of the gates to the six forward gears. A sturdy tube, running through the cockpit in plain sight, connects the shift lever to the transmission, located at the far rear of the GT1. Before driving away, a test run through the shift pattern reveals that the shifter glides through its gates with the same uncompromising precision cherished by gun aficionados in the action of the finest rifles.

Shifting the GT1 is not the smooth, gentle process found in a road car, however. The synchronizers act with lightning speed, mechanical components lock together in the blink of an eye. The right hand on the shifter senses the action of the synchronizers. With a feeling like that of a steel trap springing shut, first gear is engaged. Now, gentle footwork is called for. Driving off, all eyes are focused on the GT1 and its driver. Slight pressure from the right foot, and the roar from the rear of the car rises in pitch; the left foot eases in the clutch, and the Porsche gets underway with unexpected good manners. Many an ordinary road car requires a more delicate touch.

Between the Porsche racing department and some of our favorite roads, where we will put the GT1 through its paces, lies the everyday reality of heavy traffic on the highways, narrow village streets, and clogged city arteries. The GT1 handles all these situations with amazing calm. Far removed from its natural violence, and well off its turbocharger boost, the engine surprises us with its smooth power. Thanks to the crisp shift action, we quickly become familiar with the remarkably

Boxer with an attitude: the GT1 carries its nose in the air.

tall gear ratios. Although engine speed hovers in the solid-citizen range – between 2000 and, on rare occasions, 3000 rpm – our progress is anything but quiet.

These transit stages through the real world demand a good working knowledge of the car's unfamiliar dimensions. The GT1's overall width of 195 cm (nearly 78 inches) takes on different proportions when we consider that a slight miscalculation, resulting in contact with the carbon fiber bodywork, will cost us not only our reputation but also the cash equivalent of a middle-class sedan. The overall length of 475 cm (187 inches) is not unusual for fully-grown cars, but new perspectives are opened when more than half of this length is hidden from the driver thanks to the GT1's limited view to the rear. There is no rear window, and the two outside mirrors seem to concentrate their gaze on pursuing competitors, who apparently gather behind the car wherever there is a speed limit. Then there's the matter of the turning

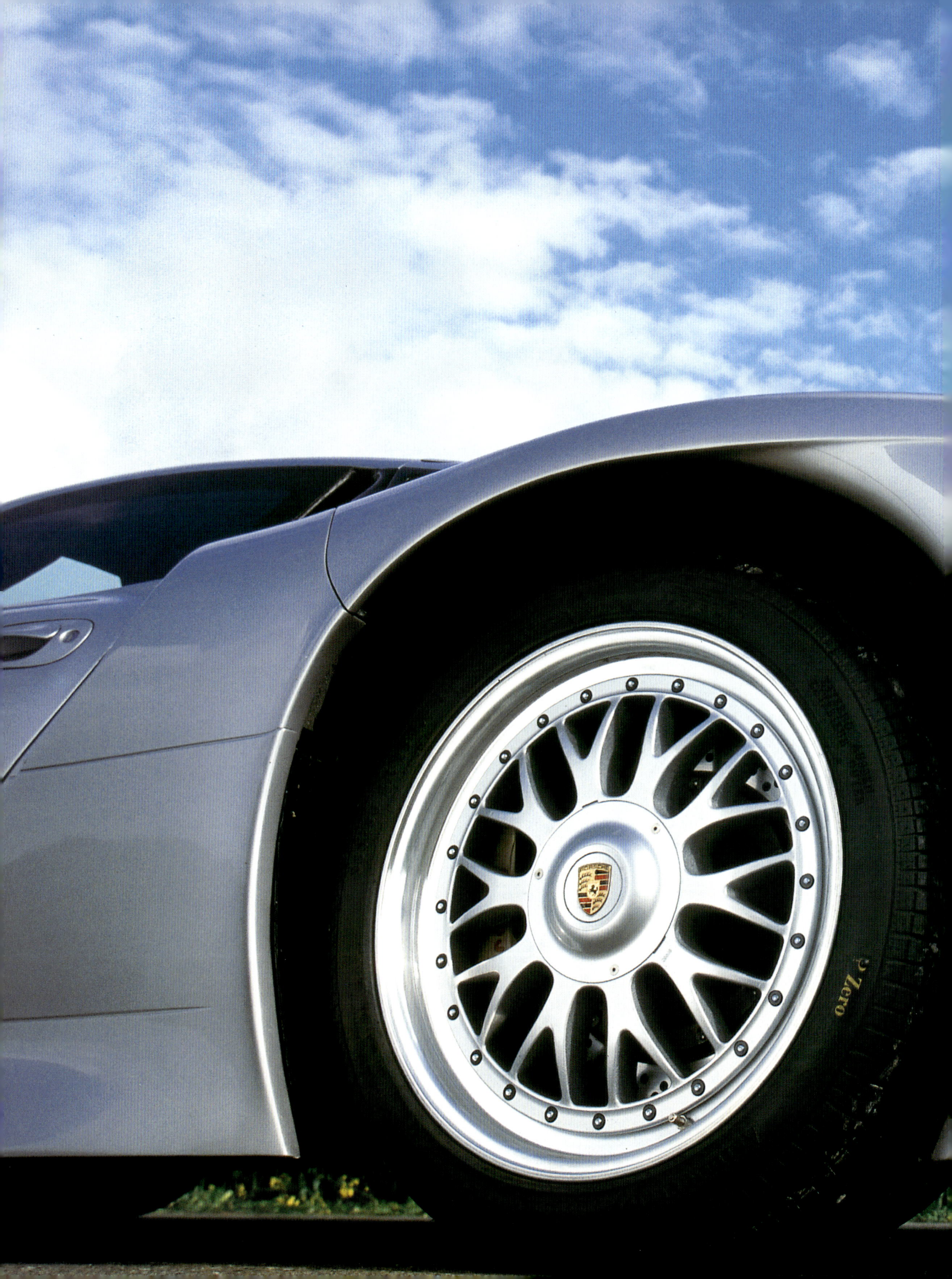
P Zero

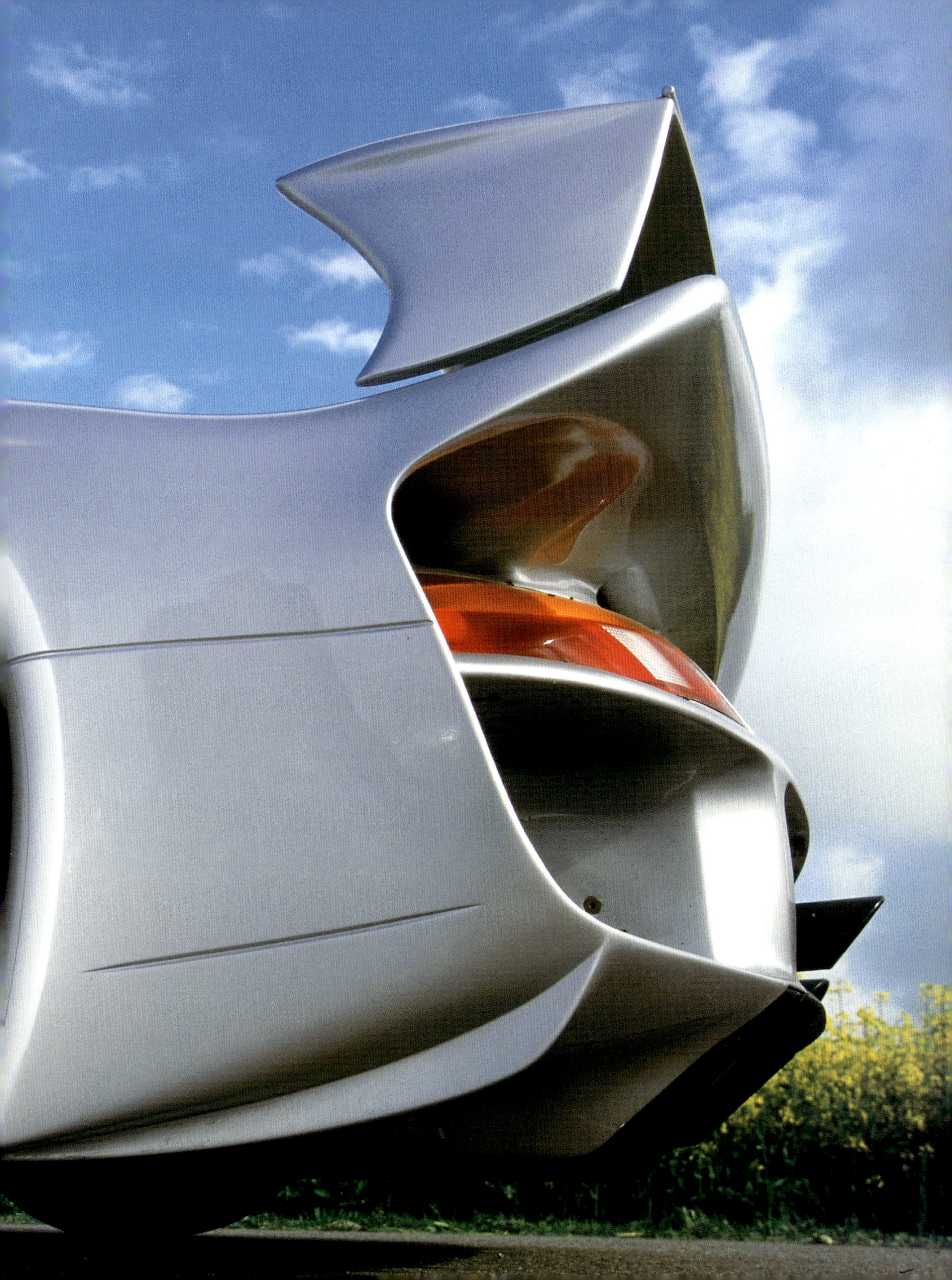

circle, which has been reduced from 16 meters (52.5 ft.) to a still-considerable 13 meters (42.6 ft.) with the introduction of the wider front suspension and added space under the fenders on the second-generation GT1. Making right-angle turns at city intersections is just barely possible, but tighter turns become a geometry problem with several unknowns.

At some point we find the open road, and suddenly the world around the GT1 changes. Time and space are warped by the power packed into this graceful one-ton car. Test numbers are inadequate to describe the effect of reaching 100 km/h (62 mph) in less than four seconds, or just ten seconds to 200 km/h (124 mph) from a standing start. Topped out in sixth gear, 300 km/h (186 mph) feels completely different in the GT1 than the same speed in a Boeing 747 at the moment of liftoff.

As soon as we submit to the power of the GT1, the world seems to shrink and roads become shorter. Straight sections disappear much more quickly than we remember, blending into braking zones in which proper deceleration is measured on the far side of one g. Turns seem tighter than before and lateral forces higher than we've ever experienced – these are the early indications of a serious addiction.

The most seductive aspect of the Porsche GT1 is the car's ability to display its performance in the most dramatic way. Instead of smoothly and systematically working the entire rev range up to 7400 rpm, the car turns every gear into a dramatic stage performance. Each power play begins with a thunderous first act; in the lower two gears, the GT1 threatens to peel the rubber from its tires. But an even more powerful thrust, eclipsing all that has gone before, begins above 4000 rpm, accompanied by howling turbos and skyrocketing boost pressure. Each horsepower is devoted to accelerating 2.1 kilograms of the car's mass. This is communicated to the driver as the impression that he and the car have been irrevocably launched, without any possibility of recall – until, in the most ambitious cases, acceleration stops abruptly at 7400 rpm when the engine runs up against the rev limiter. But human courage will seldom endure long enough to see the rev limiter, and rare indeed is the open road that would permit such exuberance.

Six gears allow the GT1 to execute six such performances between a standing start and 300 km/h (186 mph). All while the orchestra at the rear of the car underscores every excursion along the power curve with a techno symphony in a major key for gas flow and applied mechanics, a symphony that roars into the cockpit at 90 decibels. It is terrible, it is wonderful, and fortunately we aren't driving all the way to Hamburg. On the shorter legs dictated by the 73 liter (19.3 gallon) fuel tank, we travel in the isolation of our own noise. The radio, with its announcements of traffic jams or the latest from the German political scene, cannot break through to our ears. Even our cell phone leaves us in peace for a while; we never hear its hoarse ringing.

A drive in the GT1 is anything but a smooth flow; in real life, as in real racing, it becomes a succession of accelerations. Yet precisely this powerful acceleration is but the gentle side of the Porsche GT1. Under braking, it is more violent by far. Its four brake discs are 380 mm in

Getting to the point of this virtually untamed racing machine.

diameter, larger than the wheels of the first 911, and a single front brake caliper has eight pistons – as many as all four disc brakes of an early 911 combined. Without aerodynamic aids, all of this effort would be useless. The secret of the car's almost supernatural deceleration lies in aerodynamic downforce. The shapes of spoilers, wings, and undertray make this so powerful that at 250 km/h (155 mph) the car experiences a downforce equivalent to twice its own mass; theoretically, it could drive on the ceiling. At top speed, deceleration approaches 1.9 g, and remains beyond the theoretical limit of 9.81 m/secý throughout the speed range. Engineers can calculate a "negative power" for deceleration, and this brake system dissipates energy at a rate well above 2000 horsepower, about five times the actual engine power available at the drive wheels.

The aerodynamic ability to grip the road more securely as speed increases inevitably changes our attitude toward speed itself. Driven normally, obediently within the rules of the German Federal highway system, the GT1 doesn't behave any better or worse than a normal 911. No surprise, since its power-assisted steering has been borrowed from the production car. A slightly different layout, and the assistance of a few geometrical tricks, make the steering of this barely tamed race car more direct, more agile.

In the GT1, the blessing of the car's quick reactions never becomes a curse at higher speeds, which bring the calming influence of added downforce. Straight-line stability increases even during seemingly boundless acceleration. Two hands, holding the steering wheel loosely in the preferred Porsche way – gently but firmly – guide this turbocharged animal toward 300 km/h as it is effectively glued to the road. We take the fast bends of the Autobahn with unprecedented calm, the steering behavior of the GT1 putting us far beyond ordinary doubts. With so much downforce on both axles, there is no perceptible delay between steering inputs and course changes. To me, it

Direct connection: the shift linkage is clearly visible inside the cockpit.

appears as if there is an invisible curved ruler, which this Porsche is compelled to follow.

The manner in which the GT1 injects calm into rapid motoring alters one's personal perception of speed. If the road is clear and removed from all danger, 300 km/h no longer presents a challenge to the driver's skills; with my gaze firmly fixed on the horizon, we pass through that magic speed imperceptibly. My lady companion calmly announces that the 300 km/h barrier has come and gone.

In the real world, this alien encounter with a new form of roadholding takes place far beyond the limits of ordinary tire adhesion. Even when the curves are tighter and the speeds lower, and that beneficial downforce is minimal, a sensible driver still will push the GT1 a good bit quicker than he would other cars – at the same time remaining farther from the limits of tire grip. I will freely admit that I never risked more than moderate understeer in turns, matched by equally moderate correction with a gentle application of throttle.

This is the true secret of all fast, irreplaceable cars: they demand respect of their drivers, and thus are even quicker. For me, a moderate dose of 544 horsepower is sufficient; talented drivers may need more. Hans-Joachim Stuck, for example, after a victorious drive in the 1100 hp Porsche 917/30 at Laguna Seca, California, asserted that "Just as I always suspected, a really safe car needs at least 1000 horsepower."

Rueck

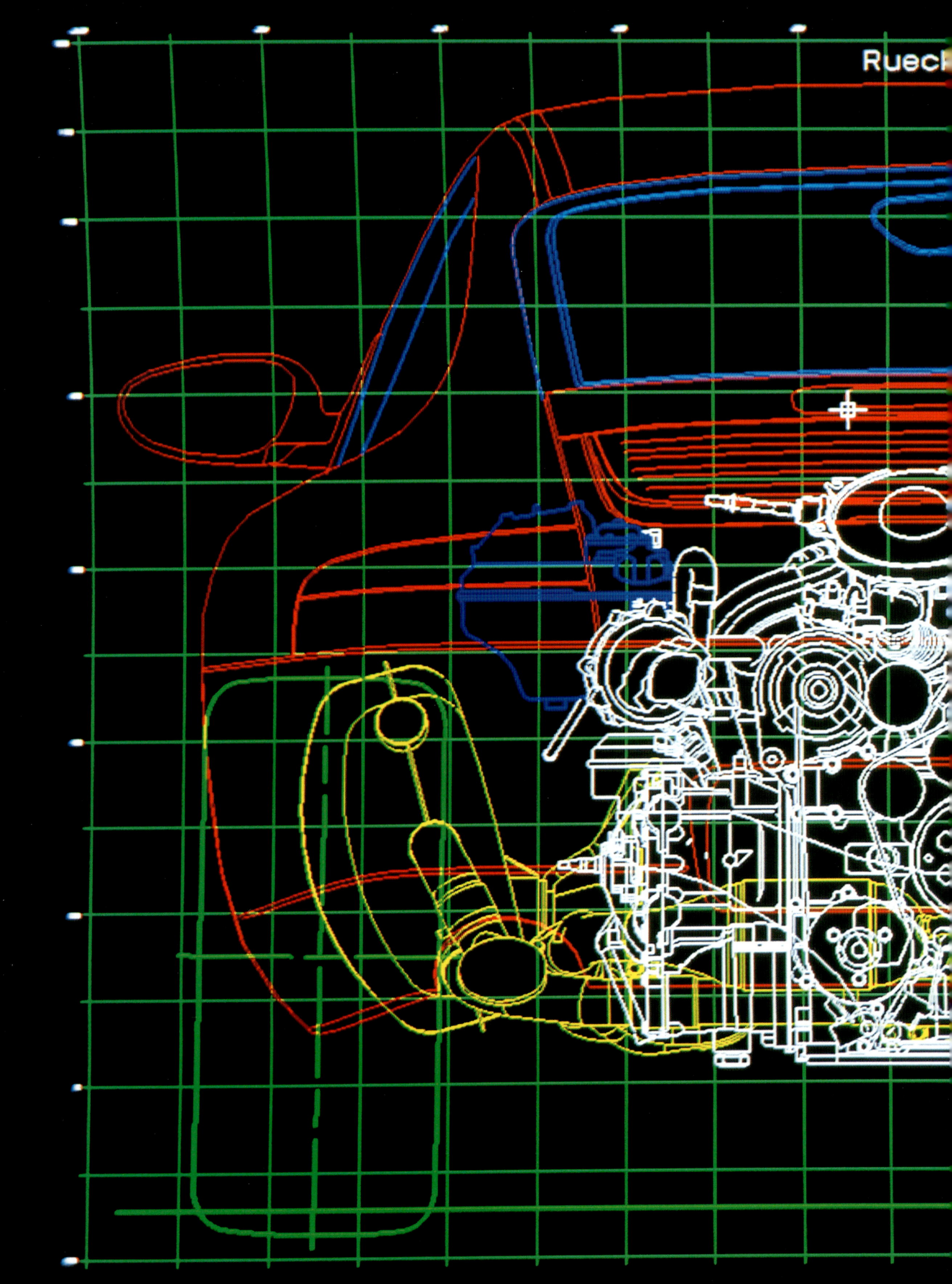

sicht

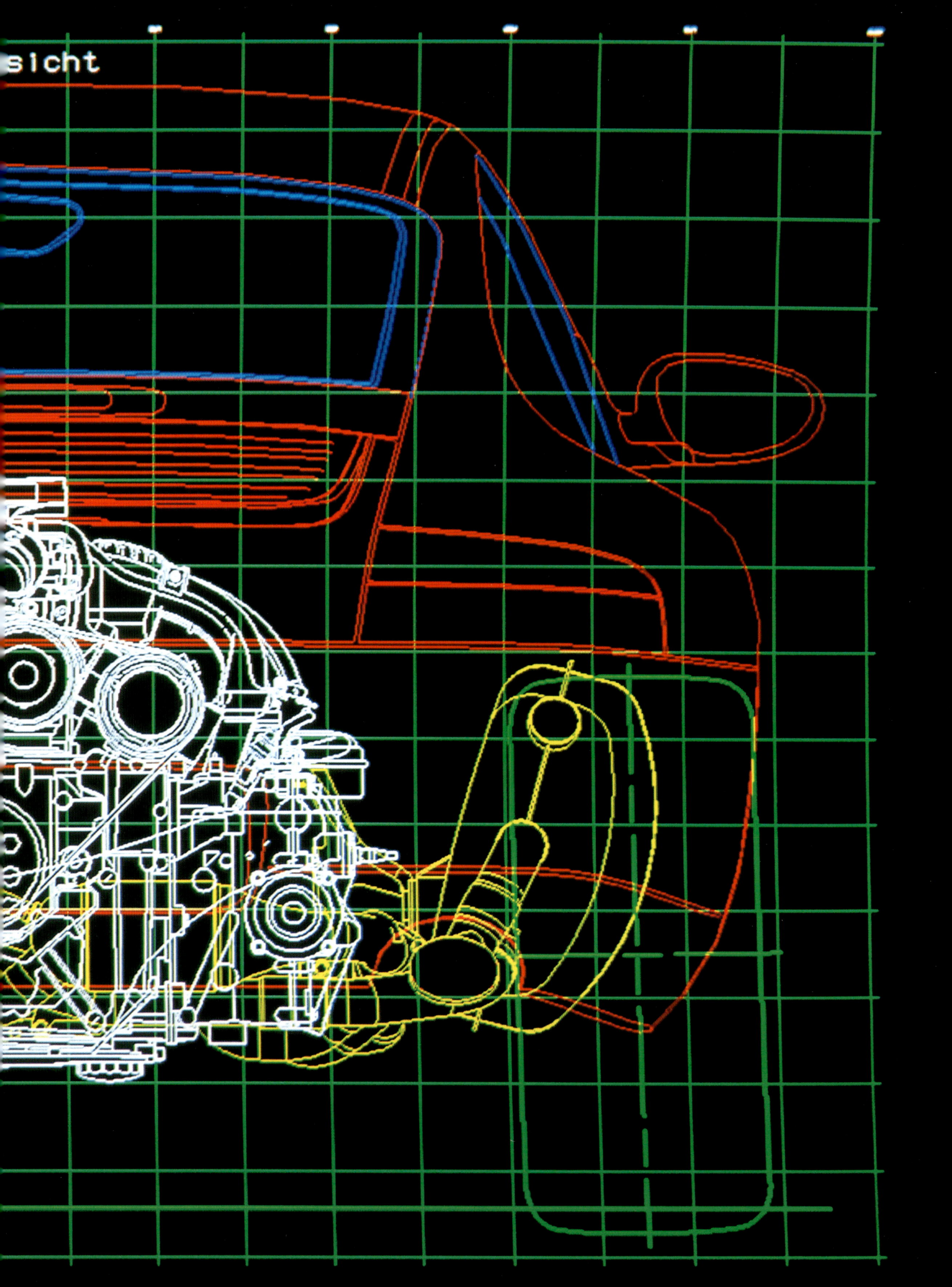

Technical Specifications

By the Numbers

The new Carrera may have less displacement, but considerably more power and torque than its predecessor. The Porsche GT1 is nearly twice as powerful as the production car.

Porsche 911 Carrera

Engine specifications

Engine Type Designation		M 96 / 015 06
Number of cylinders		6
Bore	mm	96
Stroke	mm	78
Displacement	cc	3387
Compression ratio		11.3:1
Maximum output	kW (hp)	221 (300)
at rpm	rpm	6800
Maximum torque	Nm (252x ft.-lbs.)	350
at rpm	rpm	4600
Specific output	kW/liter (hp/liter)	65.2 (88.6)
Valve diameter		
Intake valves	mm	37,1
Exhaust valves	mm	32,5
Valve timing	at 1 mm lift	
	Intake opens	15° ATDC
	Intake closes	46° ABDC
	Exhaust opens	39° BBDC
	Exhaust closes	7° BTDC
Rev limiter	rpm	7300
Idle rpm		
Manual transmission	rpm	700 ± 40
Automatic transmission	rpm	700 ± 40
Engine weight	Manual transmission 190 kg (420 lbs.)* *including dual-mass flywheel	Automatic transmission 179 kg (394 lbs.)

Engine Design

Configuration	6-cylinder aluminum alloy boxer engine, water cooled
Radiators	two for manual-transmission vehicles, in vehicle nose; three for vehicles with Tiptronic S
Crankcase	vertically-split aluminum alloy case with separate bearing carrier for crankshaft and intermediate shaft
Crankshaft	forged, 7 main bearings
Crankshaft bearings	plain bearings
Connecting rods	forged, with "cracked" rod caps
Connecting rod bearings	plain bearings
Pistons	squeeze-cast aluminum alloy
Cylinders	aluminum alloy, with Lokasil surface
Cylinder head	three-piece aluminum alloy head
Valve guides	pressed in
Valve arrangement	two parallel overhead intake valves, inclined to cylinder axis two parallel overhead exhaust valves, inclined to cylinder axis
Valve actuation	via bucket tappets
Valve train	dual chain from crankshaft to intermediate shaft, thence via separate dual chains to each exhaust camshaft. Intake camshafts driven via simple chain from exhaust camshafts.
Variable valve timing	Porsche VarioCam with 25° range in intake valve timing
Valve lash	hydraulic valve lash adjustment
Intake system	two-stage resonant induction system (composite material)
Lubrication system	integral dry sump
Oil supply	one pressure pump at front of engine two scavenge pumps in cylinder heads
Oil cooling	via oil-water heat exchanger

Powertrain

Design		Engine and transmission bolted together to form integrated drive unit. Rear wheels driven by double-jointed halfshafts	
Clutch		hydraulically actuated single-disc dry clutch, dual-mass flywheel	
Clutch disc diameter	mm	240	
Automatic transmission:			
Torque converter diameter	mm	282	
Max. torque converter ratio		1.92:1	
Converter stall rpm	rpm	2450	
Transmission		Manual	Tiptronic
Number of gears, fwd/reverse		6/1	5/1
Gear ratios			
1st gear		3,82	3,66
2nd gear		2,20	2,0
3rd gear		1,52	1,41
4th gear		1,22	1,0
5th gear		1,02	0,74
6th gear		0,84	–
reverse		3,55	4,10
Final drive		ring and pinion	
Final drive ratio		3,44	3,676
Limited slip differential		automatic limited slip, lockup factor 25/40 percent	
Traction assistance		Automatic Brake Differenial and traction control (optional)	
Body		Coupe, two-side galvanized steel unit body, lightweight design, all-steel construction. Full-size air bag for driver and passenger. Optional side airbags.	
Seating		2 + 2,	
Trunk volume	Liter	200	

Chassis

Front		independent via MacPherson struts, design optimized by Porsche, transverse arms and trailing links	
Springs		conically wound coil springs with coaxial shock absorbers	
		Standard	Sport Suspension
Coil wire diameter	mm	10,55...13,20	10,75...13,55
Coil diameter	mm	91,1...186,5	91,5...186,5
Number of coils		4,05	4,05
Stabilizer bar diameter	mm	23,1x3,4*	23,6x3,5*
		* tubular stabilizer bar	
Shock absorber		dual-tube gas pressure shock absorber	
Steering		rack and pinion with hydraulic assist	
Steering wheel diameter	mm	380	
Steering ratio		16,9 : 1	
Turning circle, wall to wall	m	10,6 (34.8 ft.)	
Turning circle, curb to curb	m	10,2 (33,5 ft.)	
Turns lock to lock		2,98	
Power steering pump drive		poly-V belt	
Rear Suspension		multi-link LSA suspension	
Suspension		independent, via five links per wheel	

Springs		one cylindrical coil spring per wheel over coaxial shock absorber	
		Standard	Sport Suspension
Coil wire diameter	mm	12,35...12,83	12,92...13,11
Coil diameter	mm	115,0	115,0
Number of coils		7,0	6,5
Stabilizer bar diameter	mm	8,5x2,5*	19,6x2,6*
		* tubular stabilizer bar	
Shock absorber		single-tube gas pressure shock absorber rebound 25%, jounce 40%	

Brakes

Service brake		dual-circuit brake system, split front to rear, four-piston aluminum monobloc calipers at front and rear wheels, ventilated disc brakes at front and rear wheels, vacuum brake power booster, ABS standard	
		front	rear
Brake disc - diameter	mm	318	299
Brake disc thickness	mm	28	24
Effective brake pad area - per wheel	cm²	127	98
Brake piston diameter in caliper		36 and 40 mm	28 and 30 mm
Parking brake		drum brake, hand-actuated	
Parking brake drum diameter	mm	180	
Parking brake shoe	mm	25	
Parking brake pad area per wheel	cm²	85	

Wheels and tires

Summer tires	
rim size front	7 J x 17 ET 55 mm
rim size rear	9 J x 17- ET 55 mm
tire size front	205/50 ZR 17
tire size rear	255/40 ZR17
Sonder-Bereifung	
rim size front	7,5 J x 18 - ET 50 mm
rim size rear	10 J x 18 - ET 65 mm
tire size front	225/40 ZR18
tire size rear	265/35 ZR18
Winter tires	
rim size front	7 J x 17 - ET 55 mm
rim size rear	8,5 J x 17- ET 50 mm
tire size front	205/50 R 17 89T M+S
tire size rear	225/45 R 17 90T M+S
	approved for use with special snow chains.
Spare tire	
rim size	3,5 J x 17 ET 18 mm
High-pressure spare tire	105/95* - R 17
Tire pressure	
front	bar (psi)	2,5 (36)
rear	bar (psi)	2,5/3,0 (36/44)
spare tire	bar (psi)	4,2 4.2 (61)

Dimensions

Length	mm	4430	
Width	mm	1765	
Height (at DIN empty weight)	mm	1305	
Wheelbase	mm	2350	
Track		17 in. wheels	18 in. wheels
front	mm	1455	1465
rear mm	mm	1500	1480
Ground clearance	mm	100	
at maximum curb weight	mm	65	
Angle of approach	deg.	12,0	
Angle of departure	deg.	13,0	

Weights

Empty weight, depending on equipment		manual	Tiptronic S
Total weight, coupe	kg	1320-1380*	1365-1420

*for ECE certification, plus 75 kg (165 lbs.) for driver and luggage, distributed 35 kg (77 lbs.) front axle, 40 kg (88 lbs.) rear axle)

Maximum axle load			
front	kg (lbs)	775 (1709)	775 (1709)
rear	kg (lbs)	1145 (2524)	1145 (2524)
Maximum vehicle weight	kg (lbs)	1765 (3891)	1765 (3891)
Roof load	kg (lbs)		35 (77)
with Porsche roof transport	kg (lbs)		75 (165)

Capacities

Engine oil	Liter	approx. 10,25 (10,8 qts)
oil change	Liter	8,25 (8.72 qts.)
Transmission	Liter	2,7 (2.85 qts.)
Automatic transmission with torque converter	Liter	approx. 9,5 (10.0 qts.)
Differential	Liter	0,8
Fuel tank	Liter	approx. 65 (17.2 U.S. gal.) reserve 10 (2.6 gal.)
Engine coolant	Liter	22,5 (23.8 qts.)
Brake fluid	cc	450 (15.2 oz.)
Windshield and headlight washer fluid	Liter	ca. 2,5 / 6,5
Power steering fluid	Liter	1,27 (1.34 qts.)

Performance

		Manual	Tiptronic S
Top speed km/h (mph)		280 (174)	275 (171)
Acceleration			
0 - 100 km/h (62.1 mph)	sec.	5,2	6,0
0 - 160 km/h	sec.	11,5	13,0
0 - 200 km/h	sec.	18,3	20,4
Standing-start kilometer	sec.	24,2	25,3
Elasticity (Manual)			
		5th gear	4th gear
80 - 120 km/h in sec.		7,1	6,9
100 - 200 km/h in sec.		18,3	17,3
Power to weight ratio			
		manual	Tiptronic S
	kg/kW	6,0..6,2	6,2...6,4
	kg/hp	4,4...4,6	4,6...4,8

Fuel economy

	manual	Tiptronic S
city l/100km	17,2	18,3
highway	8,5	8,5
weighted average	11,8	12,0

Porsche GT1 – Street Version

Engine specifications

Number of cylinders		6
Bore	mm	95
Stroke	mm	74.4
Displacement	cc	3163
Maximum output	kW (hp)	400 (554)
at rpm	rpm	7200
Maximum torque	Nm (ft.-lbs.)	600 (433)
at rpm	rpm	4250
max. boost	bar	0,95 - 1,05
Specific output	kW/liter (hp/liter)	126 (172)
Rev limiter	rpm	7400
Idle rpm	rpm	900

Engine Design

Configuration	6-cylinder aluminum alloy boxer engine, water cooled
Radiator	in vehicle nose
Crankcase	vertically-split aluminum alloy case with separate cylinder blocks
Crankshaft	forged, 7 main bearings
Crankshaft bearings	plain bearings
Connecting rods	forged
Connecting rod bearings	plain bearings
Pistons	squeeze-cast aluminum alloy
Cylinder head	three-piece aluminum alloy head
Valve guides	pressed in
Valve arrangement	two parallel overhead intake valves, inclined to cylinder axis two parallel overhead exhaust valves, inclined to cylinder axis
Valve actuation	via bucket tappets
Valve train	two double chains from crankshaft to four camshafts

Valve lash	mechanical adjustment
Turbocharging	twin turbochargers
Intercooler	in engine compartment
Lubrication system	dry sump
Oil capacity	15 liters (15.9 qts.)
Oil cooling	via oil-water heat exchanger
Exhaust system	dual-stream system
Emission control	two 3-way metal catalysts, oxygen sensors
Fuel injection	sequential control of individual injectors via DME (Digital Motor Electronics)
Fuel supply	electric gear pump
Fuel quality	Super Plus, 98 Research Octane Number

Electrical System

Voltage	V	12
Battery capacity	Ah	50
Ignition	DME (Digitale Motor Electronics)	
Firing sequence	1 - 6 - 2 - 4 - 3 - 5	

Powertrain

Design	Engine and transmission bolted together to form integrated drive unit. Rear wheels driven by double-jointed halfshafts
Clutch	hydraulically actuated sintered-metal clutch

Transmission

Number of gears	6 / 1
Gear ratios	
1st gear	3,153
2nd gear	2.000
3rd gear	1.440
4th gear	1,133
5th gear	0.941
6th gear	0,829
Final drive	ring and pinion
Final drive ratio	3,444
Limited slip differential	automatic limited slip, lockup factor 60/40 percent

Body

Two-door coupe, sheet steel and carbon fiber composite construction

Trunk capacity	liters (cu. ft.)	150 (5.3)

Chassis

Front suspension	upper and lower A-arms
Springs	one cylindrically wound coil spring per wheel over coaxial shock absorber
Shock absorbers	single-tube gas pressure shock absorbers
Steering	rack and pinion, with hydraulic assist
Stabilizer bar	tubular, adjustable
Steering wheel diameter	mm	360

Rear Suspension	upper and lower A-arms with pushrods
Springs	one cylindrical coil spring per wheel over coaxial shock absorber, pushrod actuated
Shock absorber	single-tube gas pressure shock absorber
Stabilizer bar	tubular, adjustable

Brakes

Service brake	eight-piston aluminum monobloc calipers at front, four-piston aluminum monobloc calipers at rear, individual circuit to each wheel, ventilated disc brakes at front and rear wheels

		front	rear
Brake disc diameter	mm	380	380
Brake disc thickness	mm	32	32

Wheels and tires

rim size	front	11x18 ET 63 mm
	rear	13x18 ET 80 mm
tire size	front	295/35 ZR 18
	rear	335/30 ZR 18

Dimensions

Length	mm	4710
Width	mm	1970
Height	mm	1170
Wheelbase	mm	2500
Track		
front	mm	1502
rear	mm	1588

Weights

Empty weight	kg (lbs)	approx.1120 (2470)
Curb weight*	kg (lbs)	1250 (2753)

*according to EU (European Union) standard, with 90% fuel capacity and 75 kg (165 lb.) driver

Capacities

Engine oil	Liter	15 (15.9 qts.)
Fuel tank	Liter	73 (19.3 gal.)
Engine coolant	Liter	25 (26.5 qts.)

Performance

Top speed	km/h (mph)	310 (191)
Acceleration		
0 - 100 km/h (62.1 mph)	sec.	3,7
0 - 160 km/h in	sec.	7,1
0 - 200 km/h in	sec.	10,5
Standing-start kilometer	sec.	20,4
Power-to-weight ratio	kg/hp	2,11
	kg/kW (lbs./hp)	2,87 (6.33)

Outstanding acceleration, record-setting braking

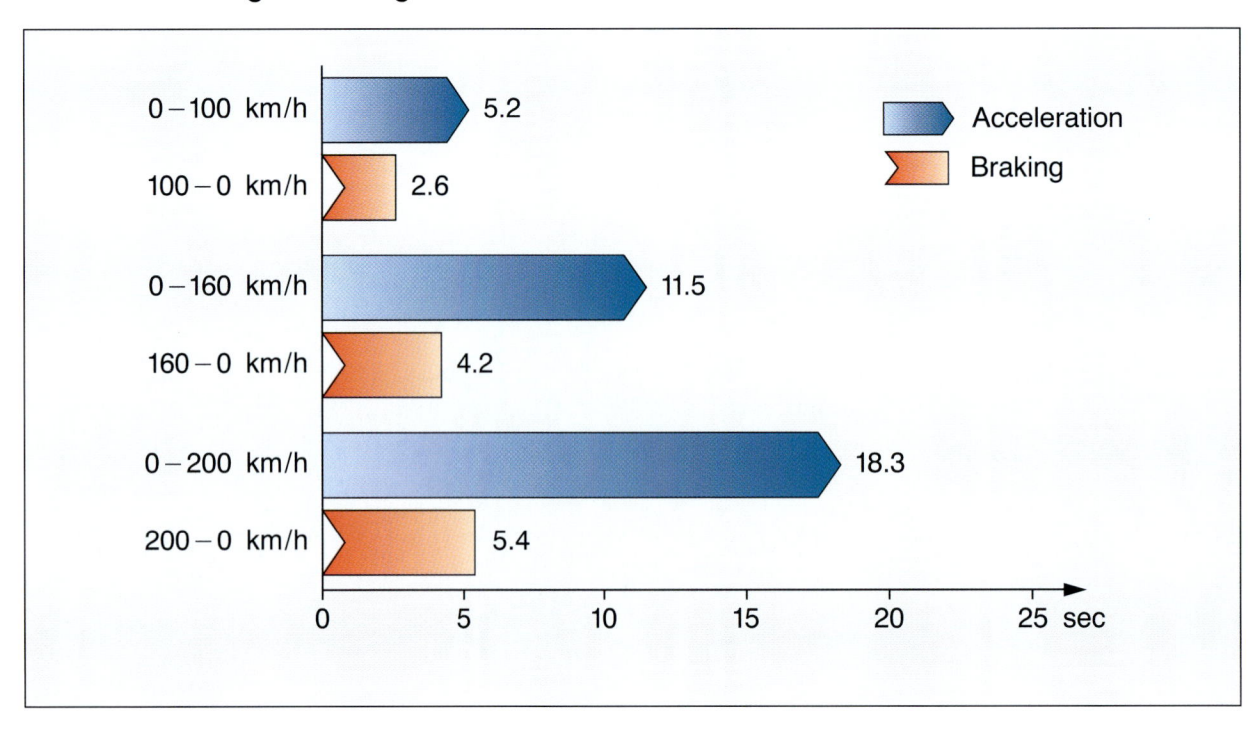

	sec
0–100 km/h	5.2
100–0 km/h	2.6
0–160 km/h	11.5
160–0 km/h	4.2
0–200 km/h	18.3
200–0 km/h	5.4

- Acceleration
- Braking

300 hp (221 kW) at 6800 rpm
280 Nm from 2000 to 7300 rpm

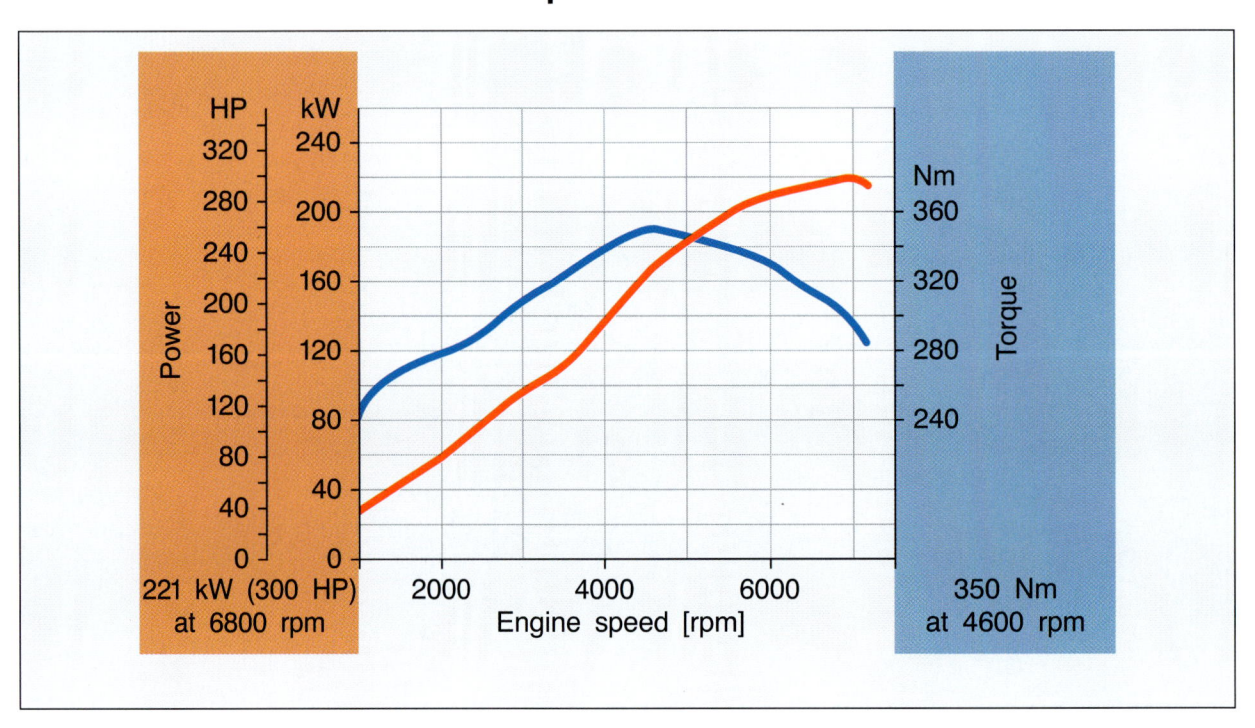

221 kW (300 HP) at 6800 rpm

350 Nm at 4600 rpm

Engine speed [rpm]

Six-speed manual transmission: the key to maximum thrust

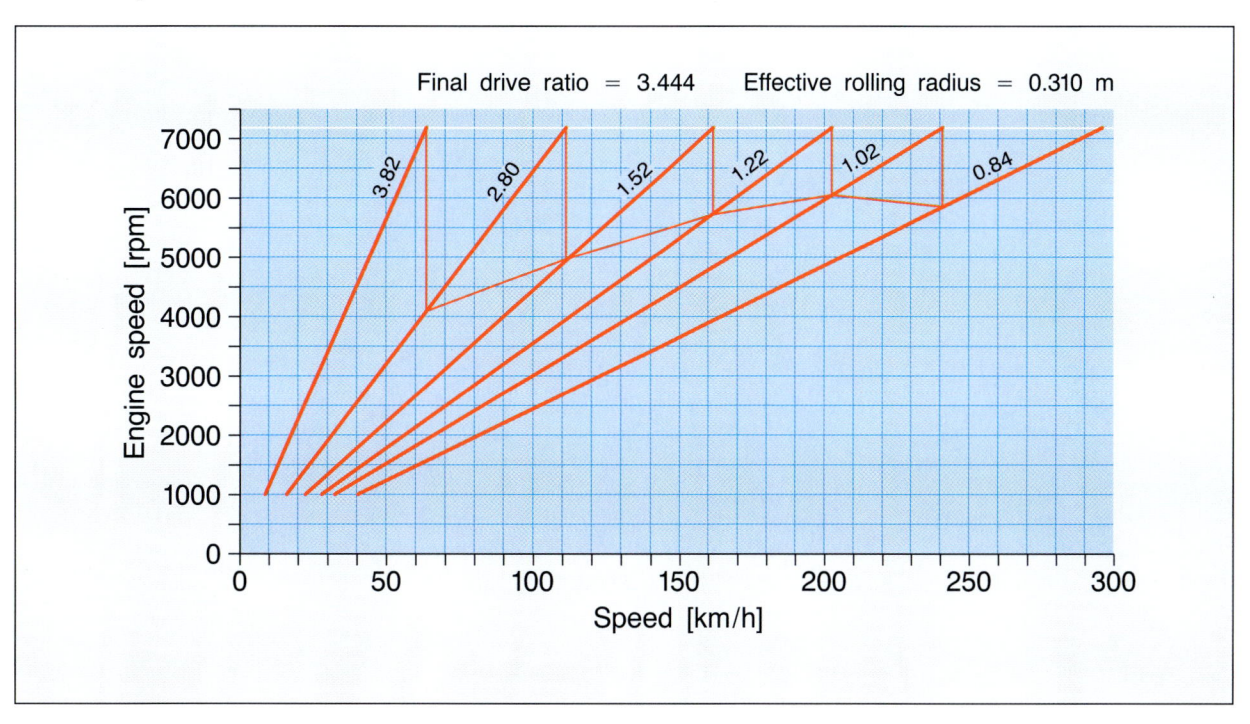

A sporting automatic transmission – the five-speed Tiptronic S

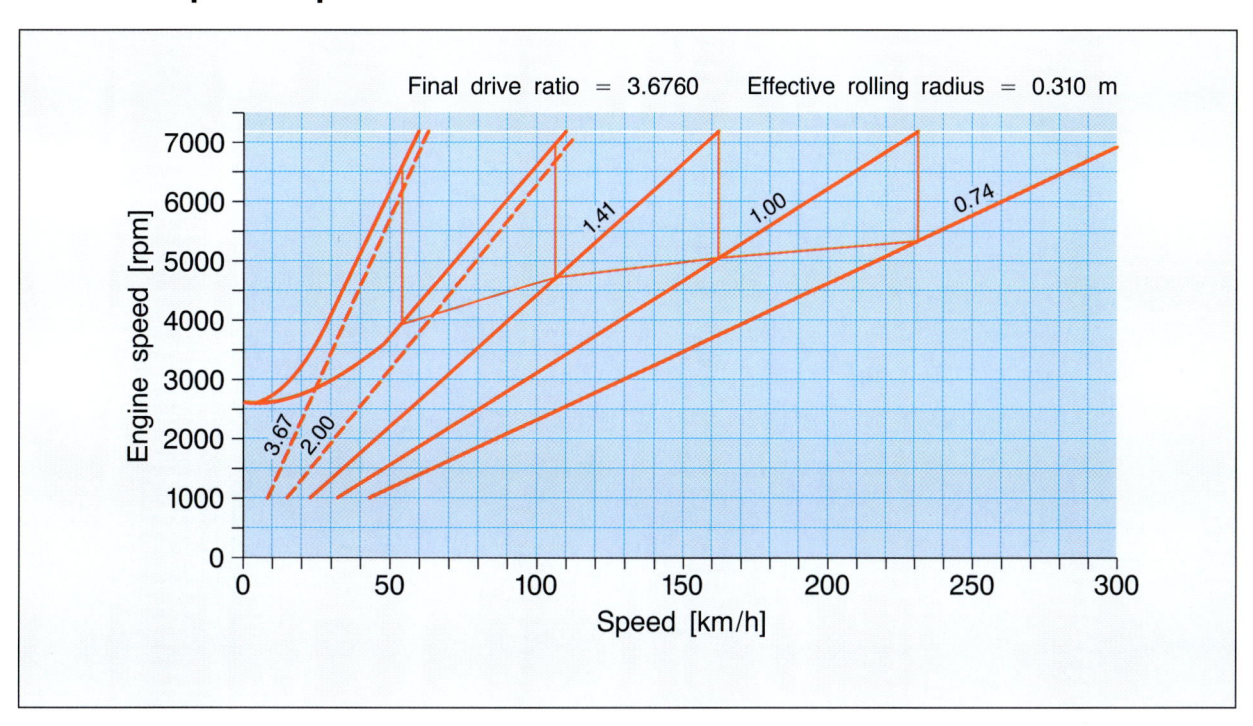

159